OTHER
DAYS
AROUND
ME

OTHER DAYS AROUND ME

a memoir by

RICHARD HOUGH

Oft in the stilly night
E'er slumber's chain has bound me
Fond memory brings the light
Of other days around me

Thomas Moore

A John Curtis Book
Hodder & Stoughton
LONDON SYDNEY AUCKLAND

British Library Cataloguing in Publication Data

Hough, Richard
Other days around me: A memoir.
I Title
920

ISBN 0-340-55221-2

Published by Hodder and Stoughton,
a division of Hodder and Stoughton Ltd,
Mill Road, Dunton Green, Sevenoaks, Kent TN13 2YA.
Editorial Office: 47 Bedford Square, London WC1B 3DP.

Designed by Sara Robin

Photoset by Rowland Phototypesetting Ltd,
Bury St Edmunds, Suffolk
Printed in Great Britain by St Edmundsbury Press Ltd,
Bury St Edmunds, Suffolk

CONTENTS

ILLUSTRATIONS

(All photographs from the author's own collection)

One of the sailors hoisted the seasick sheep onto my back, and we all waded through the surf onto the shelving pebble beach. This was the only inhabited islet of the group, and the only one named on our chart: Boat Islet. The population of two meteorologists were wild with excitement at our arrival. They had been stuck here for fifteen months, their relief several times being prevented by the almost constant bad conditions. When they were not reporting the weather they played football on the beach, or listened to the radio, cooked, ate and slept, in their hut.

We dumped the sheep on the beach, and when a sailor cut the bonds securing their legs, they stood up and sauntered off into the tussock grass and began grazing as if they had never left their Andean meadows.

Sacks of coal and drums of oil from the two whalers were being hauled to the hut above the beach, together with sacks of flour and potatoes and hundreds of tins, mostly dented, of Swiss condensed milk, apricots from Bulgaria of all places, strawberries and ham from native Chile, four dozen bottles of spirits, and other domestic needs for the replacement meteorologists.

A football match with more than two players this time was already under way. My wife and I said we were going to explore. The lieutenant smiled and shrugged his shoulders; the captain of our armed tug and his men had long since concluded we were amiably mad. 'You'll be the first to look,' he commented, and saved the football from the sea with a hefty kick.

We followed one of the sheep up a muddy runnel, pulling ourselves up by the tussock grass, the spray from the Pacific rollers crashing on the western shore already in our faces. The sheep, and we, paused as a Magellanic penguin emerged from its hole, fixed us with beady, incurious eyes, and followed us with its head as we passed by.

Others showed themselves, like householders at their doors when a procession passes, forerunners of the sights awaiting us higher up. The New Yorker *magazine had sent me to do a piece on Cape Horn. Diego Ramírez, this group of volcanic rocks emerging from the sea far south of that Cape – the end beyond the end – was an unexpected bonus, and marked one of the most interesting days of a life which, lucky for me, has not often been humdrum.*

'. . . the sights awaiting us higher up'
A drawing by Charlotte Hough

1

The Springtime
of the Year

I never saw my sister. She died in November 1921, six months before I was born. My mother told me later, 'I thought I was going to lose you, too.' My pretty fair-haired sister, Mollie, was eight years old. Our vicar and friend in Preston Park, Brighton, the poet Andrew Young, who never saw us in his church, comforted my mother and father with this quatrain:

> A flower herself to flowers she went,
> Sharer of beauty's banishment;
> She left us winter, but to her
> It was the springtime of the year.

My birth on 15th May 1922 acted as a distraction from grief, although it would have been more appropriate if I had been a girl as the last born had been Philip, age five. There was a May heat-wave that year. 'Oh dear, I was so hot carrying you those last few weeks,' my mother told me, but not complainingly. She was born Margaret May Esilman and was far from being a grumbler. She had been a Sunday-school teacher before she married my father in June 1911, and her religion meant much to her.

My father, however, was a positive agnostic, as he called it, a reaction from adolescent fervour when he had been 'a bit hysterical about God'. When my parents married, my mother, without a word, concealed her Bible and prayer book and they were seen only privately by her eyes for sixty years. Then, when my father died in his ninetieth year, they reappeared upon her bedside table, without comment, by her or me. I never asked her, but I am certain that the prayers which had been silent ones while lying beside my father for six decades were now spoken aloud again while upon her old knees beside her single bed.

My mother was always called Meg. She was a good, unpretentious woman who espoused no great cause but spread a comforting warmth about her. She was slow to think ill of anyone, except those who might hurt her family. I never heard her utter a cross word to my father. Her loyalty to him was like a hawser, though he often gave cause for exasperation, especially in his reluctance to pay out the smallest sum of money and failure to change out of his business suit before evening gardening.

Her mind was not profound nor deeply questioning but her mixed north-country and Scottish blood gave her the gift of pragmatic common sense. I loved her but appreciated fully her qualities and courage only after the death of my father, who had been such a comfort after her semi-crippling stroke fifteen years earlier.

She was born on 6th February 1887, the year of Queen Victoria's golden jubilee, but her freshness and brightness and outgoing nature were far distant from the mustiness and bigotry associated with that old sovereign. She grew up in Southport, Lancashire, the only daughter of the second marriage of Alexander Esilman, a successful chemist in Liverpool. With the death of his second wife, she became even more precious to him as companion and housekeeper.

Meg Esilman had a prosperous, middle-class upbringing, made friends easily and was good with flowers. 'I always seemed to be giggling with my best friend Effie.' There was turn-of-the-century bicycling and roller-skating. She enjoyed church, sang in the choir with her pretty but not strong voice, and loved her Sunday-school classes, first as pupil then as teacher.

When my mother was twenty-three she and her friend Effie were attracted to the idea of going on a holiday with a party to Switzerland. She had never been abroad before and was greatly excited at the prospect. It was organised by the Christian Holidays Association, known as CHA, or, with giggling frankness by these two girls, 'Catching Husbands Association'.

'My father was at first very doubtful about this scheme and didn't want to lose me, even for three weeks. Or perhaps he had overheard me talking about catching a husband.

'There were about thirty of us altogether and we were nearly all strangers to one another. There were two older people in charge to

2

look after the decorum. Effie and I were shamelessly flirtatious and made a bee-line for the best-looking young men.'

My mother told me that right from the start a rather serious young man attracted her. 'He was tall and athletic with thinning hair and a dark moustache and wore steel-rim spectacles. Effie said he would soon be bald and was too shy for her taste.'

Days among the mountains were filled with walks and climbs and trips in paddle steamers on the lakes. There was a service every evening, but also games, ping-pong being the most popular. They all slept in dormitories, simply but not uncomfortably, and of course strictly segregated.

The pairing off of some couples became more apparent as the days passed. Effie teased my mother about how far behind the main party she and George Hough (pronounced 'How') had trailed on a day-long climb. 'Who is he, Meg? Is he funny?'

My mother told her all she knew: that he was a clerk with Barclays Bank in North Street, Brighton, that he lived with two of his unmarried sisters, that he liked to philosophise and talk about books, that a man called George Bernard Shaw was his hero, that he did not attend church but that did not mean he thought there was no higher being.

'He doesn't sound at all your sort,' Effie decided.

'Oh, but he can be funny, too, and is very kind.'

In my mother's diary of that epochal holiday she begins by referring to Mr Hough who carried her bags. At the end they walk arm in arm and she writes of 'George'. Shortly after their return, to Southport and Brighton, George wrote a tremendously careful letter to Mr Esilman, giving his credentials and asking permission to propose to his daughter. The reply was not kept but it was favourable, a touch reluctantly, I imagine; and George next writes to Meg asking for her hand in marriage. After that, over the following ten months there are frequent long and expensive rail journeys from Brighton to Southport, the last one in June 1911 for the wedding.

My father, George Stanley Hough, was the younger son in a large north London – Bowes Park – family. The Houghs were descended from the Kay-Shuttleworths of Lancashire. John Kay of Bury (born 1704), whose father ran a woollen factory, possessed an ingenious mind and invented, and patented, the fly-shuttle, which more than doubled the speed of output. He also invented numerous other gadgets and machines, including a water-pumping windmill: a typical figure of the industrial revolution. But John Kay did not prosper from his ingenuity, spending too much time on litigation against weavers who failed to pay royalties, and suffering the destruction of his works by a pre-Luddite mob fearful of job losses.

One of John Kay's sons, undeterred by his father's experience, became an inventor, too, and one of his grandsons, James, added Shuttleworth after his name when he married a daughter of Sir John Marjoribanks. He became a prominent physician in Manchester and 'the founder of the English system of popular education' which earned him a baronetcy in 1850. One of his sons married a Huguenot, Elizabeth de Groot, and their daughter, Ann, married my grandfather John James Hough. My father was born on 30th November 1880.

This family was brought up austerely, with much economising and talk of thrift. John Hough was at one time a carpenter, joiner and cabinet-maker to the Queen and exhibited at the 1851 exhibition inspired by her husband, the Prince Consort.

But none of that helped John Hough's finances, and the relentless scrimping and scraping necessary to bring up seven children led him to take a dramatic and risky step that was quite against his nature. The face of north London in the 1870s and 1880s was being transformed by housing development, virtually uncontrolled and unplanned so long as it met health regulations, and they were pretty sketchy. Many builders went bankrupt before they could complete and sell their terraces of houses, and it was upon these hapless failures that my grandfather set his sights. With the aid of high interest bank loans, he began buying them at knock-down prices, some of them already up to roof level, others scarcely beyond the foundation stage.

Employing cheap Irish labour, John Hough completed these terraces and sold them rapidly. They made good purchases because he could not bring himself to take short cuts and use inferior materials. He could certainly have made more money out of the business but he did transform the family's finances, without observable effect on their standard of living.

Through my grandfather's banking connections, my father was found a job at fourteen as a trainee clerk with Barclays Bank. 'I had finished my elementary education two weeks before, so that makes it August 1895. I was told that Pater couldn't afford to keep me at school any longer. I walked to Bowes Park Station and from King's Cross I walked over a mile to Camden Circus and the bank.'

My father was under strong religious pressure during this sensitive period of adolescence and became introspective and fearful of the powers of his body. He admitted to me once that he had been agonised by the conflicting (as he saw it) demands of Christ and his sexual awareness, though he put it more circuitously than that.

For a while religion was in total command. He became a member of the Boys' Brigade, wrote intense Gospel verse, and altogether got himself into a fine old state. I suppose it was common at the time that he neither expected nor received any sort of guidance from his parents – Pater and Mater – or anyone else. He later reckoned that Bernard Shaw, the Webbs, and that lot saved him from what he regarded as the hysteria and hypocrisy of orthodox religion.

The reaction was violent and he had not fully recovered from it when he met my mother, the first woman to whom he felt able to talk freely.

In the wedding photograph my mother looks touchingly vulnerable and innocent, her frail prettiness contrasting surprisingly with her inner strength, patience and resolution, all of which were often called upon to deal with this confused, prejudiced but decent man of thirty.

It was soon evident to my mother and their friends that his love for her was without tremor or blemish, condition or compromise. It was to remain so until he looked up into her eyes from his deathbed.

They honeymooned in the Lake District, not far from Southport, by Derwentwater for the first week, and then Ullswater for the second week. She knew this area already, but for him it was a revelation and began his lifelong love, which I was to inherit, for the fells and becks of this beautiful part of England.

After more than a decade of bachelorhood in Brighton, the long journey in the train down England with his bride at his side to the house they were to share evokes a sentimentality and tenderness in my mind almost as if I had shared the compartment with them instead of being as yet ten years unborn. It was a minute semi-detached house with an attic for the living-in maid, a prerequisite for all but the working class in 1912.

This house was off the Dyke Road, Brighton, and the nearby tennis club became the centre of their social life. My mother's only anxiety was for her father, but he had found himself a housekeeper and occasionally visited his daughter in Brighton. My father walked off to his bank every morning, as he was to do all his working life, even walking back for lunch if business permitted. It was a commonplace life, but healthy and happy with long walks on the South Downs at weekends, interrupted shortly before their first child, Mollie, was born in 1912.

When the war began my father volunteered but failed his medical. The doctors discovered the scars of a patch on one of his lungs, which he would not confess to. Years before, while he was still working in the basement at Camden Town, he developed tuberculosis, not surprising considering the foul air and high content of coal dust in which everyone in London worked and lived. He regarded his rejection as a dreadful slight, and an embarrassment which he suffered all through that long, bloody conflict. He looked so strong and tall and fit, and in a way this made his position among their friends all the more awkward.

Barclays Bank, in its paternal way, had taken full responsibility for my father's health and sent him away to a sanatorium in 1898, and when he had recovered, despatched him to one of their branches in the clean sea air of Brighton, where he lived in splendid health for the rest of his life. As one of the first in Kitchener's Army, he would very likely have been killed, so Barclays can be said to have twice saved his life. But they got no credit nor thanks from him. He affected to denigrate his profession – 'Pah! Bankers! Nothing but bloody usurers' – claimed to hate his work and despised himself for lacking the courage to break free from the tyranny of a secure job and take up market gardening on his own. He was a man of many and curious contradictions, with hyper-sensitive pride a strong ingredient. In fact, he was considered good at his job, was soon promoted chief clerk, and then a manager before expectation.

Like many other families, the Battle of the Somme with all its terrible slaughter, led to the conception of another child, and his birth in 1917. This was my elder brother. He was christened Philip Stanley by the Rev. Andrew Young. This family of four moved twice into larger houses, the second time to a hideously ugly 'semi' in Cornwall Gardens, Preston Park. Gardening, tennis, walking and bridge were the recreations of this typical middle-class couple living in the suburbs of this middle-sized English provincial town.

The Houghs were known as a cheerful, contented and unpretentious family, with a living-in nursemaid supplemented by a daily maid-of-all-work and a washing woman who came on Mondays and filled the house with steam.

But orthodoxy was not total. Their closer friends were aware of my father's socialist views and controversial stance on a wide range of subjects, like against capital punishment but for the Russian Revolution. Surprisingly, he once felt duty bound to improve his position among the business community in Brighton by becoming a Freemason. He bought all the right things to wear at meetings and the special case to contain them but was so appalled at their activities that he only went a few times. 'All that bloody mumbo-jumbo and signs and nonsense – like savage rites!' The case and its expensive contents lingered at the back of a cupboard for years.

What George preferred was the Freelancers, an informal gathering of mainly professional men who met and debated subjects of the day and gave occasional papers – my father's first on, of course, George Bernard Shaw. They sometimes went hiking all day in the country and had beer and sandwiches at a pub. They exchanged 'baccy' for their pipes and came back glowing and covered in Sussex Weald mud for tea. Later, some of them joined the Left Book Club, and exchanged copies among themselves, earnestly debating the contents of books extolling the virtues of life in Russia and condemning the horrors of capitalism, by which they all appeared to prosper.

At home in Cornwall Gardens, books were almost never bought, my father frequenting the public library, my mother, for her lighter tastes, Boots Lending Library. But there were in the one bookcase the complete works of you-know-who and the novels of Mary Webb. Also some Hugh Walpole novels, read because of their Lake District setting and by me for the saucy bits. 'A bit of a bookworm, our Dick,' my father would comment not entirely approvingly. But I got a 'William' book at birthdays or Christmas sometimes, and earlier there had always been Beatrix Potter books about the place.

'At the time I knew I was going to have you,' my mother once recalled, 'we were very happy. The horrors of the war were over and we thought we would complete the family – make it three and no more. Then in November 1921 Mollie was taken ill with appendicitis.' She did not often talk about Mollie, but when she did there was always an unshed tear in her eye.

There were complications, which one shot of penicillin would have cured today, but within eight days she was dead. All through my childhood we visited her grave on Sundays, but never entered the beautiful little Norman church. We replaced the flowers in jam jars, raked the gravel, from time to time brought thermos flasks of hot water to scrub the headstone with its gothic lettering.

As usual in family life my brother, five years older, meant more to me than I to him. He missed his elder sister dreadfully and early on when he took any notice of me it was to tease. I remember him as redder-haired than I suspect he was, immensely strong and peerlessly brave. He could break sticks I could scarcely lift, he could throw a ball as far as the eye could see, he ran like the wind, swam like a dolphin. He fearlessly climbed trees of stratospheric height, a distant figure in shorts, briefly glimpsed through the branches while my mother stood pale and paralysed with fear beside me, urging me not to look up.

Philip carved model planes and 'flew' them, in his hand, for hours in order to break endurance records. He once flew a Bristol Bulldog from Scotland to London, holding it in his aching hands for the entire journey in a big Wolseley tourer. Mysteriously challenged by him one day as to whether or not I loved him, I perversely and quite untruthfully declared that I did not. The effect was cataclysmic. He burst into tears. I was shocked and horrified at this first ever proof of *my* power. Later, he confessed he wrote poetry and showed me some. He also pursued butterflies with a net.

Phil went to the local grammar school in the Dyke Road. He was not happy there, and was bullied. One evening our house was seized with the tight grip of hushed drama. Something awful had happened to Phil at school and he was in the bath recovering. I believe it was no worse than a drawing pin in his bottom, but this and similar events led to a momentous parental decision that was to affect us both later.

At six, in the late summer of 1928, I was sent to Lourdes Convent, Preston Park. My father gave no hint that his principles might thus be compromised. The choice was governed by convenience and economy as the grounds flanked our garden and it was very cheap. It took boys up to the age of eight, with a minimum of religious teaching, but there were few of them and the climate was over-whelmingly feminine, and musty with the smell of incense and nuns. Not only were these unfortunate creatures forbidden from exposing their bodies, even to themselves, but they bathed in-frequently, in their special combinations, anyway. Boarding girls were allowed a bath a week, presumably naked.

At Lourdes Convent, I was puzzled by all the garish figures of the Holy Mother in corridors, classrooms and even on plinths in the grounds, but my questions at home were sidetracked. The lowest class, from which I never graduated in three years, was taught mainly by lay women. Nuns took the stickier subjects like mathematics, and in their dark hoods, not altogether clean white waistcoats and designer-stubble, filled me with terror. At first, I could not understand why the Mother Superior, a Basque and the ultimate terror, was so dark, small and drab by contrast with her highly coloured likenesses on plinths about the place; and where was her baby in swaddling clothes?

There were more heroic moments than listening to the girls whis-pering about the peculiar night activities of the nuns; there were football injuries to take home in mixed pride and horror. And there was the day of the crash, 13th June 1930. Sir Edmund Segrave was killed spectacularly hitting a log on Windermere while attempting the world water speed record. All the convent boys were thrilled and simulated the crash in the playground, rolling over and over with shrieks and bangs. But I was the only one whose parents were by chance on the fells overlooking the lake when the crash occurred, and I let everyone know, loudly. It is my first memory of showing off, a weakness that was mainly, but not entirely, eradicated during the Second World War.

Out of the convent, friends were few. They were not discouraged by my mother, but there was no time that I can remember when friends were sought out for me, and I spent many hours alone in my workshop or on my bicycle. This made my friendship with the Cox family so vivid and precious. They lived in a gaunt 'semi', almost as hideous as ours, up the road. It was a house full of racket and enterprise, the sound of shoes on bare boards, bicycle and wireless parts, big, lovable, smelly dogs, and a cat called Beldam, though bedlam would have been more appropriate. There was brown bread and Marmite for tea, with plain cake, for the budget was tight. There were chickens all over the garden, pecking at the few remaining humdrum plants (all very different from home), and a rough pony somewhere, in confined circumstances but rich in the love of all the Coxes. My mother called them 'genuine', a much favoured accolade, but I don't think she completely approved of their hugger-mugger life style.

Dr Cox had been a doctor at the front in the war and, ironically, had been chlorine gassed after it due to a faulty X-ray machine and had to be treated very gently. He coughed a great deal but never complained. I can scarcely recall his appearance but I know he had saintly as well as heroic qualities, and his family loved and cherished him, but he died before all his children grew up.

Mrs Cox was 'a tower of strength' (another favourite), resourceful, capable and loving, with a jutting chin and strong hands for cooking, gardening and generally managing the household and its animals, strays included.

John, the youngest Cox, was my contemporary, phlegmatic and kind, the ideal companion for elaborate car games round the house. Next, two years older, was Nancy, into dolls rather than cars but always willing to oblige. Then there were the big boys, Philip and Bobby, as sweet-natured as the rest.

They all went to church on Sunday, packed into an old open Morris. Sometimes, they called in on us on the way home, and I wondered a little enviously what it had been like for them, so self-sufficient, free of doubts, in a row, kneeling in prayer, breaking into chatter again in the porch as they left: 'Goodbye and thank you, Vicar.'

Philip Cox, two years older than my Phil, was a great hero of mine. Tall, strong, with a deep laugh, he did all the right heroic things, joining the RAF, going to Cranwell, growing a moustache, Brylcreeming his swept-back hair, putting up his wings and flying Bristol Bulldogs. Later, he shot down one or two Messerschmitts in the Battle of Britain and then was shot down into the Channel himself while leading his squadron. His younger brother, Bobby, tousled hair, always cheerful, went to sea and survived until 27th August 1944 when his minesweeper hit a mine and sank off Cap d'Antifer near Le Havre. He saved several of his crew but then disappeared. John joined the Army and – thank goodness – survived; while Nancy, a trained nursing sister, worked more or less without a break for the entire war. What a family!

Among my parents' friends were the Kennards, Ken and Mary. He was another great hero, and friend, even surrogate father sometimes. He was another pilot, in the Royal Flying Corps in the Great

War. He had ended his flying crashing from a great height, which had been the cause of his protuberant eyes – or so I believed. He seldom talked about his experiences. But once, in very old age, he recounted with unexpected lyricism, finding his way back to Cairo in evening mist, flying a Martinsyde. The evening sun reflected scarlet on the mosques while the three great pyramids, tops jutting out into clearer air, pointed the way to his airfield.

'Uncle' Ken was full of good cheer and jokes. He was a one-man estate agent, and far too nice to be much good at it. He really made his modest living as a rent collector, but from time to time his board was to be seen outside a house for sale or to let, and then my heart would swell with pride. N. T. Kennard had a diminutive office in Station Road with one or two photographs of freehold bungalows at £350 in the window. The inside smelt of the gasfire and his pipe.

Ken did not look right in a blue suit, in my eyes. He looked better in weekend sports jacket, patched at the elbows, and grey slacks. He looked best of all in white tennis clothes at the Preston Park Lawn Tennis Club. Here there was no need to search for his name. Here on the Championship Board it was 'N. T. Kennard' year after year as men's single champion: '1925 N. T. Kennard', '1926 N. T. Kennard', 1927, 1928 . . . And as joint champion in doubles finals too.

Here at the tennis club the name was respected, and admired. 'Ah, here comes Ken!' 'Evening Ken!' 'Who're you playing this evening, Ken?' The voices called out from the line of deckchairs outside the timber and asbestos pavilion. Inside, tea was being served from a big urn on the table beneath the roll of honour. '1929 N. T. Kennard.' And never an immodest word.

As he went inside to change, Mary would sit down among her friends and fellow spectators. She was full of unmalicious gossip and ever on the alert for a new recruit to the cause of spiritualism. 'A cup of tea, dear? You must need it.' She worked Saturday mornings as well as the weekdays. She was the only woman there with a job. Her wage as nurse at Allen and West's factory in the Lewes Road was essential to supplement Ken's meagre earnings. She went off at the crack of dawn on her bicycle.

We bought our first new car in 1926, a bull-nose Morris Cowley, winsomely named 'Suzanne' after my father's tennis heroine, Mme Lenglen. It could manage a little over 40 m.p.h., but was usually driven at around 30 m.p.h., not very well and irascibly by my father. There was a certain amount of fist-shaking and cursing, especially at motor-cycle combinations with the family on board which were 'hogging the road'. 'Really, George, your language!' I think a serious crash was avoided because there was so little traffic.

'Suzanne' was part of the family, tenderly cared for, oiled and greased, washed and polished, every weekend. On Sunday mornings the Hotchkiss engine would be cranked into life, Mother would climb into the front seat, Phil and I into the back, Father adjusting the rear Auster screen to give us some sort of protection. Often we took the Kennards, too. 'How's the old bus, George? You do get a good shine on her.' A walk through muddy woods, perhaps chucking a ball about, a chorus or two of 'Raggle-taggle gypsies, oh . . .' A pause for Phil to climb some immensely tall beech tree. A longer pause at a village pub. Much cleaning of shoes on return to 'Suzanne', ending with a rub on the running boards' mats, fitted to the cheapest cars at that time, like boot scrapers outside gentlemen's residences in town.

Bella Robson came into our lives around 1929 as general factotum, expected to bath me, clean the house, prepare, cook and serve the food, though my mother did most of the serious cooking. Bella was an involuntary emigré from the north-east, daughter of an unemployed miner in Morpeth. Like thousands of her class and generation, she was sent to the relatively prosperous south-east, her name on agency files as 'Trainee Maid-General'. Bella was at first paid 10s a week, with full board, then £1, the single banknote drawn with awesome reluctance from my father's wallet every Friday as she cleared lunch. She was a round-faced, happy Geordie who tickled me and let me listen to Henry Hall on the kitchen wireless in my pyjamas in front of the Ideal boiler, where my love for jazz was born.

There was plenty of room in the house for Bella. The year 1926, of coal strikes, lockouts, the General Strike, was also a year for our family of mighty domestic decisions. First 'Suzanne', who gave us unheard-of mobility; then the new house, giving us unprecedented spaciousness. My father grew vegetables on a plot of land on the other side of Cornwall Gardens. In 1926 he negotiated its purchase and prepared plans for a house on it. What excitement, what crises with architects, what rows with builders about estimates! My father's pride demanded that it should be the biggest house in the road. It was never *quite* that because the Harts at the north end, opposite the Coxes, had a near-mansion with a tennis court. But they were 'rather common' and the house was ugly and almost concealed by trees, so it somehow did not quite count. (They also had a ferocious Airedale who scared the wits out of me.)

Anyway, number 14, named 'Marecote' after Father's favourite Swiss village, had an integral garage – very modern – a billiards room, doubling up as our playroom, two lavatories (one outside for Bella), and central heating. This supposedly came from the Ideal boiler but I do not remember it ever doing better than taking the chill off, and Father tended to turn the radiators off anyway before leaving for the bank.

In wondering amazement I watched this house go up brick by brick, floor plank by floor plank. Plumbers, electricians, carpenters, 'brickies', all became my friends. At just five I could mix cement with the best of them, jersey, shorts and long curly fair hair spattered by bedtime. The roof went up, including several dormer windows, the floorboards stained, linoleumed or carpeted, coal delivered, the Ideal boiler lit for the first time, the furniture moved across the road. First meal in the kitchen, and then in ecstatic excitement the first bath and to bed in the room shared with Phil.

After breakfast my father was crossing the ample hall to prepare for the bank when the ceiling fell down. I mean *all* of it: not an inch of plaster remained. We ran out in dismay at the noise, and there he stood, a raging snowman. No greater affront could have been inflicted upon him, and many furious telephone calls were made, and letters written to solicitors. 'Poor Daddy – oh dear!' murmured Meg.

2

P.R.

A school called Frensham Heights came into our lives in 1928 and remained the dominant influence, first for my brother and then for me, until the summer of 1940. It was a progressive co-educational school established soon after the First World War. It had much in common with its near-neighbour, Bedales, but its brief lineage was through St Christopher's, Letchworth, a pioneer in self-government, self-awareness, experimentation and advanced ideas on almost everything. Like Bedales, St Christopher's, King Alfred's and others, Frensham was part of the backlash against the tidal wave of conformist *nouveau* public schools established to cater for the children of the new Victorian middle class.

Frensham is a turn-of-the-century neo-Elizabethan mansion poised high above Frensham Ponds in Surrey, with distant views over gorse and heather and pine trees (intermittently on fire in tinder-dry summers) to the heights of Hindhead. It was built for a brewer called Charrington who was also a cricket fanatic. The twenty-two original bedrooms on two floors accommodated the two teams, who battled it out on an adjacent field, returning to champagne and billiards. It was converted into a hospital during the First World War, and put up for auction after it, with 300 acres of parkland and woods, failed to meet its reserve, and then bought by Mrs Edith Douglas-Hamilton for £40,000 privately. Edith had married into the Scottish ducal family and had been a Wills, daughter of Sir Frederick of the Imperial Tobacco Company. Frensham Heights School can be said truly to have been founded on 'beer an' baccy'.

In my time boys played on the cricket pitch where once Dr

Grace had shown off his cover drives. They occupied one floor of dormitories; the girls played lacrosse and slept, strictly segregated, on the other floor. Earnest 'Morning Talk' (rather than prayers) was conducted where the more frivolous after-dinner chat of the brewer's guests once rang out. The panelled smoking room became a library, the orangery the juniors' classroom, the billiards room complete with tiered seating, the juniors' recreation room. The palm court ballroom became a combined theatre, ballroom and music room. Over in the stable block, the stalls were converted into classrooms, the hayloft into an art room, including weaving, while printing, carpentry, metalwork and engineering were carried on elsewhere. The courtyard became filled with roller-skaters of both sexes during break and at weekends.

Luckily for Phil – and me – the Grammar School headmaster in Brighton had advised our parents that we would benefit from the enlightened style of this new school. So when I was coming up to six and about to begin my experiences with the nuns of Lourdes, my eleven-year-old tree-climbing poet brother was taken to inspect Frensham Heights.

What really mattered at Frensham was not its beautiful setting and grounds, the fine equipment, the emphasis on arts, crafts and athleticism, nor its many other qualities. What mattered was Paul Roberts, the greatest headmaster in progressive education. P.R. was bald, portly, hesitant in speech, benevolent and ever-optimistic in outlook; modest, wise, considerate and tolerant. Anyone today who was at Frensham during his time, 1928–1949, should consider it one of the great fortunes and privileges of his or her life.

P.R. would have been hopeless at an orthodox boys' public school. St George's Harpenden was considered progressive in the early 1920s but the boys were beaten for misdemeanours in the traditional way. P.R. had been there as a master and when it became necessary to beat a boy, he would put it off for as long as possible, sometimes to the very end of the term. 'It was hell,' an old boy told me recently. 'Much worse than what we wanted and was usually applied – a beating at once and get it over.' There was no beating at Frensham. It was a stroke of genius, or amazing good fortune, that he should be selected as headmaster. I think it was luck, for the governors who had appointed P.R. very soon after threatened him with the sack because of what they considered his over-liberal principles and failure to attract more pupils. Only by the joint efforts of a defence committee formed by my parents and several others was Paul Roberts, and the school, saved to survive the difficult years of economic depression.

I had overstayed my time with the nuns by a full year and felt gawky in my overlong shorts, an object of ribaldry among the girls. I suspect that I was held there for three extra terms as a measure of economy. It was not the first nor the last time that I was embarrassed by my father's reluctance to spend money before it became absolutely essential.

For the first time, two trunks were strapped onto the rear luggage grid of the car for the journey across Sussex and into Surrey. In my trunk were grey Aertex shirts, shorts, green blazer, overcoat, raincoat, underwear and football boots. On my head I wore a green cap emblazoned with the Frensham eagle. I was speechless with awe at my situation, unbelieving that there would ever be a more important occasion in my life. Some instinct told me that Phil would provide me with no fraternal comfort, which was as well because as soon as we arrived he was swallowed into his lofty world of seniority, for which he could bear no blame.

On an afternoon in late September 1931 I stood in the middle of a long linoleum-floored passage, with dormitories opening to left and right, lost in a vacuum of non-comprehension, like a man about to go under for a serious operation. Before me was my mother, wearing a long tweed skirt and buttoned jacket, a fur clipped about her neck, a small tilted hat on her head. I had never before experienced her *leaving* me; I mean seriously leaving me, not just to go shopping, but for ages, perhaps for ever. My father reluctantly wore his banker's blue suit, adding to the solemnity and formality of the occasion. He was anxious to be off. My mother was talking to the matron, who was stout, in starched uniform, white at the cuffs, thick white hair.

'Goodbye, dear, you'll be all right. Don't worry.' And from my father a firm handshake. 'Goodbye, old son.'

They disappeared down the corridor with the speed of the white rabbit. But, unlike Alice, I was unable to follow; instead the white queen took me to my dormitory and helped me unpack the new clothes that were suddenly as comforting as old friends.

*   *   *

16

It was not possible to have a more tender introduction to boarding school life than Frensham's. A motherly Miss Jones looked after the junior juniors, and Paul Roberts was as distant from Mr Murdstone as St Paul from Josef Stalin. In fact, we saw more of Mrs (Enid) Roberts than P.R. She was beautiful, South African born, with a commanding presence and (I was to discover) less flexibility in her discipline and a greater resistance to special pleading than her husband. But she was equally kind even if you 'could not fool around with Mrs P.R.', as I later discovered.

The P.R.s' quarters, quite properly, were the old Charrington suite, overlooking the great cedar of Lebanon that dominated one end of the front terrace, and the tennis courts.

The only discordant note in this chorus of concern and kindness was struck by a Miss Field, head of the junior department, a vixen-like, grey-haired woman not much given to smiling nor to words of encouragement and praise. Perhaps it had been decreed that there should be a few drops of angostura to offset what could have been the 'surfeit of the sweetest things'.

The diet of education at Frensham, with the emphasis on the arts and crafts, was consumed between many and almost excessive periods of physical endeavour. The day started with a one-mile run in shorts and vest, in all weathers, through the woods and park-lands, and back to ten minutes of exercises in the one-time ball-room. Then a cold bath and an austere-ish breakfast at eight. There were games every afternoon and boxing twice a week, conducted for the boys by an Army sergeant who came over from nearby Aldershot in an ancient Clyno car and taught us between sessions of filthy story-telling in the Army tradition: very un-Frenshamian but good fun. There were school sports and cross-country runs over the rough and undulant terrain, strong competition for the cricket nets and tennis courts at weekends. Physical fitness was the very stuff of our lives, *mens sana in corpore sano* would have been carved into the oak panelling that was everywhere if we had not been so self-conscious about such things. I soon took it as normal to bicycle to and from school at the beginning and end of every term, forty-nine miles over 800-feet Hindhead and the South Downs.

Young show-off once attempted the journey before breakfast to surprise his parents, an apple in his pocket. I got beyond Henfield before I ran out of 'fuel' and collapsed from exhaustion beside the road. I managed to hide the bicycle in the ditch and thumbed a ride to Preston Park. Pride led me to pretend the gears of my bicycle had failed, and when later my father took me back, a surreptitious adjustment to the Sturmey-Archer appeared to prove the point. *What* humiliation!

The masters and mistresses at Frensham were mostly as robust as we were, and almost had to be to survive. The six-foot-four nineteen-year-old Adonis, Martin Rivers, came to us from Bedales, after a brisk course in Sweden, to teach gymnastics. Stephen Hogg was a deft hockey and tennis player; Sam Counsell, an Oxford blue, taught games relentlessly. Even the grey-haired ancient (probably forty-year-old) second master, Lewis Weedon, raced about the sports field.

Only one or two amiable intellectuals stood out against all this frantic activity. The only evident exercise of Rex Warner our classics master, also novelist, poet and translator, were gentle walks in the woods with Cecil Day Lewis, pausing to study the bird life through binoculars. Then there was dear, willowy Sydney Carter, later to become a notable folksong composer and performer, who exerted himself as little as possible but was once or twice seen, awkwardly, with a hockey stick.

From the mid-1930s, Frensham Heights was infiltrated by an increasing number of German and Austrian Jewish children, mostly boys. Some had arrived penniless with their parents after hair-raising hardships. One boy had seen his father beaten as he scrubbed the pavement in Vienna before escaping. Others arrived with plenty of money, equally thankful to be away from the insane tyranny of Nazism.

These boys and girls brought double blessings to the school. They helped the school's finances, and they introduced a deeper measure of intellectualism. It did not matter – in fact it was a rather good thing – that they contributed almost nothing in the sporting field. They were, on the whole, not much good at running and hitting balls, but, my goodness, they knew about music and the arts. Ferdy Mayne, arriving with no English, was playing Caliban at the end of his first year. Claus Moser was only one of several pianists whose magic rang out from the music rooms from which we had mostly heard painstakingly rendered scales and practice pieces. There had always been music at Frensham, every morning at 'Morning Talk', and at weekend concerts, but this renaissance sweetened the lives of all of us.

Some of these boys, with their thick accents, physical awkwardness, heavy boots and *lederhosen* were teased, but not much and not for long. At a tough traditional public school they would not have lasted a week. And another thing: in the 1930s there was still quite a lot of middle-class and subdued anti-semitism. My tolerant father was not guiltless. But working, living and playing with them for eight months in the year extinguished any latent anti-semitism in us, once and for all.

Funnily enough, and a bit anachronistically, no one took a deeper and more patriotic interest in the 1936 Berlin Olympics than most of the Jewish boys, avidly following the triumphs of the blond aryan athletes in the pages of the *Berliner Illustrienen Zeitung*. They were, I suppose, poised between cultures and loyalties. We did not much mind but sports captains would have welcomed this measure of enthusiasm from them as spectators at hockey matches against Bedales.

I don't know whether we lost academically more as a result of our love affairs than the traditional single-sex school from their pashes and homosexuality. It is obviously not calculable. But after the age of thirteen or fourteen, affairs were of prime concern, either in practice or gossip. We were prepared for them, as if by some tribal initiation rite, by junior school lessons in the nude, outside and in the sun only, but often enough to be able to scrutinise, year by year, the pubic development processes. After that there was naked swimming in the pool, segregated but only nominally so.

Another incitement to early lust were the Saturday evening dances, where the shapeliest girls were in keen demand, while the wallflowers had as partners only the occasional kind master. The greatest test of nerve was the obligatory dance with Mrs Roberts, when sex was sublimated to the avoidance of treading on her feet. In my last year, with war raging, dances were made yet more vivid by the need to ventilate the ballroom from time to time by opening the windows and drawing aside the black-out curtains, which called for extinguishing all lights. How the announcement 'The next dance will be a blackout dance' sent the pulses racing!

Most of these affairs were notable for their brevity. There could be two in a single term, a pair of friends perhaps partner-swapping around half-term. Others were long-lasting, assuming almost a marital status so that the eventual break-up was like a celebrity's divorce in the big world. My first lasted a full year and was a very joyous business. Absurdly long letters were exchanged during school holidays, eventual marriage was taken for granted (it nearly always was), and she came to stay with me at Preston Park, strongly approved of by my parents. There were a lot of shorties after this, and finally one who did become my wife, though she threw me over for a couple of miserable terms and I thought I would never get her back again.

These affairs were conducted with incredible innocence. I think there was a bit of hanky-panky between a French boy (of course) and a statuesque girl, which led to the removal of both, and David Knowland, a close friend and great seducer, proudly showed me a French letter one day but never told me whether he used it. Otherwise it was mainly companionable stuff, with a bit of lying together and discreet kissing and touching, incomprehensibly mild today.

Academically, the girls were brighter than the boys up to about sixteen, when the boys began to catch up. The standard of teaching was not brilliant, competition restrained and with few exceptions there was little encouragement to excel. I was not the only one to fail the fairly simple Oxford and Cambridge certificate first time, to my father's severe displeasure because it meant more school fees when he expected me to be earning my living well before eighteen, like himself.

My last year at Frensham, '39–'40, was the most eventful, memorable and confusing of all my nine years there. Everything seemed to happen. I had by now become a prefect – or counsellor as we were perversely called – and wore a grey blazer with initials sewn into the top pocket, signifying prowess in some sport or other. I suddenly became rather good at running, and partly because some of my nearest competitors left early, found myself winning almost everything. I particularly enjoyed the cross-country, which took us downhill by any route we liked three miles to Frensham Great Pond, and back again uphill, soaking wet from half-jumped ditches and streams, to the finishing line. Here, cheering on their hero, were the girls and a more solemn huddle of freezing staff.

I recall, immodestly, breaking all but one of the school running records, and being entered for the inter-county sports championship. It did my self-confidence a power of good, and a pretty American girl insisted on carrying the trousers from which one stepped before a race.

The teachers, who changed quite often because of the poor pay, become over the last years more clear-cut in memory. This is hardly surprising, but men like Rex Warner, Sydney Carter and above all Martin Rivers, would have stood out in any crowd. Martin Rivers was the archetypal hero for any schoolboy, and in our case for any schoolgirl, one and all falling head-over-heels for him. Luckily, it was the girls' gym mistress he went for, and how she was envied! He preferred to be called Martin rather than Mr Rivers, and was ceaselessly full of ideas. Under his inspiration, a squash court was built by the senior boys in spare time in a single term. An outdoor theatre, at the same time and sponsored by another master, got bogged down (partly because of its absurdly wet site) after three years of struggle – compulsory at that.

Then there was the matter of renewed war with Germany. We were, relatively, a politically minded school, and decidedly left wing. The English master, Stephen Hogg, obliged us to précis the leading articles by Kingsley Martin in the *New Statesman*, which helped to nudge me to the right later. There were one or two boys and girls from conservative homes, but the hot debates in our 'parliament' were between communists and socialists. All the Knowland boys were communists, despising their father who paid their fees thanks to the profits from a substantial restaurant business. Apart from Mr Weedon, all the staff, too, were left in politics, and we even had an anarchist in Signor Baldelli, an amusing Italian with a fund of filthy stories equal to the Army sergeant's, and more subtle. (He was carted off to a camp in the Isle of Man the day Italy entered the war.)

Pacifism walked proudly arm in arm with leftism, among staff and pupils equally. We would have backed Foreign Minister Halifax to the girl and boy if he had got away with his truce plans after war broke out. And the intellectuals like Wystan Auden, Aldous Huxley (his boy was with us for a while), Benjamin Britten and his mate Peter Pears, who found it more convenient to be in America, were highly regarded.

In my case, the fashionable school attitude towards pacifism, which I adhered to in a confused sort of way, was further complicated by my earnest wish to join the Royal Navy, which one had to presume would be involved in the fighting in the event of war. Some boys become obsessed with stamps or football stars; I became obsessed with fighting ships. I carved models of the world's warships, learned the statistics of the world's navies, down to the thickness of a Brazilian battleship's armour plate. I read Taffrail and Bartimeus and recited Newbolt and Kipling. My seeming bloodthirstiness and, later, my determination to go to Dartmouth as a naval cadet, appalled my poor father. Then he, rather surprisingly but actually cunningly, offered to take me away on holiday in 1938:

just the two of us in a little German cargo boat, across the North Sea to Norway – by chance in the period of the equinox.

As was intended, the sea was so rough and I was so seasick – unconscious for three days and nights – that all thoughts of making the Royal Navy my career faded astern like the odious funnel fumes from the SS *Latona*. I was deeply disappointed by this decision, but it did simplify things a bit. I was now able to conform comfortably with current school thinking.

As the war started to become more serious, convictions at first never wavered. We were conscious – how could we not be? – of epochal events across the waters when first Norway and then France fell. The securing of an air raid siren on the bell tower was accepted but not the posting of senior boys and male staff up there with rifles to wing descending German parachutists. This refusal to defend our country by joining the Local Defence Volunteers (later Home Guard) muddied the school's local reputation even further, the population of Farnham and its environs being mostly retired colonels with expensive complexions. But passive defence was all right, and we redeemed ourselves slightly in local eyes by helping to dig an immense ditch along the Farnham by-pass to act as a tank trap, and filled a great many sandbags.

But while the war remained out of sight, our little world remained little changed: committee meetings, exams, love affairs broken and sealed, swimming in the evenings after cricket and sports practice, concerts at the weekends, exeats on bikes with picnic lunch. Staff and pupils alike hung onto this frail network of security, awaiting the millionth chance that might preserve our way of life for ever.

The fantasy began to break up after Dunkirk. Suddenly, to the soothing sounds of a Frensham summer was added a new note, of aircraft, not all of them friendly. By early July white vapour trails distantly patterned the sky with whorls and the hectic lines of pursuit and evasion. Once or twice in early July the tearing-calico chatter of machine-guns could be heard far away. At night we were awoken sometimes by the air raid siren, and hurried down to the school's ample cellars. The sense of outrage amongst us was not widely discussed, but it was strong and grew rapidly. We were, after all, pacifists, some of us members of the Peace Pledge Union. But the poison of war was seeping into us, from the sky.

Martin Rivers suddenly packed his bags and joined the RAF to protect us. That had a massive shock effect. Sydney Carter joined the Quaker Friends' Ambulance Unit to pick up the bits. Talk of careers among the senior boys was switched to the choice of service, Army, Navy or Air Force. When we were old enough, in a few months, there was no doubt that most of us would be following – even flying with? – Martin Rivers: the old squash court gang, high in the sky in our Spitfires, our one-time gym master leading us into battle, silk scarves whipping in the slipstream? None of us liked to admit to the relief, tempered by apprehension, that the decision for war gave us. No more doubts – or not many.

In the last days of July 1940, almost nine years after I had first climbed the stairs behind my mother and father to stand forlornly as they said goodbye, I went up the same stairs to say goodbye to Paul and Enid Roberts. I was head boy, six feet tall, fit from the school regimen, somewhat indifferently educated, finding women easier to get on with than men, a bit sentimental and lacking in the resiliency and worldliness of the traditional public school product.

Whatever I was, merits and demerits, warts and all, I owed to Frensham Heights, and that meant Paul Roberts. His gently expressed wisdom, sense of justice ('but don't expect life to be fair – it is *not*'), belief and confidence in all under his charge, were marvellous to witness. At Frensham Heights it was impossible not to be caught up in the all-embracing affection and gratitude for this man who governed our lives, beating a straighter path for us through the undergrowth of adolescence than we could possibly have done without him. None of us would forget the sincerity with which he gave his total attention to you over advice or just general discussion. Even the most stony-hearted amongst us left school the better for his philosophy of tolerance and kindness.

The Robertses were having mid-morning coffee in their drawing room. Paul got to his feet from his deep armchair to greet me, an undertaking for a man of his weight but an act of courtesy he never missed.

'Well, Dick, it was nice of you to remember us. So you're really off?'

'Yes, sir. And thank you for everything. It's funny to think I'll not be coming back.'

'I hope you will,' said P.R. 'Please come and see us, and give our warmest regards to your parents.'

I looked at that familiar round face for what might be the last time, the kindly close-set brown eyes, the broad mouth, a little turned down at one side, the dear bald pate, then turned to Enid, crocheting away, one eye half closed against the rising cigarette

23

smoke. We had had a few dust-ups, Mrs P.R. and I, but I had always felt respect and affection for her.

'We'll miss you, Dick. You're bicycling home, I expect. Watch how you go.'

I shook her hand and thanked her, and when I closed the big panelled oak door behind me, I experienced the same sense of apprehension at leaving behind the familiar to face the unknown as I had – only yards from this spot – in 1931 when I had first arrived. For whatever else Frensham Heights had inspired in me, it was not, I'm afraid, the self-confidence that sees most public-school educated boys through the early years of adult life.

3

The Delectable Mountains

When I arrived home on my bicycle from school on 21st July 1940 bad news awaited me. There was to be no family summer holiday, for the first time ever. Phil had chosen farming as a career, with my parents' warm approval. He had been to the appropriate colleges and my father had negotiated a loan to cover the equipment and the first year's rent for a farm on the borders of Oxfordshire and Gloucestershire, near Lechlade. His first harvest was imminent and we were all going off to give him a hand.

These summer holidays had been decently long, never less than three weeks, and they entailed a night each way on the journey, none of our destinations being attainable in one day – not at an average of 27 m.p.h. The exciting preliminaries included two days of packing, the old trunk being dug out of the attic, and slowly filled from a list written in my mother's rounded clear writing. Down in the garage, the grease gun would come out of its box and special attention paid by Phil and me to the car's every nipple. Brasso on the radiator, car rugs aired in the garden, the leather straps got out and greased, ready for the ceremonial act of securing the luggage on the grid.

By 1931 'Suzanne' had been superseded by a Humber 14/40, a bit up-market from the Morris Cowley and hand-built like every-thing in those days, tremendously heavy in weight and to drive, with a devilish gearbox. Several months passed before my father achieved top gear. On every journey, he would try two or three times, his silent rage contrasting with the noisy crash of cogs, then give up. Neither he nor his family uttered a word, pride being desperately at stake. Then one day it slipped into fourth gear, like

25

the proverbial hot knife through butter. To have offered congratulations would have suggested previous failure, so we still remained
silent.

But by now, all was well, and we nosed through the Brighton
traffic, heading for the Lake District some three hundred miles
away, speeding at up to 50 m.p.h. at times on the A23.

Earlier holidays had been spent in Devonshire and Cornwall,
when I was only five to seven or so. As a consequence, Phil was
bonded to Devonshire for life and later bought a farm there. But
for nearly sixty years, the Lake District has possessed my soul, and
a year seems empty when I have not visited it. The first bond of
loyalty was secured on this holiday, when I was nine, and the love
and excitement began to surge when I first saw from the back seat
of our 14/40 Humber the rise of the fells from the road from Kendal
in early August 1931.

This was the first time I had seen mountains. Of course, by Swiss
standards, even Scafell Pike, at 3,200 feet the highest in England,
is only a pimple, but for a boy brought up in south-east England
it is a giant, rising above other giants in the central fells. I stared
about me in wonder as we passed Windermere on our left, Bow
Fell distantly behind, and then Rydal Water. Today in summer
the traffic is sometimes stationary along this road, for miles in both
directions. Sixty years ago, a pony cart might hold you up briefly,
and open char-à-bancs passed from time to time, but you could
park anywhere without fear of obstruction.

In the event, we did stop beside Lake Grasmere as it came
into view ahead. Father said, proprietorially, 'Have you ever seen
anything like that before, eh?' And Mother said to Phil and me,
'Now you know why we came here for our honeymoon.' The water
spread out before us, a little grass island in the centre with a stone
shelter and one or two sheep in it. One man in a boat was fishing.

It was stupefyingly beautiful, as different from the green undulat-
ing Downs of Sussex as the Rocky Mountains from the plains of
Middle Western America. The dry-stone walls traced their way
haphazardly across the grass and bracken of the fellsides, the sheep
grazed or lay with their growing lambs in groups, and the smell of
the heather and bracken was heavy on the still evening air.

'Last lap,' remarked my father, pressing the starter (no more
cranking with the Humber). 'Mrs Wilson will be waiting for us.'

He halted the Humber beside a stone and slate house called
Easedale Lodge.

'Well, here we are.'

'I do hope it will be all right, George.'

It was. We were greeted by plump Mrs Wilson and shown our parlour and the two bedrooms upstairs. This was ours, for tonight and twenty-one days, an infinity of time. That evening we walked back into the village. Mrs Wilson had told us that it was rush-laying Saturday at St Oswald's church. Mother, without hat, tied a handkerchief over her head and we joined a small group of villagers and tourists. I recall candles, solemn music on the organ, singing and white-cloaked figures advancing down the aisle, bending to cast armfuls of rushes on the flagstones. Afterwards, Father remarked, 'Very interesting. I am glad we caught that. But what primitive balderdash, eh Meg?'

We walked back to our new home in the dark. It was a still night and the only sounds were the harsh raps of our studded shoes and the lap of the ghylls and becks – exciting new words to me* – that brought the fell water down to the River Rothay. We did some boating and swimming on these Lakeland holidays, but unless the fells were covered with low cloud or it was raining heavily – and oh how it could rain here! – fell walking and climbing was the first daily occupation. We would drive out to some other valley or pass, park the car, sling our rucksacks with sweater, raincoat and sandwiches onto our backs, and step out.

Phil's and my fit-making routine at Frensham stood us in good stead for these interminable climbs, up, up, up, along heather, sheep-cropped grass, screes and boulder-scattered tracks. Summits that proved false time and again were always ahead, until magically the cairn on the real summit came into sight, and we huddled round it in the whistling wind to savour the view and eat our sandwiches.

But in 1931 my legs were only half developed, and I had not yet been through the arduous body-building routine of Frensham Heights. In the evening, my whole body ached, but I was too much in love to care – in love with every aspect, every shape, every changing colour, every challenge, of these fells: the roan trees clinging to the brink of the gorges filled with pure racing water you could drink, unlike muddy Sussex streams, the sound of the sheep

---

* Beck, from the Old Norse bekkr; fell, fjall; ghyll, gil. Vikings occupied this area around 900, burying their boats in the valleys, clearing the land and farming, as do their descendants today.

high up where grazing was sparse, the collies rounding them up to the whistles of a distant figure poised on a scree, the little ghylls that spilled over into the tracks in wet weather, even the nail scratches on the rocks which, in cloud or mist, reassured you that you were on course.

Harrison Tickle, Sergeant Man, Pike O'Stickle, Dove Crags, Pillar, Great Gable, Lingmell and many more – these fell names were recited like some climber's litany every evening by the light of the oil lamp after supper. The map was spread out, routes and peaks for the next day debated. 'If it's an east wind we don't want it in our faces on this ridge. Better approach from this side – follow the beck to here, then . . .'

The enchantment was total, the sound of every fell and ghyll magic to my ears. These were the happiest moments of my childhood, when admiration for my father was unconditional, when he was at his best. These peaks were conquered as if we were pioneers forging new trails, filling in the *terra incognita* on the chart.

There were to be three successive holidays with Mrs Wilson at Grasmere, at the end of which there were not many peaks left to conquer, and Phil and I were beginning to leave even Father behind – he was fifty-two now – while Mother tended to limit herself to shorter walks. Then early in 1934 father said, 'I think we ought to make a break. We've never been to North Wales. Let's give it a try.' So we did, and it was very much like the Lake District except the local people talked a strange language and in some places did not even understand English, and there were some marvellous expansive beaches. We had a new Morris Oxford saloon this year, dark green and black, very swish, with an art-silk anti-dazzle blind for the rear window, operated by the driver through a cord. It had many other features which could, and did, go wrong, to Father's fury, for we were already entering the era of shoddy workmanship and poor quality control in the car industry.

The Morris had not only a rear blind, but also a smoked glass sun visor, electrically operated lit-up trafficators, to warn of turns, which flicked up out of the door pillars, little circular mirrors aimed to check whether these trafficators were working, folding tables let into the back of the front seats, a lockable glove box let into the veneered mahogany dashboard, which sported any number of dials, and other comforts and aids, including a switch to dip the head-lamps, and a 'sunshine' sliding roof.

But – and here was the ultimate refinement and precaution against Father's gear-crunching – our Morris had a 'free-wheel' which could be operated by turning a knurled knob. This allowed the car to be driven without using the clutch so that you changed gear up and down simply by moving the gear lever and relied exclusively on the brakes for decelerating.

My father said one day, 'Do you want to take her over?' He was talking to *me*, not Phil who was already driving properly, with a licence. I was twelve. We were on an enormous smooth sandy beach. The prospect was stupendous, yet also alarming. But assuming a casual air (I thought), I said, 'Thanks, I do.'

From my father's lap, I had often steered our cars along Sussex lanes and had become reasonably accomplished. I had even been allowed to change gear once or twice. But now. The whole great machine under my command! I climbed into the driver's seat where I had for many years, in imagination, driven up Honister Pass in record time and led the Brighton Speed Trials time and again. Nothing I could do now could match those triumphs, but at least this was no daydream.

Up and down I drove, from the rocky cliff at one end of the beach to the fenced-off fields at the other end, swinging noncha-lantly round picnickers, close enough so that I was certain they could see me, changing down, pursuing another car full of children in the back – that was a bit of luck – and passing it at 40 m.p.h. There were piles of seaweed awaiting collection at one place, and I zig-zagged in and out, with the hint of a skid. Mother, Father and Phil were busy with the picnic when I returned, pumping the Primus stove, unwrapping the sandwiches. None of them looked up when I halted, pulled on the handbrake, switched off and got out.

'Hullo, dear, did you enjoy that?' Mother asked.

'Quite good fun.'

Father did not approve of the movies. 'Nothing but filthy sex.' My Mother wanted to take me to *One Night of Love* with Grace Moore because she had heard it was so beautiful, but Father would not hear of it. 'All slush and rubbish.' Instead, Bella was allowed to take me to slide travelogues in the Aquarium on Brighton front, *Glorious Switzerland, Bolivian Peons of the Andes*. Phil took me, illicitly, to *Ben Hur* and that made a stunning impression, and he also took me to *The Mummy* with Boris Karloff. The coming back to life scene haunted me for weeks.

But Father over the years took me to one or two films, and rather an odd selection they were, too. *Modern Times* was OK in his eyes because Charlie Chaplin was left wing and anti-capitalist and funny. Another was *Queen Christina* at a flea-pit in Porthmadog. I cannot imagine what had impelled him to take us all to this movie, and, of all times, when on holiday. Perhaps he had heard that Greta Garbo, so serenely beautiful and alone, would not be sexually corrupting. More likely, my mother had read the rave notices of this film everybody was talking about and begged to be taken. Anyway, the cinema was jam-packed and Phil and I had to sit in the aisle, and Mother soaked her handkerchief to the last shipboard fade-out.

We went back to the Lake District three more times in the 1930s, staying at first with Mrs Zanazzi in her house overlooking Derwentwater. 'Nothing's changed, has it, George, since our honeymoon.' They had been married twenty-five years, and the one change was that they now had hulking boys of fourteen and nineteen, an age difference that seemed less than earlier. Ours was in no way a spiritual relationship but happily based on physical endeavour and 'things' – cars, cameras, bikes, and now, here in the Lake District, mountains. Fifty-five years ago, our capacity for climbing seemed limitless, though Phil could still outdistance me. There were triumphant moments on the more obscure peaks, basking in sun above cloud, and not a soul in sight. There were scree runs, down a thousand feet in less than a minute, and times when, temporarily lost, we were more than an hour from home in high winds and rain that could penetrate any garment.

I often took out Hugh Walpole's dog, Bingo, a jolly fox terrier. Walpole lived above Manesty overlooking the lake, next to Mrs Wills of the tobacco fortune, who took her own dogs out, a dozen or more golden retrievers who ranged over the slopes of Cat Bells. My father did not care for dogs. They disturbed his thoughts on walks and ruined the garden. I had to be content with temporary ownership, and had intermittent care of another terrier at school, which strayed from its home in the nearby village, and to the fury of its owner I indulged disgracefully. Young family life is incomplete without a dog and I have rarely been without one, mostly sheepdogs which I find so beguiling and easy to train.

4

An Atmosphere
of Awe*

The Battle of Britain, like Phil's harvest, was still in its opening
phase when we arrived at the farm. His new combine har-
vester, the only one in the neighbourhood and the object of much
local scepticism, was cutting a swathe in the big field of wheat
beside the old farmhouse with its even older cedar tree in its garden.
There was a sense of pioneering in the air, as if this might be a first
ever harvest in New England in the seventeenth century, instead
of the most recent in so many thousands in old England. Phil
worked all hours, especially conscious of his responsibilities now
that Mother and Father were there.

Phil showed me an old Morris Oxford, similar to our family
model long since superseded by first a terrible Canadian-built
Chevrolet and then a more staid Rover. This Morris had a wide
near-horizontal rake secured to the front axle, with metal-tipped
tines set at an angle to slide along the stubble after the combine.

'Your job's to collect the straw,' he told me. 'It'll pile up in front
of you, and before it starts falling off, drive it to the rick and reverse
out.'

'How fast can I go?' I asked. I was old enough to drive on the
road with an 'L' plate now.

'Very slow,' Phil said firmly. '10 m.p.h. maximum. Otherwise
you'll break a tine. There's a bonus for you if you get through the
harvest without a break.'

It was weary but physically undemanding work, mostly in a
cloud of dust – harvest dust which led to the harvest bug creeping

---

* 'A schoolmaster should have an atmosphere of awe, and walk wonderingly, as if
he was amazed at himself.' Walter Bagehot

under my skin all over my torso. Oh, how I itched! And there was little sleep at night. I hated farming while appreciating, and to some extent sharing in, Phil's pride and excitement as the grain piled high in the drier and the men worked late into the twilight. As darkness fell we became aware of the sound of German bombers, easily identifiable by the unsynchronised note of their twin engines, heading for the industrial Midlands and north, or farther west to South Wales.

The skies were rarely silent by day or by night in this beautiful summer of 1940. There were training airfields all around, single-engine Harvards at Brize Norton a few miles away, many varied types at Little Rissington to the north-west – Ansons, Blenheims, Airspeed Oxfords and some Mohawks from America. They flew quite low, practising formation flying and carrying out navigational exercises in the cause of the long war that lay ahead. Through the open roof of my car I caught glimpses of them in spite of the dust, and wondered how long it would be before I could be one of the pupils, and whether I would be any good at it.

Towards the end of August and during the first days of September, the Battle of Britain was at its climax. The morning news-papers told of heavy German losses, sometimes of over one hundred, with Spitfire and Hurricane losses perhaps one quarter of the German figure. Nothing was said of the serious damage to British airfields, the knocking out of radar stations, and worst of all the severing of communications, the defence's lifelines.

We were on the fringes of the battle and saw little of it, but Brize Norton a few miles away was bombed on 16th August and hangar explosions led to the destruction of almost fifty aircraft, though we were not told about that either, and they did not figure in British losses. I got a letter from Martin Rivers one morning. 'This is the life! Flying is wizard, the most beautiful thing in the world to do. I did aerobatics every day last week. Soon I'm off north to learn to fly Hurricanes. Maybe I'll be in time for the fun. Hope you're enjoying toiling on the soil!'

'The fun!' I ruminated. Shooting down enemy aircraft was not on the Martin Rivers agenda a year ago. Nor was 'wizard' a word we ever heard at Frensham. But this letter heightened my impatience and made straw-sweeping seem very mundane. There were Hurricanes at Brize Norton, and we sometimes saw them overhead. I thought they *must* have shot down some of the German raiders. (They did not.)

I had letters from other Frensham people. David Knowland, who had had cartoons in *Punch* while still at school, was at art school in Bristol. My closest friend, John Liversidge, 'Thistle', with whom I smoked and listened to Duke Ellington records, had gone to sea as an apprentice, and my last girlfriend, Charlotte Woodyatt, with whom I corresponded every few days, was with her mother at Bushey in Hertfordshire. 'Come and stay as soon as you can get away. Mummy would love to meet you.'

At the end of the first week in September, with most of the harvest in, I left for London by train from Lechlade and took the Green Line coach to Bushey. Charlotte and her mother, Helen, were temporary tenants in a modern house in this suburb, awaiting a cottage nearby which would soon be ready for them. Down the road lived a spinster aunt, Barbara, whom I at first found rather intimidating. This set-up was seemingly humdrum, but in fact it was as impressive as it was welcoming. The conversation seemed immensely amusing and intellectual, full of references to contemporary artists, poets and novelists. Rather guiltily, I recognised this was not at all like home. Aunt Barbara was a close friend of Hesketh Hubbard, the painter and lecturer and founder of the Print Society, and had nearly married him. The names Frank and Marjorie Whittington often came up. Next door was the foremost painter of trees; Lucy Kemp-Welch lived opposite the church, and her friend Alice Woodward, who was a friend of Beatrix Potter, had a studio on Chalk Hill.

All these artists had been to Hubert von Herkomer's art school, which had thrived before the First World War and, long after his death, was still partly occupied by his less successful ageing students. Then there was Charlotte's half-brother, Roger Roughton. Helen had married first Thomas Roughton at the beginning of the First World War, and he had been killed right at the end of it, leaving through his 'soldier's will' his considerable fortune to his only son when he became eighteen.

All this I learned later, as I discovered that the war widow Helen Roughton had rather reluctantly married again in 1923, with a view to having a sister or brother for Roger. The marriage did not prosper and Helen left Henry Woodyatt within a few months, but there was no divorce. Even sixteen years later he thought she might come back.

He was quite unforgiving of Helen for abandoning him and had many chips on his shoulder. He was a doctor, the youngest child

in a large family and there was no money left for public school so
he went to the charity Graycoats and never got over it. He began
as a naval surgeon-lieutenant, quarrelled over a woman, switched
to the Army, quarrelled again but served throughout the First
World War before taking a practice in the New Forest. There he
met Helen, and quarrelled. Until he was too old he drifted in and
out of locums, rowing with landladies. He contributed nothing to
the cost of Charlotte's schooling or upbringing, although the two
got on well when they met. Helen had minuscule private means but
was one of those women who, in their style, clothes and hospitality
somehow give the impression of being quite well off.

Roger, whom I never met, was a revolutionary communist, poet
and intellectual. He would have gone down rather well at Frensham
Heights. Instead, after leaving school he threw himself into young
Fitzrovia, with people like Giles Romilly, Churchill's nephew,
David Gascoyne, Hugh Sykes Davies and Dylan Thomas. In the
late thirties he divided himself and his newly inherited money
between the *Daily Worker*, surrealism and a very smart magazine
he started up, *Contemporary Poetry and Prose*. In 1938 he drove a new
yellow American Cord, his one concession to capitalism, and lost
almost all his money. The Russo–German pact of July 1939, putting
hated fascism in the same camp with beloved communism, nearly
killed him with grief and disillusion, and when the war came a few
weeks later he disappeared to Dublin.

I knew nothing of all this when I first came to stay in Bushey. I
felt liberated and happy, in love with Charlotte, picnicking over
the fields, swimming, playing records, reading from a range of
books the like of which I had never seen in a house. The air battles
seemed more unreal and distant here, though we saw plenty of the
action, including a big raid on nearby Hatfield with much fighting
while we were swimming at the Spider's Web on the Watford
by-pass. The sky was peppered with the grey puffs of anti-aircraft
fire, and we could see, very distantly, the RAF fighters harrying
the bombers.

There was no question of my settling down to a career, but I
had to have something to do and make some money before I began
my training. Through my schoolmaster cousin, Raymond Cooper,
who had joined the Army, I got an interview with a Mr Farnfield
who ran a school uncannily like Waugh's Llanabba Castle called
Bickley Hall in Kent. I had no qualifications beyond School Certificate, no training or experience in teaching. But Raymond had

been a great hero there and that gave me a good start. After an hour's chat in the headmaster's study, all oak panelling and countless brown photographs of football teams, this agreeable man put me in charge of a class of eleven-year-old boys, the whole lot of them in *all* subjects – Latin, which I had given up at fourteen, maths which I had failed for the certificate, ancient history (better), French (worse) and so on, even football, which we hardly ever played at Frensham. The salary was £50 a term, less laundry.

I discovered that only the headmaster was qualified, and all the staff were rather elderly, time-servers to the man, with grubby black gowns and mortar boards and whisky on their breath. I had no idea this sort of place still existed, and it was certainly as far distant from Frensham as a holiday camp from the Gulag. There was plenty of beating and slapping of heads with a ruler to discourage slacking. Why in heaven's name any parents sent their sons to Bickley Hall was incomprehensible to me. But the parents of 'my' boys were greatly admiring of the place, put their absolute trust in me, even took me out with their boys to local hotels for Sunday lunch, much welcomed as Mrs Farnfield did not manage very well with the food rations and was an indifferent cook at the best of times. 'How's Jack's geography getting on?' 'Oh, it's really improving.' Even a broken shin on the football field, due to my impatience, seemed to pass off without any rebuke.

The old lags in the staffroom filled their pipes and drank their beer before mid-day dinner and shorts – quite a lot of them sometimes – in the evening. They were kind to me. I offered no competition, and it would have been difficult at any time to find replacements at the sort of money, and conditions, Mr Farnfield offered; with the war on, quite impossible. Anyway, I would be off soon – off to the war they were too old for. They were, one and all, immensely helpful over the subjects I did not know and had to teach. 'Tell 'em a story if you get stuck. They always like that and it keeps them quiet.' They knew I was writing stories for *New Writing* and *Lilliput* (none published).

The matron was very kind, too, and as I had no heating in my attic and she had a gasfire, I used to huddle in her room while she darned boys' socks and listened, rather uneasily, to my record of Ellington's 'Black and Tan Fantasy'. Above us, while the daylight Battle of Britain faded away with only scattered darts at London at an almost invisible height by very fast fighter-bombers, the night blitz began in earnest. The boys and all of us were down in the cellars at least a part of every night, the noise of guns and exploding bombs was indescribable, and in the morning, in pyjamas and dressing gowns, the boys scoured the crater-peppered grounds for the largest bomb splinters. It was just like conker time all over again.

I went up to London *en route* to Frensham one Saturday. It was astonishing that any trains at all were still running and large areas, some still burning, were like the film of Wells's *The Shape of Things to Come*. At school I adopted the usual rôle of old boy, with tweed jacket and scarf, flashing my cigarette case and no doubt being odiously patronising. But it was nice to see Charlotte, which was why I had come.

Teaching was not my métier, and the boys were beginning to rumble me. Story-time got longer and longer as the time came to start on logarithms and algebra, neither of which I had begun to understand at Frensham. I had signed on for just one term, but Mr Farnfield asked me once or twice, obviously for reassurance, 'Will we have the pleasure of seeing you back here in the new year?'

'I think the RAF will have claimed me by then, sir.'

It did not, however, and for a number of weeks I worked as an ambulance driver in Bushey. Charlotte and her mother had moved into their cottage, but there was no room for me there, so I lived a moderately primitive existence in one of the old Herkomer studios, which had neither reliable floors nor ceilings, nor coke stove for that matter.

Every third evening I would usually have supper with Charlotte and her mother. Helen always managed to rustle up something tasty from the increasingly stringent rations, just as she managed to create a sense of luxury out of the simplest of material. Coal fires burned in both of the little downstairs rooms. Here we talked and listened to records or the wireless, and I read aloud the whole of *Great Expectations*. Charlotte was going to a secretarial college and later got a job as secretary to Arthur Watt the literary agent.

The pleasure of these evenings was abruptly cut off by a telephone call from Dublin. As Helen answered it upstairs, the tone of her distant voice told unmistakably of tragedy. It was a long call. She was cut off and reconnected. When she came downstairs her face was ashen. 'I knew it would happen . . . I knew it would happen,' she kept repeating. It was the first time I had seen a grown woman crying. 'I must go and see him. I must go tomorrow, poor darling boy.'

Roger was dead. In my embarrassment, I wanted to leave them to their grief. This was not my world. In some inexplicable way, I had slipped into it as a temporary guest and could do nothing to comfort them. But Helen said firmly, 'Don't leave us – not now – please stay.' So I did, trying, at an immature eighteen, to offer comfort. Then Aunty Bar turned up and she was equally insistent that I should form part of the defence line against grief. I no longer found her intimidating, and remained fond of this generous sweet-natured woman for the rest of her life.

That evening, plans were formulated for the next few days. The village lawyer was telephoned at home, and he promised to deal with all the details the following morning: how to deal with the Irish authorities, how to apply for permission urgently to leave the country, and a hundred other things. Suddenly, subtly, I was drawn into this family; really doing nothing but sensing that I had serious masculine responsibility for the first time in my life.

As sharp confirmation that childhood was slipping behind me, I got my RAF papers a few days later. There were a lot of them, including a railway voucher to Weston-super-Mare in the west country. 'You are instructed to report to . . . the medical examination will last approximately from . . .' There were notes about swearing loyalty to King and Country in order to become a proper airman. Already Paul Roberts's kindly smile was disappearing in my consciousness like the grin of the Cheshire cat, and the peremptory voice of military authority was sounding distantly and ominously.

In the train my mind was filled with old doubts and now rusting principles. Voices from the past murmured about the evils and futility of war, the sanctity of human life. Intellectually, Sydney Carter had been my guide and mentor, while Martin Rivers was the masterly hero of school. Their ways had divided, but should I, after all, have followed in the trail of Sydney's ambulance rather than the flight path of Martin's Hurricane? Perhaps there had been too much introvertism at Frensham. If so, it was coming out now. I had only hours to decide, and to confuse things even further I felt a twinge of good old-fashioned fear creeping over me. Then I thought of my boyhood hero, Captain Albert Ball VC, fighter ace of the First World War. Forty-four victories! But a few days after his last, he was killed, I also recalled.

Then, would I ever live with the shame of backing out now? I thought not, climbed down to the station platform and strode out, back straight, to do my duty. I was fit all right. I raced from doc to doc, pausing with the optical doc only long enough for him actually to exclaim at my sight – 'Well, young razor eyes – off you go.' And the swearing-in process at the end of it all was got through with unseemly haste, I thought. My hand was on the Bible for perhaps one and a half seconds – 'next please'.

My mood going back to London on the return journey was quite different from the doubt-ridden outward trip. I looked round the compartment, crowded with middle-aged anonymous men and women, and already felt the smooth touch of the silk scarf, glanced down to the undone top button indicating fighter pilot, and the golden splash of the wings above my top left pocket, medal ribbons shining below – well, perhaps not medals quite yet, but soon. I experienced a slight flash of resentment that these civilians about me had not recognised they were in the presence of the Captain Ball of World War II or soon to be anyway. After all, I had volunteered, hadn't I? A word of acknowledgement, please.

I went down to see my mother and father at Brighton. In the selfish way of an eighteen-year-old, I could not make out their attitude to my decision. My father had not thought much of me through adolescence, seeming to disapprove of more or less anything I did. I once plucked up courage to show him one of my stories. He handed it back without a word. Once he remarked, as I wrote, 'At your scribbles again!' The tone told all. He thought my purchase of a lightweight portable typewriter a ridiculous extravagance, and said so. The loss of his respect and affection was a considerable deprivation, and one of the reasons why I preferred the little cottage in Bushey to Marecote, Cornwall Gardens, Preston Park. Now, he appeared to disapprove of my being in the RAF as much as he had disapproved of my being in ARP, partly, no doubt, because I had hurt his beloved Meg by living with another family.

It was an awkward but mercifully brief occasion. My mother was as sweet and affectionate as ever, and while not uttering approval or any nonsense about 'Good luck – we're proud of you' in front of my father, was clearly apprehensive about my future in the air. Well, so had I been, once. I tried to put the fate of Philip Cox out of my mind, and think about Captain Ball VC, and returned to Bushey. A few days later orders came to report to ACRC Regent's Park, London. Suspecting that they did not do much flying in the

Royal Parks, I packed some basic human comforts, as ordered, in brown paper, which, I was told, must be retained 'for the return of your clothes'. It might have been hospital I was going to for an operation, and it felt about the same.

5

Young Man
Goes West

When I folded my clothes, wrapped them in brown paper and tied the string, I felt I was despatching for ever my former life. All I had now to remind me of my civilian past was my watch and wallet and washing things, and they became disproportionately important in their familiarity.

In St John's Wood we lived in requisitioned luxury flats overlooking the tree-lined canal and the hundreds of acres of Regent's Park. As far as was practical, these flats, each costing hundreds of thousands of pounds today, were made fit for war and the lowest form of human life, RAF cadets. The windows were bricked up and we could only glimpse the park through a vent. There was no heating or lighting and the lifts were inoperative. In the lobby the only lighting illuminated ferocious notices about KRs, which turned out to be King's Regulations, which in turn prohibited almost everything at the risk of suffering awful punishment.

If life was fairly austere for the cadets, it could not have been much fun for the corporals who had direct control over us, in flights of fifty, and the penguin, or wingless wonder, officers whose sole function was to supervise the corporals and the ever-flowing river of young humanity, or semi-humanity. We were at ACRC to be card-indexed, intelligence-tested, kitted out, inoculated and kept out of mischief until we were despatched to our initial training. Flying was still months away so we got only the standard issue boots, long coarse underwear, two shirts (one in the wash once a week), uniform blue trousers, jacket, overcoat, cape (airman for the use of) and gas cape (airman not for the use of, we hoped) and service gasmask.

Looking around at the young men of my flight, I was puzzled and dismayed by their variable quality – in appearance, physique and intelligence. It certainly cut down to size any conceit you might have enjoyed after passing through medical and interview so far. It was not until later that we learned that only about 13% of these cadets ever got into the air. A good many of them were eliminated even here, before the beginning of their training. Many came from the industrial north, Glasgow and Liverpool where conditions between the wars, and unemployment, did not offer much of a start in life. Many also seemed to talk in a foreign language, and for this reason Geordie, Scouse, Welsh and Scots tribes quickly formed, and went out birding and boozing in the evenings. There was a scattering of public-school boys, future officer material, who were as swift to spot their own kind and took taxis into the West End for an evening at Hatchetts.

Rugby and Harrow, secondary schools on Tyneside and the Clyde, all prepared their pupils for this sort of rough institutional life better than Frensham Heights did. If there had been beatings at ACRC it would not have bothered them in the least. At a time when class divisions had scarcely begun to collapse, I had willy-nilly been excluded from working-class life and habits, just as the self-confidence bred into public-school boys had been alien to our Frensham creed. Gently nurtured, that was me.

On the other hand I was much better equipped physically than many of these working-class lads. We marched a great deal to kill time, we did PT in the park and on Primrose Hill, we lined up for indescribably ghastly food at the zoo, for ninety minutes or more, and there were always several who fainted from revulsion or hunger. One day we marched to the members' pavilion at Lord's cricket ground, no less. There we lined up beneath the baleful gaze of W. G. Grace, dropped our trousers for venereal check, and received several jabs, too many for some, who collapsed to the sacred floorboards.

Intelligence tests eliminated more cadets, and like a bomber squadron's breakfast table after a bad night over the Rühr, there were many empty gaps after the first ten days. But what did the authorities think they were up to? Surely a more stringent check when signing on would have saved all this waste of time?

It was a brief spell at St John's Wood, and I shall remember it for the cry of the baboons and wolves, the eerie call of the hoopoe birds, the smell of the greasy food and unclean blankets, and the murderous crash of the 4.5-inch guns on Primrose Hill a quarter-mile away when raiders came over during the short summer nights. But, above all, I recall my miserable state of mind – and downright feebleness – at suffering a period of almost total non-communication with my fellows. Not a very good start. Captain Ball VC indeed! *He* had lots of friends.

There was less cause for grumbling and self-pity at the next destination. On a sunny summer's day, we marched from our St John's Wood 'barracks', kitbags on our right shoulder, to Paddington railway station. 'You're going to 'ave a nice 'oliday by the seaside,' declared our flight's corporal, introducing the element of sarcasm junior NCOs felt obliged to include in every observation, comment and rebuke. In this case, the sarcasm was somewhat misplaced, however. We might well have been a troop of Boy Scouts off to summer camp in fair Devonshire, kitbags instead of rucksacks and 'Eskimo Nell' rather than 'One man went to mow . . .' on our lips. At Babbacombe station we piled out of our train with many a friendly obscenity, but we could not complain about our camping site. No canvas and duckboards for us but a very nicely situated three-star hotel with views over the shimmering sea.

Like our previous place, carpets, curtains and other luxuries had been removed, but at least there was glass in the windows, hot water and lighting, and a recreation hall with ping-pong table. A verandah overlooking the garden and sea evoked middle-class holidaymakers taking tea – 'Indian or China, ma'am?' – Phyllis still in her Jansen costume demurely half-concealed by beachgown.

Our flight's success or failure, happiness or misery, depended on our corporal. Corporal Jones was a short, dark Welshman, not fearsome of mien, but as we quickly discovered not to be treated disrespectfully. For a year and a half, almost since the beginning of the war, he had been dealing with a new green lot of cadets every eight weeks and had learned his lessons well, especially the lesson on *how far to go* at suitable moments for relaxing discipline and becoming matey. We all pronounced him a success at the finish of the course.

At Babbacombe No. 1 Initial Training Wing we worked a near twelve-hour day, seven days a week. Sunday morning Church Parade for RCs and C of Es: anyone else and especially agnostics scrubbed the mess and kitchen floors on the principle that if you did not want Godliness there was no escaping cleanliness. The rest of the time we had lectures on armament. Stripping and reassembling the Lewis gun, sighted and then blindfold, seemed an odd exercise though it had heroic implications. Aircraft identification, with models suspended from the ceiling, seemed more relevant to the needs of a fighter-pilot, and so did clay-pigeon shooting. This provided the great majority of us for the first time with the heady scent of spent explosive as well as sorting out the sharp and less sharp shots. I was below average. Morse code, by lamp and flag, air navigation which included vectors and drift and magnetic and real north and other tiresome terms, seemed equally irrelevant. Captain Ball flew by the seat of his pants and that was for me, too.

A number of our lot were failed before halfway through initial training, and seconded – poor fellows – to GDs or general duties, which could mean anything, like scrubbing the mess and kitchen floors *every* day. A great deal of time was spent square-bashing in the neat little Babbacombe parks with lobelia-lined flower beds and retired colonels reading the *Daily Telegraph*, not best pleased with all the row we made. Then little Corporal Jones strode out ahead of us on route marches around the hilly little resort. We were encouraged to sing, and in my bourgeois self-consciousness I hoped we would not break into 'She'll be coming round the mountain when she comes . . . She'll be wearing silk pyjamas when she comes . . .' We always did.

We might end up, like the Boy Scouts, with a bracing swim from a cove, naked with a guard on duty. We really needed a lifeguard, too, as only a few of the posher cadets could swim and it was an interesting example of class distinction seeing the nobs far out in the Channel before returning with elegant crawl through the splashing Geordies and Cockneys in the shallows.

Our flight was further fined down as the weeks passed and we began our exams. 'Now boys,' Corporal Jones addressed us in his powerful Swansea accent, 'you have been treated fairly and we've been good friends.' He cast his eyes over our ranks, standing at ease after a five-mile march. 'I want you to do well in these exams, for your sake of course, boys. But also for mine as good results reflect well on me as well as your instructors.'

Jones got a fair result and only two or three failed. We went out to celebrate and I became quickly and abominably drunk on gin. It's the wrong drink for early excess and I was sick onto the floor by my bunk. The next morning, feeling ill, came the culminating moment of the course, when we were promoted from Aircraftsman

Second Class to Leading Aircraftsman – 1338428 LAC Hough, R.A. Five bob a day instead of two.

I was beginning to feel a smoother-turning cog in the system now, and my letters home and to Charlotte were less complaining. However modest my achievement, I had succeeded where others had failed. I began to look differently at my contemporaries and made one or two friends. And then, as material confirmation that we were soon off on our first scramble to Angels Ten, we were issued with our flying gear.

Photographs of RAF pilots beside their Spitfires showed them wearing white overalls. Very chic. But here before us on the Stores counter, it looked as if we were going to fly open cockpit 1917 Sopwith Pups in a new dogfight with the Red Baron. First you slipped on a roughly contoured dark brown eiderdown, then another layer over it and finally the Sidcot Suit, an all-enveloping neutral coloured garment with zip pockets for maps and a very fancy fur collar, actually not for warmth but to protect the ever turning neck searching the sky for the enemy.

For the protection of hands on joystick and throttle at high altitudes, the order was silk linings, woollen gloves and great fur-lined leather gauntlets. Equally beautiful and of the same high quality were the thick woollen socks and wool-lined leather flying boots. And finally, with beating hearts, we handled our lined leather flying helmets, with goggles which included a hinged smoked glass panel to help to watch for the Hun in the sun.

One of the informal lessons we learned at No. 1 ITW concerned RAF slang. Just as trades and professions, especially the medical profession, had developed a jargon of their own to reassure themselves in their exclusivity, so the young RAF, twenty-three years old, had created and relished its slang. 'Wizard prang!' exclaimed Corporal Jones. 'You must know what that means. It means a bloody bad crash.' 'And Harry clampers, Corp?' 'Bad weather, too bad for flying. And a wizard prang probably means you've had it, or gone for a Burton or gone for the chop.'

Anxious to be seen as veterans, we absorbed all this new language, and used it, too often at first. 'What's the gen [or intelligence]?' we would ask one another. There were three sorts of gen. Gen, duff gen and ace gen. Only the last had any sort of truth behind it, the second you did not bother to listen to, and the first you treated with grave suspicion.

As the time came for our departure from our summer seaside

holiday, fit and brown, the gen began to fly. We were going to Cambridge, South Africa, Canada, and surely duffest of duff gen, the USA. Before that we would have no leave, forty-eight-hour leave, seventy-two-hour leave. In desperation one of us broke into the CO's office and extracted the ace gen from his desk. It proved to be the duffest gen of all.

In the event, on 3rd October 1941 we were all packed into a trooptrain and despatched to Wilmslow outside Manchester where an enormous transit camp had been built, seemingly endless rows of Nissen huts, linked by duckboards (just as well, for it never stopped raining), a parade ground, officers' and NCOs' quarters, and admin offices. All transit camps are about the same. Some are dirtier than others, some have less unspeakable food than others, but none can be expected to show much individuality or provide much useful occupation.

For the twelve days we were at Wilmslow, there were three occupations according to the time of the day. In the morning we were sent to Stores, where in turn we were issued with Arctic kit (most elaborate), tropical kit, and kit. Finally, as if we were about to be discharged already or perhaps seconded to MI5, we were kitted out with civvy clothes, from trilby hat to black shoes, white shirts, coloured tie, 1 for airman's use of, double-breasted suit and a very long Nazi Party-like belted raincoat. Correct size was not a high priority. One or two of us looked like Max Miller, mine was decidedly on the short, cramped side. Finally, a cheap, bookie's fibre suitcase was thrown at us, with orders to put the whole lot in it. Thousands of these gents' suitings were issued at Wilmslow. Whatever happened to them all? In the evening we went out and drank beer. For twelve days, Captain Ball VC seemed more distant than ever, but by 15th October we were back in another troop train, with suitcase and kitbag. The ace gen was that we were embarking in a troopship.

Rail travel in Britain in 1941 was a slow and speculative business. The whole system was overloaded because of the needs of war, and bombing had disrupted lines, and anyway it all had to be conducted in almost total darkness during the night. We rattled and puffed our way north through the night, and I awoke when the train was crawling up Shap Fell in the Lake District. Rising and falling in the half-light, far into the distance, were the fells which I could recognise and which I had climbed in those comfortable holidays of peacetime. The sight was so poignant that I was tempted in one mad moment to step from the train, away from the unknown and back to the known and loved. Everyone else in the compartment was asleep, Mrs Wilson at Easedale Lodge was a day's walk distant, and I could climb up by Sour Milk Ghyll, smell the bracken, listen to the music of the sheep and, above, the mournful cry of the buzzards. The coarseness of service life would slip away and I would be as I used to be, in shorts with a rucksack on my back, free to do whatever I desired.

Our train breasted the summit of Shap, and at once picked up speed, faster and faster, with the pace and inevitability with which I had been drawn, without fully understanding why, into the gigantic machine of war. Others woke up with the increase in speed and the rocking of the carriage, and in a few minutes the new normality of life, the obscenities and cigarette lighting and grumbling and speculation, took over.

In the late afternoon, our trooptrain rattled to a halt in the shattered dockland of Glasgow. All about us was the devastation of a city bombed night after night during the previous winter and spring of 1941. Enough of the nearby quay had been cleared of rubble to accommodate a mighty liner alongside. We were not out of our seats before the gen began to flash along the length of the train. She was the *Louis Pasteur*, a French liner built to snatch the Blue Riband from Britain, still uncompleted at the fall of France, delayed by communist strikes and sabotage and with a kink in her keel leading to cork-screwing at speed. A real devil, ran the gen, with accommodation so frightful that Canadians and New Zealanders had refused to sail in her. Now we were to be put to the test. Would we pass? If I had known what we were in for I would have become the Fletcher Christian of any mutiny.

Sixteen months later, Jock Colville, the youngest of Churchill's Secretariat, sailed to South Africa to learn to fly under similar conditions to ours. When he arrived, he despatched by diplomatic bag (he was a very privileged cadet) a letter of stinging complaint to Clementine Churchill, knowing she would show it to her husband. Investigations into troopship conditions, revealing the contrasting luxury of officer accommodation with the animal-like living of the lower ranks, led to his return passage as a pilot officer being almost as uncomfortable as the outward journey as a lowly cadet, hoist with his own petard, as he confessed.

We were packed into the messdecks of the *Louis Pasteur* in three layers, in hammocks above the mess tables, on the mess tables, and on the teak deck under the mess tables. Seasickness was rampant before we had left the Clyde Estuary and continued throughout the ten-day passage. The stench was frightful, the tedium almost unbearable. Apart from our sleeping space, there was nowhere to go except the open decks above. There were buckets and taps of seawater, the lavatories were lengths of horizontally disposed tree trunk above a trough of ceaselessly mobile excreta. When a storm blew up, I dug myself a nest in a large pile of potatoes and went into nauseated hibernation for two days and nights.

As the days passed the gen ran that there were even worse conditions down in the scuppers below. A couple of us descended steel ladders and discovered several thousand Canadian troops living in the twilight of a Hogarthian hell, smoking those dreadful Canadian caporals, drinking beer and Bourbon, and playing interminable poker. If this had been an east-bound passage they would long since have mutinied and taken over the ship, these tough Canucks from the northern farms and forests told us forcefully. But these troops were going *home*, discharged for compassionate or medical reasons, and not a complaint crossed their lips.

Our great liner cork-screwed herself west, officers and nurses and a handful of civilians occupying some of the state cabins (the others were bolted), dancing at night to a string quartet whose music sometimes filtered down to our slums. One or two of their menus filtered down, too, stoking the fires of mutiny. For a while we had a battleship and a half flotilla of destroyers to escort us, but the destroyers could not keep up in the storm, and the battleship left us, too, five hundred miles out of Halifax. It was only five months since the *Bismarck* and *Prinz Eugen* had been loose in these waters, and the U-boat war was approaching its climax. The *Pasteur* now pushed up her speed to 33 knots (the gen had it) and the yawing was worse than ever.

We docked at Halifax on the evening of 25th October. This commonplace Canadian port and city at once assumed the guise of peacetime Blackpool or Coney Island. After more than two years of blackout in Britain and a crossing in darkness, 'the light that never was on sea or land' – the street lights, the lights of homes, factories, offices and dockland, the lights of buses and cars moving along the wide streets – was blinding and almost shocking. The train awaiting us, a great snorting beast with cowcatcher and massive smokestack, was equally unreal, with deep leather seats, spittoons, a smoking car and velvet curtains. Without delay, we thrust off

48

into the darkness through forests and fairy-tale log cabin villages.

At 3 a.m., with much masculine huffing and panting, we came to a halt at the first large station since Halifax. RCAF officers and redcaps were on the platform and soon had us organised into flights. The gen was that we were now going to march to our barracks. Fantasy descended upon us like the snowflakes which had just begun to whisper to the ground about us. We began marching off into a forest.

No one was quite sure where we should be going but we had utter trust in Canadian efficiency and hospitality. We had been told there was no welcome like a Canadian welcome, our friends in peace, our allies in war. Very wet and cold, three-quarters of an hour later, we heard the faint sounds of hammering and the calling of many deep voices in the darkness. We stumbled into a patch of light, and also into one of those traditional fairy-tales in which an army of gnomes builds a fairy queen's palace overnight. Ahead of us was a scene of controlled chaos and industry the like of which I had never seen.

Arc-lit in the night, a township was going up before our very eyes – a township of wooden huts in rows, of a main street and what might have been municipal buildings. The fronts of the half-completed buildings looked like façades, and as we got nearer the fairy-tale effect faded and the scene was more of studio workers hurrying a movie set to completion before the star arrived. But we, the cast of thousands, were already there, and well before our time. The great new Royal Canadian Air Force Transit Camp at Moncton was not yet ready for its guests.

There was not much Authority could say except to advise us to make do as best we might. A scratch meal would be served in the half-roofed mess hut in about one hour, we could go into town and seek hospitality there (at 4 a.m.), or settle into some of the more complete huts. Several of us opted for the last course. The carpenters, hammering and sawing away like men possessed, had lit fires of plank offcuts on the floor of the huts they were working on. I recall collapsing exhausted dangerously close to one of these, and sinking into a deep sleep with the scent of sawdust in my nostrils, and snowflakes brushing my face.

For three days and nights a thousand or more airmen led a life of nomadic improvisation. The local people treated this unexpected arrival of young men from the old country with amazing hospitality. Many of us slept between sheets in their spare rooms or in their cars. Others built themselves huts in the woods, making free use of the timber intended for the camp. Bacon and eggs on a scale we had not seen since the days of peace were piled up for us, free in the homes, at special prices in the drugstores. There was even time for a seduction or two among the more ardent cadets.

On the third day an order, the only one given at Moncton, spread that we were to assemble on the muddy clearance that would one day be a parade ground, with our kit. An officer then walked slowly through this mob dividing it into two groups, one twice the size of the other. By the grace of God, I found myself in the smaller group of some three hundred, for the word spread like a forest fire in a gale: we were destined for the USA. Nor was it duff gen or gen; it was ace gen. America, a land of peace and plenty, of pretty girls and pretty big steaks, of skyscrapers, giant automobiles and world famous hospitality. Nothing, surely, could add further spice to my luck. But, oh yes it could. A very tall Canadian Flight-Sergeant with a bunch of folders under his arm barked at us, 'Form yourselves into flights of fifty – and make it smart.'

And so we did, awaiting our fate, while the sergeant, arbitrarily selecting a commander of one flight, thrust a folder into his arms. 'You're for Oklahoma – get moving', 'You lot – Alabama – you lucky people, if there are any survivors I'll eat my boots', 'Tyrell, Texas, for you, the good Lord help you', and at last to us. He eyed us doubtfully, selected a tall, rather serious old man of fully twenty-three and handed him a folder clearly marked CALIFORNIA. 'Your train leaves in half an hour.'

'Where's Lancaster, Flight?'

'In a valley outside Los Angeles. And you really *are* the lucky guys. Yours is civilian run. Most of the other schools are run by the Army Air Corps, and, boy, are they tough!'

The other, larger group of some seven hundred cadets was being similarly segregated and assigned to Canadian flying training schools. We felt very superior. What we had seen of Canada and Canadians was reassuring all right, but could not compare with the pulsating excitement and mystery of Texas or Alabama. As for California, the related words sparkled in the grey Moncton sky of early winter: Los Angeles, Beverly Hills, Hollywood, Sunset Boulevard, film stars, Goodman playing at the Hippodrome . . . Never had an RAF flight marched so eagerly, with a song on our lips and a gleam in our eye, to the next destination.

6

Per Astra
ad Ardua

On 29th October 1941, our mighty trans-continental train steamed into Los Angeles main terminal. It had been a really comfortable and pleasant five-day journey, across the plains of Iowa and Nebraska to Salt Lake City, then over the Rockies, across the deserts of Nevada and down into LA. There was some trouble with French-Canadians in Montreal when we left the train for a drink, and again in Chicago with the Irish, but otherwise we were warmly received, especially in Salt Lake City. We dutifully but not altogether seriously changed into our civvy suits to cross the frontier in order to avoid offending the American Neutrality Act, looking at once like an ill-dressed bunch of schoolchildren close to riot. Then we resumed our old guise, in which we were variously mis-identified as Guatemalan firemen on a spree and Mexican frontier guards.

There was no confusion at LA. Here we were received on the platform by a large body of women with their daughters, a welcoming party with touching little presents and visiting cards – 'Just call us any time, honey, and we'll meet you and take you to our homes.' There was only one way to deal with this and that was to mark the cards according to the attraction rating of the girls, and it had to be done rapidly as we were bidden to another train, a snorting beast with cowcatcher of the type much used in Westerns, one imagined, to take us out to the Mojave Desert, Lancaster and our airfield.

I found myself driving through Lancaster recently, and there was nothing of the old small town left. It had become a city. Fifty years ago there was main street, a saloon, post office, grocery store, drugstore with juke box ('Chatanooga Chou-Chou', 'I Don't

51

Want to Set the World on Fire'), saloon and that was about it. Most of the long-distance trains charged straight through, sirens moaning hauntingly, firebox glowing. On still nights the sound faded slowly until, once again, the sound of the coyotes took over.

On that first evening, a coach awaited our arrival and we piled in for the six-mile drive to No. 2 British Flying Training School, feeling distinctly un-British by now but quite glad about the name. The wonderfully named Polaris Flight Academy was one unit of the Arnold Scheme set up under Lend-Lease to train RAF pilots away from the hurly-burly of war and the unfavourable climate of Britain. I cannot recall the loss of a single day's flying during the seven months we were there. There could be sharp desert frosts at night but at 3,000 feet above sea level, the days were balmy even in mid-winter and the clarity of the atmosphere was wonderful for flying.

Not until the following morning did we become aware of the nature of our Academy, and what we saw we liked, very much. The camp was made up of chalets which were arranged, like the much larger single-storey classrooms and admin, recreation and dining blocks, around a large lawn. In the centre of all this there flew from a single pole the flags of the USA and RAF, in that order to emphasise who really owned the place.

A short distance away, like brooding sentinels, were two large hangars, with the control tower between them, while in neat lines sat the three classes of training planes we were to fly. At last, after three months and 6,500 miles, and about time too, here was the real thing. I felt distinctly Captain Ballish now, especially as the open cockpit biplane primary trainers, all struts and wires and doped canvas, looked as if they had been designed to fight the Red Baron.

Next, we followed the heavenly breakfast scents to the dining block. I stared down the length of it. Behind the line of shining hot plates, cookers and tables stood a team of chefs, white hats bobbing as they tossed wheatcakes, broke open eggs single-handed with electric speed, scooped up sizzling strips of bacon. Their wisecracks were as fast as their cooking and they were all smiling . . . our minds inevitably swam back to the less fragrant corridors of London's zoo.

Before we got to the cooking part we were invited to load up with individual packets of cereal, great jugs of cream (proper cream, the sort you cannot buy in America today in case you get a heart attack), toast, honey, piles of butter and individual bottles of milk.

We were evidently not going to starve; nor, we discovered later, were we going to suffer the full rigours of discipline. This Academy was presided over by a squadron-leader and flight-lieutenant, officers of infinite goodwill and amiability, as well they might be in this billet of ultimate remoteness and privilege. Equally gentle, liberal and kindly were the ground instructors loaned from the learned corridors of UCLA, University of California, Los Angeles.

By contrast, and some contrast, were the flying instructors. These tough, scarred veterans had been either crop-dusters or stunt fliers from the movie studios and were accustomed either to flying below twenty feet above the farming acres of southern California, or simulating aerial dogfights or gory crashes following combat. Accustomed as they were to informal wear, Authority had issued them with khaki uniform and little silver wings, which fitted about as well as our civilian gear. They swore and spat a great deal and could fly like angels, but their patience with pupils was not infinite. A Mr Gordon took me in hand. Mr Gordon was of the crop-duster breed, sandy-haired, with a broken nose, close-set eyes, deeply lined skin in which it appeared there had settled the dust of his calling since 1927. Like his stature, his fuse was on the short side, and he used 'goddam' like Australians use 'bloody'. 'Goddam it, I'm going to throw you around the goddam sky,' were his first words to me.

'Air experience', this first flight was called, and some experience it was. Like an ancient public rite, it was clearly given to every cadet to see if they would crack, the principle being, I suppose, to sort out the men from the boys before wasting time on the timid. Every flying evolution conceived since the Wright brothers took to the air, spins and chandelles, inverted flight and lazy eights, flick rolls and (even worse) slow rolls. If Mr Gordon had not piled it on so heavily I should certainly have been sick as a dog, but the sheer speed and the terror the performance caused me drove out any idea of airsickness, though it was all I could do to hold it down as I staggered towards the locker room after landing, leaving dreams of Captain Ball high in the blue sky.

The Stearman PT13, the standard American primary trainer, was the student pilot's friend, forgiving yet responsive, vice-free and tough. It could be stalled at ten feet on landing and take no offence. It could equally be stalled at 5,000 feet and the gentlest pressure forward on the stick brought you out of it. I came to love it second only to the Tiger Moth later which was a touch daintier but not so strong. After more than eight hours of 'goddamming' from Mr Gordon he told me to 'stay in the fucking cockpit' when we landed. It was his method of telling me to solo and he appeared to have extinguished any further interest in me.

The emptiness in the forward cockpit matched that in my stomach, but war, as I was to discover on rather more critical occasions, consists mainly of doing involuntarily ridiculous things you would never dream of doing if common sense still ruled. I did not want to take this goddam Stearman into the California sky *all by myself.* I knew now that this thing Mr Gordon called a ship took off all too easily and once that had happened it was a matter of getting it down again, which was a great deal more difficult, or taking to the parachute. What was more, the whole of my course, many of whom had already been through this ordeal, were lined up on seats in the sun watching my every move. I knew exactly when their interest would be sparked. Not at take-off, too easy; not in the circuit, which was routine; but at the *landing*.

Their interest accorded with mine. Up over the boundary fence, scrubland below, level off when the altimeter registered 1,000 feet, bank-and-turn left, left again, shrug off the loneliness, parallel with runway, and beyond, clearly identifiable, the little figures of my mates, agog for the culmination. Over the familiar farmstead which marked the turn in, back with throttle, glide in, steady now, peaceful without Mr Gordon's goddammits coming through the tube, but too high and then too low, a touch of throttle.

As everyone knows, the act of landing an aeroplane consists of causing it to travel progressively more slowly until it can no longer support itself in the air and has therefore to be supported by the ground. The switchover of responsibility must, as far as possible, coincide with the wheels being close to the ground. If you lose momentum too early the aeroplane drops through space, too late and it bounces up again eager for more flying.

My first solo landing was unique in the annals of aviation because it combined both misjudgements and led to *three* rapidly successive landings. My memory, even immediately afterwards, was dim because my eyes were tight shut. However, I lived and the wheels were not crushed, and later I was even able to taxi the good, brave old Stearman back to its parking place.

'Not bad – three for the price of one!' crowed one of my mates who had soloed perfectly after six hours.

Just as at Frensham Heights School our latest love affair was often a distraction from other things, like lessons, so at the Polaris Flight Academy, even when in the air, our thoughts were never far from Los Angeles, Beverly Hills and Hollywood. Out here, with the San Gabrielle Mountains separating us from our Mecca, we had nightly evidence in the glow in the southern sky that all was well in movieland. For big first nights, like the one for *The Birth of the Blues* starring Bing Crosby and Louis Armstrong, searchlights patterned the sky with their beams, just as they had at Wilmslow during raids on Manchester, for less celebratory reasons.

The first real friend I had made in the RAF was a dark, slim, good-looking boy called Allan Palmer. We had conspired together on the subject of gaining social entry into movieland but before we could effect anything, Hollywood opened her arms wide and invited our entire course to a welcome-to-movieland party. It came in the form of an inflexible embossed card and in the name of 'Ronald Colman and his friends', and was two Saturdays hence. Worth waiting for, so we decided against a pre-emptive strike.

At mid-afternoon a coach turned up at the Polaris Flight Academy and we piled in, looking unusually well scrubbed and shaved. Almost two hours later, after following the pass over the San Gabrielle Mountains, a road that was to become as familiar as Oxford Street, heading down Sunset Boulevard and climbing again into the exclusive heights of Bel Air, we halted outside the clubhouse of the Golf Club. Cicadas chirruped, the moon peeked down at us through the palm trees, and from within we caught the sound of dance music played by – who else? – Ray Noble.

Our hosts and hostesses, mostly British, had wisely arrived well before us in order to tank up for the ordeal they faced. What, they must have asked themselves, what, in the name of God, were they going to do with some fifty British youths between 7.30 p.m. and the time they could decently claim they had done their duty? Whatever it was to be, it would, they had reasoned, be less difficult with a few very dry martinis under the belt.

A chorus of welcome greeted us. The music ceased. The Duke of Beverly Hills, Ronald Colman himself and his beautiful multi-sequinned wife Benita Hume were at the door. 'It is great – really great – that you could come.' 'There's scotch, gin, or beer, not like the old country's beer but the best we can do out here in the colonies . . .'

I looked about me in wonder and awe. I was nineteen, exceedingly raw and unsophisticated, without social training beyond what a progressive co-ed school had provided. What I now faced was an extravagant set from one of those movies starring Melvyn Douglas and Myrna Loy. And, to add verisimilitude, who was that over there, smiling that familiar dimpled smile, but Myrna Loy? And next to her – could it be? – yes, it was Charles Boyer.

It was like turning the pages of a fanmag. Never, since, have I been to a major beanfeast at which I knew everyone. There was that old trouper Edna Best, that wonderful old joker C. Aubrey Smith, wiping the beer froth from his grey moustache. And gorgeous, mysterious Kay Francis, Alan Jones the singing chap, Artur Rubinstein poised suitably over the ivories of his Bechstein, and, representing that 14b Baker Street duo, Basil Rathbone impersonating Sherlock Holmes and Nigel Bruce puffing on Dr Watson's pipe. Ida Lupino and Maureen O'Sullivan fought for my favours, Maureen winning the contest and taking me by the hand to a corner by a window, a martini the colour and size of a tumbler of cold water in my other hand.

The sequence of events was never clear, even immediately after this party, but some of them stand out in my memory (supported by surviving letters to Charlotte) fifty years later.

Tall and very British Brian Aherne was heard calling out to Alan Jones, 'Come on, Alan, let's have it.' And his new petite wife, Joan Fontaine, who had just won the Oscar for best actress in *Suspicion* with Cary Grant, backed him up. So did her sister, flawlessly elegant, Olivia de Havilland.

What were we to expect? Alan Jones should give us what? I should have known, and soon did when Chief Host and Benign Ruler of all things British in Hollywood, Ronald Colman, gave his ruling support: 'I say, Alan old boy, I think you ought to give it to the troops.'

This decided things. With a little help from his friends, like putting him onto Artur Rubinstein's piano and steadying him when he was up there, Alan Jones broke into 'The Donkey Serenade'. 'There's a song in the air and the sweet señorita . . .'

Another monster dry martini had slipped down my throat, and I was now behind the curtain on the window seat with Maureen

O'Sullivan. 'Isn't this cosy?' she commented, and I agreed. The scent of Chanel and Booths gin floated over me. 'Who would you like most to talk to just now?' she asked, and before I could consider this very fully, thankfully added, 'Anywhere in the world, because you see I am very good on thought transference.'

Like the crass dolt I certainly was, I said I'd like to talk to my fiancée 6,500 miles away in war-torn Britain. She thought that was not difficult, so long as we held hands very tightly. I did my best.

Other happenings worth recording were dancing with my Maureen, talking cricket with C. Aubrey Smith who ran the famous Hollywood Cricket Club and was short of players – 'This damn war's taking away all the best youngsters, though God bless them,' he added hastily. Then listening in awed silence to an amazingly drunk Reggie Gardiner doing (several times) his rendering of a 4-6-4 LMS locomotive drawing the 10.45 Glasgow express out of Euston, up the famous incline past the Roundhouse, and into Primrose Hill Tunnel – first the skidding and then the steady straining, clickety-click, clickety-click over the points, gathering speed, the strong whistle before going into the tunnel. How he was cheered! Good old Reggie.

Brian Aherne slipped me a card. 'Joan and I would love to have you for the weekend if you can spare the time.' And he did not seem as drunk as the others either. 'Thanks most awfully.'

'You said earlier you were looking for John Collier. I'll see if I can find him and bring him along.'

Somehow, as they do, the evening drew to a close. Our bus was outside, looking ridiculously prosaic, ready to take us and our light baggage to the YMCA for the night. The moon was setting, the dawn was not far away. Oh Lord, I'm not going to any boring YMCA, I said to myself with unaccustomed grittiness. All around bidding us farewell were white mink coats and the inevitable sequins and leading men in black tie who had told them of their love on a dozen silver screens. 'Terribly decent of you to come, Dick,' declared Ronald Colman. And Benita added, 'We'll see more of you.'

I was especially aware of one lovely dark figure gliding towards me on a slightly zig-zag course. I intercepted her. It was gorgeous Kay Francis, with whom I had earlier danced several times. She had seemed rather melancholy and I had tried to cheer her up. Now I said to her (rather pointedly, come to think of it), 'Do you by any chance know of a cheap hotel near here where I could spend the night?'

This was not strictly speaking a cheap hotel area but Kay was not in the least put out. 'My dear boy, you must come home with me.' And she took my arm and I navigated her towards the biggest Cadillac I could see. I was right. Her black chauffeur advanced to meet us, took the other arm as if not for the first time, and we both bundled into the vast interior.

We purred up the canyons of Bel Air glimpsing the lights of distant mansions between the palms and scrubs. 'Wasn't that a swell party, Dick darling?' I agreed vehemently as her gloved hand patted mine. The hiss of tyres on tarmac changed to the crunch of gravel, always a reassuring sound, especially if it lasts quite a long time, and it did. At length a white mansion of acceptable dimensions hove into view. What was next on the agenda, and what was my expected rôle? With mixed relief and disappointment, I saw a figure spring from the shadows of the porch, and he spoke not as a manservant.

'Kay darling, you *have* been a long time.'

'Oh God, I need a drink,' was the prompt response. The dignified black chauffeur assisted his mistress to the ground and the young man, who took not the least interest in me, helped Kay inside.

Our young friend, who I now saw was quite Levantine in his good looks, did the honours behind the bar, and Kay told him all about the party, and what sweet boys they were, and how brave to be fighting for their country in war-torn Europe. This last mighty highball drove me through the garrulousness of Phase II into Phase III silence but it did not matter. Kay, suddenly practical, took my hand and said she was taking me to the attic. I did not resist. 'Most of the bedroom suites are filled with my furniture. You see, Dick darling, this isn't my real home. I've borrowed it while my new one is being completed.'

My hostess chattered away, now walking straight and purposefully, proving that last drinks can steady you, through several drawing rooms furnished and decorated in various European periods – no shortage of space down here – and up one of those wide and gentle staircases Ginger Rogers and Fred Astaire used to dance down. The room was about the size of the airmen's mess at Wilmslow, but nicer. The bed, a mock Elizabethan four-poster (or it may have been the real thing) was turned down, and on the bedside table was a cornucopia of fruit and a tray of whisky, soda and water.

'That's if you get hungry or thirsty in the night,' she prattled on, 'and there's the bathroom.' There it was indeed, gold, sunken and large. I felt her lips brushing my cheek. 'Come and have breakfast with me in the morning.' And she was gone.

I was awoken at 10 a.m. by a solemn black manservant who informed me that my breakfast would be served in Miss Francis's room, and he gave me much-needed directions.

A heavily alcoholic sleep had finally dispersed all belief in the reality of last night's fairy-tale. Yet here was Queen Titania again, and lovelier than ever, I saw, when I had covered the quarter mile to her reclining throne. No sign anywhere of our fellow from the Levant. Her face that millions idolised looked up at me from the silken pillows and her lovely white arms were spread wide in welcome. Before her on a bed-width tray lay her breakfast – a measure of tomato juice in a dainty cut glass.

'How did you sleep in the attic, Dick dear?' she asked in her deep rather husky voice and as if in regret that I had been alone.

The manservant brought in a man's breakfast, flapping open a sheet-sized Irish linen table napkin across my shaking knees.

Kay was overwhelmed with regret that she was busy today, and would I take one of the cars and drive myself about, perhaps to the observatory or Griffith Park Zoo. 'Pick yourself a girl – they'll clamour to meet you,' but she did not tell me where to find them, just 'There're thousands about this city.'

'Tonight I've fixed for you a pretty chorus girl at Earl Carrol's. She'll pick you up about seven. You'll have fun.'

I might have had more fun if this blonde did not have a chaperone in the shape of the manageress, who watched us as closely as the chorus line on the stage. It was all novel and faintly surrealist but the conversation did lack brilliance, even frequency. Later, back in Bel Air, to which Kay and I separately returned at around midnight, life became curiously interesting again. The young man from the Levant had not reappeared and the staff seemed to have the night off. She led me to her bar and she began to show me how to make Americanos, selecting with steady hand the required ingredients from an extremely wide range of bottles.

As we chattered away, sitting at stools which had become quite adjacent, I began to feel the same symptoms of a metamorphosis, from reality to fantasy, I had experienced the previous evening with all those stars of the silver screen. Admittedly, alcohol may have had some influence in the process but not all that much. And now, after quite a sober evening, I felt it coming over me again strongly.

I was, quite simply, taking part in a scene from a film. There were no cries of 'Action!' 'Camera!' but this was a celluloid world, not the humdrum world of everyday boring life.

In this film world everything was much more intense and fast-moving. As with the stars of the party, sentiments were expressed and actions conducted within seconds of meeting which would normally take weeks or months, if at all. In my bourgeois world of Preston Park, Brighton, you did not call somebody 'darling' *absolutely straightaway*, nor hold hands, tightly, behind curtains, nor brush lips across cheeks and that sort of thing at first meeting. And on the strength of a couple of dances, it was unusual to invite a young man home to what was seemingly an empty house.

So all this was clearly film-acting, and perhaps some time the director would step forward and call 'Cut!' But not yet. A soft hand was on mine. 'Dick, darling, do mix another of those divine Americanos.' No sooner said than done. We talked movieland gossip for a while, she asked me did I have a steady date back home, and the script extended to love and its pitfalls, specifying some of her let-downs and unhappinesses, which was indeed the case, as I learned later.

I lit her another cigarette from the bar lighter, just as David Manners would have done in *Man Wanted*; and she smelt just as she had done in that scene, no doubt, a blend of musk and Chanel. She drew in the smoke deeply, and spoke huskily: 'Do you think we should have just one more – a nightcap?'

I did not disappoint her – a couple of decent tots of vermouth, same of Campari, then the essential gin, stir vigorously, glancing up to give Kay a brief smile, then in with the ice.

'You are quick, Dick darling!' She raised her glass and pouted a kiss.

Later, she said, 'Tomorrow I thought we would lunch at Romanoff's.'

'You are kind, really you are.'

We drove off in the Caddi at 12.30 p.m. after a lazy morning round the pool, Jonah (as the big chauffeur was named) chatting away democratically from the distant driving seat. His favourite subject was movieland gossip which, not surprisingly, he knew more about than most. That morning it was mostly scandal about young Veronica Lake, the one with the blonde hair over one eye.

Romanoff's was dark, discreet, heavily curtained, and boasting air-conditioning, not so commonplace in 1941. It was the venue of the really great stars and their guests. No extra would ever get past *this* door. Count Romanoff received only top-billing actors and actresses (like Ronald Colman, the words 'movie star' never crossed his lips). And they had to be decently behaved, and perforce very rich.

Kay and I were quite early, but Salvador Dali was already slumped over the bar doodling on a menu and disregarding Kay's gay greeting. 'He's often like that at this time of the day,' she commented to me cheerfully and quite loudly. 'Especially when he's working. He's doing the scenery for an MGM movie.' Perhaps he uses the menu for roughing out ideas, I surmised, but said nothing as we were led to our table.

Others of our party began to filter in, peering in the half-light to recognise friends. Like night fighter-pilots, you needed good vision in movieland where all the nightclubs and restaurants were so dim a candle was required to read the menu.

'Do you know Joan Bennett, Dick? Joan, this is my British airman hero.'

'Merle, I think you've met my airman, Dick Hough, from England. He's staying with me – isn't that fun?'

Merle Oberon smiled sweetly, pecked my cheek, and asked Kay where Ginger was. From another table a voice called out from the darkness, 'She's gone to her ranch.' It was, I could just see, Errol Flynn. What a cast this film 'At Romanoff's' had! I learned later that it was Errol's last admission to Romanoff's. He was inclined to be rough in his ways and knocked someone out, a frequent occurrence in the evenings but he was not usually so drunk at mid-day.

A few others from the golf club party turned up, too, the Charles Boyers, Herbert Marshall who was at once besieged by enquiries about his very pregnant wife, and one or two others. It was a long lunch and the cutting room would be strewn later, but I would not have missed a single clip. Talk about ace gen (though of course they did not), by 3 p.m. I must have been the most genned up RAF airman in California about movieland gossip. This stretched widely from seven-year contracts ('Non, non, non – nevair touch!' exclaimed Charles Boyer) to Judy Garland's drinking capacity, and I just hoped I was covering up my eagerness to miss nothing.

From time to time, I was brought into the conversation with great tact and kindness, mostly about the Battle of Britain and the bombing and how ghastly the food rationing must be. Herbert Marshall, who had lost a leg in the 1914–18 war, expressed the earnest hope that RAF bombers were giving the Hun a touch of his own medicine.

Afterwards, learning of my interest in jazz, Herbert Marshall and Merle Oberon took me across the street and gave me carte blanche in a record store. Remembering how I had to save up for a record back home, I settled for Bunny Berigan, Fats Waller and an Artie Shaw, all twelve-inchers. 'Well, you're a modest lad,' commented Herbert Marshall, and nodded towards the salesman. Credit cards might still be years away but in Beverly Hills where every face was familiar, that's all that was needed for credit.

Reggie Gardiner of the train noises strolled into the record shop, twirling a silver-tipped stick and looking every inch the Beverly Hills *boulevardier* under his own steam, so to speak. He was very cheerful, and after greeting the others took me by the arm back towards the tempting racks. The salesman did not have to ask what he wanted, and out came another twelve-incher, 'Trains, by Reginald Gardiner'. 'Gosh, thanks,' I articulated, and he asked to see my other records. 'Very good taste, too,' he commented with a flashing smile.

Later, as we purred back to her Bel Air mansion, Kay said, not unkindly, 'You should have asked Reggie to sign it.' I went hot at my gaucheness and apologised. She put her gloved hand on mine. 'Never mind – perhaps you'll see him again.'

My next clanger was a good deal worse: an ace clanger, in front of all people, Ginger Rogers. 'Would you like to come with me for drinks with Ginger?' Kay asked me the following weekend.

By no means blasé (I never became so, either, in this star-studded other life), if one was attempting to grade the elevation of these unbelievably famous figures of the golden screen, then to me Ginger was the Mount Everest, the *ne plus ultra*, of them all.

I think I managed not to whistle through my teeth and indicated by simple words 'Yes, please.'

Ginger's gloriously beautiful, familiar face lit up sweetly as I was introduced, '. . . straight from war-torn England.' She was sucking through a straw an immensely complicated super-ice cream soda topped with fruit. Behind her there reared up like a golden Würlitzer the machinery for mixing her concoctions. Beneath it on shelves were the many-coloured jars and bottles of flavours, an ice cream dispenser and an ice-making machine. Nearer to hand, to

which Ginger often stretched one for a grape, was a colossal cornucopia of fresh fruit: not only acme of beauty, acme of health too.

'So you're a flier, Dick. Tell me about flying.'

Well, I had fully twenty hours in my logbook. Of course I could
tell her about flying. I told her of loops and Immelmanns, spins
and rolls, and generally hinted at my dexterity with the joystick.
'And to spin off the top,' I continued implacably, feeling suddenly
very Captain Ballish, 'you ease the stick . . .'

Ginger smiled, a tired smile. Of course she was tired. The Fred
Astaire pictures, I had been told, had almost killed her. Such a
perfectionist he was. Dancing, dancing, dancing. And she had only
just finished another picture. Eight pages of *Life* magazine were
given up to it that very week. I had not missed seeing that. But
there was something else my keen airman's eyes should not have
missed.

Like Baron von Richthofen diving from out of the sun, another
figure was coming up from astern, thumb, so to speak, hovering
over his gun button. I continued my graphic account, innocently
unaware: '. . . and of course you often black out when you pull up
from a steep dive . . .'

Then I saw Ginger's tired eyes shift from mine to some point
behind and above me. 'Hullo!' she said, her voice on a rising note
of affection, her eyes as alert as mine should have been.

'Ginger!' It was a deep voice, manly, authoritative.

I turned on my stool, and there at point-blank range stood a tall,
formidable figure, chest emblazoned with wings and a veritable
kaleidoscope of medal ribbons.

'Dick, do you know Wing-Commander Stanford-Tuck?'

'No,' I gulped, leaping to my feet and remembering all those
Huns he had downed in the Battle of Britain. 'No, *sir!*'

He did not know me either, and quite right, too. If he had
acknowledged my existence it could only be to ask what this imitation airman was doing here at all – with *his* Ginger, this erk who
had never seen a Messerschmitt in his sights, nor as much as baled
out over the white cliffs of Dover.

I slunk away in search of cloud cover like a shattered Dornier.
There was a boozy end to this bar, I was relieved to see, and the
patrons seemed to be in splendid form.

Nigel Bruce withdrew his pipe, took a good swallow of bitter, and
asked in his husky voice, 'What about a round of golf tomorrow, old
boy?'

'Good show,' remarked C. Aubrey Smith, stroking his grey moustache. 'And he's promised to play cricket next weekend.'

'Magnifique!' was Charles Boyer's comment. French cricket? I mused.

Joan Bennett slipped me a Bloody Mary and came up comfortingly close, too. 'Are you having fun?' she asked.

I nodded mutely. And once again there stole over me the feeling of being suspended above a desert of disbelief – just like my first solo – and would soon have to come to earth.

Once, we got ten days' leave, and I could not impose myself on Hollywood hospitality for all that time. So Allan Palmer and 'Titch' Tull and I, hitched up to Yosemite Park where we gasped at the waterfalls and went up to 10,000 feet on the ski lift and tobogganed down again.

There was no trouble in getting around, and the friendliness and generosity of the people were amazing. Not content with picking you up and driving you several hundred miles, they would invite you into their house, introduce you to their family and give you a drink or even a meal before sending you on your way. Their curiosity and eagerness were a revelation, and my love affair with America and the Americans was solidly founded during the winter of '41–'42 in the country and towns of California.

There was still a lot of poverty around from the Depression, and while the aircraft plants around Los Angeles were prospering on British Lend-Lease orders before Pearl Harbor much of industry had not yet recovered from the '29 Wall Street crash. The greatest suffering around the Bakersfield Valley and other farming areas was among the Hispanics and white farm smallholders – the 'poor whites' – who lived very primitively and sold the produce from their own little patch at the roadside – as much orange juice as you could drink for 5 cents, for instance. Nearly all of them had some old jalopy and they were as willing to pick you up as the limousine owner. To them we always made a contribution towards the cost of the gas. In small towns like Lancaster and Mojave, Tehachapi and Rosamond, you got the raw feel of frontier America. The men carried guns, and the bars were straight out of Western movies, complete with hip-swinging whores and the drunks squatting in the shade on the wooden sidewalks. Nothing, it seemed, had yet changed since the 1870s. But it was especially fascinating to witness the beginning of the revolutionary change which brought unprecedented prosperity and development even to these remote small communities as a result of Pearl Harbor and the Second World War.

I was staying at the home of an elderly film producer and his wife at a house overlooking the Pacific Ocean at Santa Monica when the news came through on the radio that the Japanese had attacked Pearl Harbor. It took a great effort to avoid seeming patronising while observing the impact of war on these cheerful if slightly excitable people, especially in the highly charged world of movieland. An invasion was hourly expected, the National Guard called out, and the mild and inaccurate shelling of a small oilwell by a Japanese submarine sent an almost seismic shock up and down the State.

Later in the afternoon, my host drove me back to the railroad station in LA, and in places the sights were straight out of H. G. Wells. The citizens stood in anxious groups on the sidewalks, crossed the boulevards regardless of the signals, and stared at abandoned automobiles. Some of these had crashed as the drivers were listening to the news on their radio, while the drivers of others (so we read in the newspapers the next day) had suffered heart failure.

The railroad station was like Paris's Gare de l'Est in May 1940 with whole families piling into the trains to escape the yellow peril. I had the greatest difficulty getting onto the Lancaster train, and it was hours late leaving. Back with my own kind at the Polaris Flight Academy late that Sunday night, we all expressed quiet relief that we had a proper ally at last, while mocking the Americans for what we regarded as over-reaction to bombing 2,000 miles away when we had been through the blitz almost nightly for three months or more. But the spirit among us all, cadets, lecturers and flying instructors, on Monday morning was, 'Well, we're all in it together now.'

Coinciding with this world-shaking event, I was promoted to monoplanes, from the stringbag biplane Stearman to the 450 h.p. Vultee Basic Trainer with closed cockpit, and after a decent interval, decided to extend my Beverly Hills social life. After all, war or no war, films still had to be made, and so far there was not much sign of austerity in this golden land.

7

Birthday Honours

B rian Aherne answered my call. 'By all means, old boy. Regard this as your second home. It'll be good to see you again. I'll be in San Francisco until Saturday, but I'll tell Joan. She'll be frightfully thrilled.'

Flying ceased mid-day Friday, for the convenience of our commanding officer who liked to get away early, and I scrounged a ride with one of the mechanics, contributing a dollar to his gas. With almost no expenses, thanks to American generosity, our 'Twenty-one dollars a day once a month' (as the popular wartime song went) was quite adequate.

I made my way first to darling Kay's mansion as she, too, had invited me and I wanted to explain. There was absolutely no public transport (only sketchy elsewhere) in Bel Air, but rather high-class limo-hitches. 'Darling Brian, you'll have fun there,' Kay commented and ordered her chauffeur to take me.

I was greeted with some puzzlement by the Filipino butler, Frank, at 703 North Rodeo Drive. Joan Fontaine was playing the part of a WAAF in *This Above All* at that time, opposite Tyrone Power, and went off early every morning in RAF blue. I was clearly not Ty Power but also dressed in this same quaint uniform. Frank took that as sufficient authority to let me in.

Joan had not yet returned from work so I had a good opportunity to examine the place, which was modest compared with Kay's, but with a nice pool, nice plants, domestic, decidedly British, and homey. There was a welcome pub influence about this movie-star bar. Dark oak panelling, leather-topped bar stools, hand-embroidered cushions on a sofa, copies of *Punch* lying about, pewter mugs lined up on a shelf ready for the noggin.

Only one wall was very un-pub-like. It was covered with signed portraits of matinée idols and notable women of the theatre and celluloid, each photograph lit to flatter facial cragginess, and signed Basil, Errol, Doug and Nigel. The women – Norma, Greta, Miriam, Marlene and co. – were equally narcissistic. And, funnily enough, there was a huge bowl of dozens and dozens of narcissi on a table under them.

I heard the merry sound of my hostess's arrival and nipped back to the drawing room, pretending to read *Life*. Joan came in with a light bounce, a chit of a girl of twenty-four, in slacks, sandals, loose blouse, and with her face plastered in make-up. I had never before seen a WAAF looking *quite* like this. 'Hullo, old chap,' she greeted me. 'So glad you've come. Let me mix you a drink.'

She did so with great dexterity, a Pimms with many fruity ingredients, and slid it across the bar to me. She put her hands up to her white-plastered face. 'Whoops! I must get this horrible stuff off. Make yourself at home. Relax. Have another drink. Play the piano or write dirty things on the walls.'

I attempted a manly laugh and buried my nose in the mug as she tripped away. Half an hour later I heard her dialling the telephone in the drawing room. 'I'm just calling up Brian,' she shouted at me. 'He's in San Francisco. Help yourself to drinks.' Then, 'Operator, I want . . .'

Brian Aherne, I later learned, was forty. He had married Joan only recently. For both it was the first time and they were madly in love. I had seen on the grand piano a photograph of them, he tall and manly, striding out of the church, she petite and floating beside him, whitely diaphanous.

'How are you, darling?' asked Joan in that appealing vulnerable voice the whole world had succumbed to in *Rebecca*.

'I miss you terribly.' There followed a lot of gossip, especially about Darryl Zanuck. Darling Darryl, to whom she owed so much.

After a quarter of an hour and a distant protest at her extravagance, Joan said a little sulkily, 'But darling, who's making all the money?' The answer was, alas, she was – 1,500 dollars a week, which was not bad for a comparative newcomer to the business. And Brian was not actually making a film at that time. If I had been more worldly I might have spotted future trouble here.

Joan Fontaine had style. She also had pace and self-confidence and a decisive masculine manner which brooked no nonsense and concealed a generous heart. If she had been brought up under more orthodox circumstances she would have led her guide troop with panache and made a killing of the rosettes at the pony club gymkhana.

In fact she had been born in Tokyo, like her elder sister Olivia who she had followed to Hollywood before the outbreak of war in Europe. She had worked in the rather menial task of chauffeuse, make-up girl and general aide-de-camp to famous film star Olivia until David Selznick had recognised her appeal and offered her the lead part opposite Laurence Olivier in *Rebecca*.

The call had come on the fifth day of her honeymoon, to the despair of Brian. And the petite, fun-loving wife – described later by Brian in his memoirs as 'young, pretty, gay and utterly charming' – became a major film star overnight. Neither her elder sister nor her husband was too pleased about this.

In Brian's absence Olivia turned up to spend the night at 703 North Rodeo Drive as a sort of chaperone as it was, I surmised, thought unseemly for young, blonde, beautiful film stars to be sleeping alone in Beverly Hills mansions with young airmen. Hedda Hopper, who was even bitchier than Louella Parsons, had got her hat-pins into the de Havilland girls at that time and it was deemed politic to reduce to the minimum any opportunities to attack them. In fact she did all the same and in a vitriolic paragraph linked poor Joan's name with a British airman – 'pleasures for the troops', something like that.

Olivia was chubbier, slower and less electric than Joan, and she had surrendered to an American accent which Joan kept at bay for almost all her Hollywood career. I knew nothing about their relationship but did notice that they appeared to be rather guarded with one another and not noticeably sisterly. But they were both vivacious and polite and kind to me, asking the usual stuff about poor old war-torn Britain, what flying was like, where I lived, did I have a girl and all that jazz. There was a good deal of booze and I remember being kissed good night as if I was a nephew to whom they ought to be kind, although in fact Olivia was only six years older and Joan four years older than me.

Olivia's bedroom and mine were separated by a bathroom which we shared, with a good deal of prearranged knockings and lockings. I had never shared a bathroom with a film star before, nor heard one at her ablutions. They were impressive and prolonged, and when I got the double knock it was after midnight. Inside, the air was heavy with scent and bath-salt emanations and steam. There was powder on the floor and jolly panties lying around. It all seemed a long way from the Wilmslow latrines, vomit-stained blankets and troopship odours.

Brian arrived from San Francisco later the next day and Joan threw herself into his arms. He was tall, tanned, fit and hearty and offered me the same warm welcome that Joan had given me – nice, casual, matter-of-fact hospitality. And this continued, weekend after weekend, and sometimes for longer, including parties at home, parties at the Ronald Colmans, parties at Ginger Rogers', a constant round broken by ten-pin bowling and tennis and swimming. Oh, what a lovely war!

And yet, now that America was in the war, there was plenty of news of it, especially in the Pacific where things were not going at all well. As to home, both Bushey and Brighton, it is difficult to recall my feelings, except the love I felt for Charlotte, whose photograph in my wallet was a great comfort. I used to write to her a lot, too, but the distance was so vast, and the length of separation so long that I think most of us became acclimatised to this life of flying and playing in the sun as if it would never cease. While longing for Charlotte, and determined to marry her as soon as possible after my return, my love for Joan increased with every visit to North Rodeo Drive. She was so pretty and vivacious and spontaneous, and so sympathetic and interested in *me* – or so it seemed.

Yet it was a funny sort of love, like on the one hand an adolescent affair at school, and a sentimental motherly love and admiration, matched by a paternal affection and admiration for Brian. After all, I had been at school at eighteen and was still only nineteen, and a rather unworldly nineteen at that.

Joan and I sometimes sat up late at the bar, with the early-retiring Brian upstairs in bed. Heaven knows what we talked about but I do not remember either of us being short of a word. We talked several times about marriage, and one night I confessed more or less total ignorance about birth control.

'Oh, you'll manage all right,' she reassured me in her decisive manner.

We moved reluctantly towards the hall and the stairs and I kissed her passionately and held her as tightly as had Laurence

Olivier in *Rebecca*, only this was the real thing, I told myself, not play-acting. 'Oh Joan, I do love you!'

We parted upstairs, but not for long. Before I had time to undress, she was back again, smiling brightly. 'Now this is what you'll need, Dickie,' and she held up an improbable and similar little roll of rubber to the one David Knowland had so confidentially shown me at school.

'Oh, I see,' I remarked nervously, 'I sort of roll it on, is that right?'

'Exactly,' said Joan. There was a pause, the first silence between us of the evening. Then she turned, taking her French letter with her, and left the room quite quickly.

That was kind of her, I thought, and did not think much further of it at the time.

I forgot all about the Vultee BT-13 as soon as I ceased flying it. All I can remember today is that it was a lumpy ship with no character, the fixed undercarriage not helping, and that it was the first plane I flew at night. It was never fully dark at our airfield. Even when a dim-out was instituted in LA (no more searchlight first nights and every other street lamp extinguished) there remained an encouraging glow to the south. Besides, the runway lights were so powerful there was never any doubt where you were.

Our instructors *hated* night flying, and the rare sight of a distant cloud was enough to call it off. But I was excited by the idea of it, and loved it when we eventually did it. I had decided at school that I had good night vision, and wandered the school grounds, with or without a girl on my arm, in the dark without any difficulty on the darkest of nights.

Some time towards the end of January 1942, my instructor, now a Mr Riley, took me up for the first time in the dark. I could see that he did not enjoy the experience and came in to land, rather badly, after ten minutes. To my astonishment, I was immediately sent off on my own. I stayed up for over an hour, navigating from township to township, skimming low over the railroad line and making dummy attacks on a train. The new Captain Ball, I decided, would be a night fighter pilot. My cocky manner on return irritated Mr Riley, who put in a report that I was over-confident – true, too.

A cadet from a senior course overheard me complain about the

Vultee, and he chipped in, 'Never mind, it's only for a few weeks. And the Harvard's worth waiting for – you'll see.' His name was Johnny Baldwin, a nice-looking fair-haired fellow already with a veteran's air about him.

Baldwin was right. The Harvard advanced trainer was fun to fly, with style and speed, cruising at 150 m.p.h. and capable of around 180 straight and level. Fuselage and wings were unpainted natural alloy, the under-carriage retracted, and the big Wright-Cyclone engine emitted a characteristic howl when directly over-head. Allan and I used to go off together and rendezvous the other side of Lancaster and show off to one another, competing for the best flick roll or Immelmann, and then dummy dogfight.

We also practised formation flying ahead of the official dual instruction so that we managed the near impossible feat of getting a word of praise out of our instructors. Cross-country navigation took us down to the Colorado river and the Mexican border. There was a grass strip just into Mexico and we landed on it in formation, remaining long enough for me to photograph a mounted border patrol, which took not the least interest in us. 'Allan,' I said one evening over a map. 'Look at this. Called Salton Sea.'

'So what?'

'What? Don't you see, it's 230 feet below sea level. Let's watch our altimeters go below zero. We'll never do it anywhere else.'

So we did, the very next day. Navigation in southern California was the easiest thing in the world, and as we discovered later to our dismay, not at all like northern Europe. First there was scarcely ever any cloud, except over the mountains, visibility was often limitless and always excellent, the roads and railways ran dead straight most of the time from town to town, and additionally there were navigation beams for the passenger airliners which you could tune into. These sounded a steady note which became a series of short or long notes if you wandered off course.

In any case, you could spot Salton Sea from fifty miles for it was a sea of white salt, shimmering in the sun and dead flat. As soon as we reached it we lost height gingerly because it was difficult to gauge altitude by the eye, until our racing shadows became visible. Very stupidly, we tested one another's nerves by competing for negative altitude until our shadows were almost as big as our planes'. With hoods thrown back we grinned at one another, glanced at our altimeters; then Allan pulled up at full throttle and we climbed to 10,000 feet where, even in April, it was freezing cold.

Our fuel registered worryingly low as we navigated back over the Mojave Desert, so we put down at a newly built training field, twice the size of ours. We exchanged notes with our American counterparts, who had no knowledge of the Polaris Flight Academy, signed a form and flew home, rather guiltily.

A few days later a rare storm blew up over the mountains to the east of us. It caught some twenty Harvard AT6s from this base which were out on an exercise, and five of them, each with an instructor and pupil, had failed to return. Ever since it was opened a year earlier, the Polaris Flight Academy had not suffered a single casualty, or injury, and only a few landing mishaps. We just flew happily around in the sun, enjoying and improving ourselves. This was the first evidence any of us had experienced that flying could be dangerous. Now, half a dozen senior cadets, including me, were sent off to search the mountainous area of the brief storm for any sign of the missing planes, and life took on a grim aspect.

I was assigned an area of the Sierra Nevada foothills and conducted a low-level square search above the rocks and scrub. After no more than ten minutes I was attracted to the glint of raw alloy just below the snowline, descended to a hundred feet and circled the splash of wreckage and the stain of oil. No one could have survived that crash and if they had bailed out they would have contacted their airfield by now.

There was a group of cowboys not far distant, and I drew their attention to the plane by waving to them and diving towards the wreckage. As I flew thoughtfully away, they were heading towards the spot.

On one of my early visits to Joan and Brian at 703 North Rodeo Drive, there was a lovely lunch party. Joan, casual as ever, was shampooing her little dog Nicky when the first guest arrived. He was Jon Hall, with long black hair for his lead in *Aloma of the South Seas*. Then came another temporary 'single', John Loder, fit, lean and talking golf hard. Then the Herbert Marshalls, she looking as if she was going to give birth before the pre-prandials.

Heather Angel was as pretty as could be, but not as pretty as Joan, her hair in short pigtails, I told myself loyally, though I doubted if Joan could match Heather's capacity for Pimms. Whether or not George Sanders had been invited was a subject for some speculation. Mrs Marshall, reading *Punch at War* while swinging in a hammock, expressed her grave doubts to me. But certainly the coterie of little starlets he had in train, now settling around him like chattering parakeets, had not been on the invitation list.

'Always late at the studio,' Mrs Nigel Bruce divulged to me. 'Such a trouble, poor George. Not a *proper* actor really. He reads his part, you know, from blackboards,' she whispered to me over her pewter mug of Pimms, and paused to check the lie of the land. 'He is quite improvident, too, you know, Dick dear. Spends all his money just now on toy trains – would you believe it?'

I could believe anything by now but resolved not to say so.

After a few hours and delicious cold lunch and many more Pimms, guests began to drift away. Charles Boyer gave me a little Gallic bow. '*Sans doute* we shall 'ave the pleasure of seeing you once more chez Colmans tomorrow for the drinks?'

I looked blankly at him until Brian came to my rescue. 'Yes, old man, we'll all be at the Colmans.'

And so we were. Joan, dressed in a baggy Chinese-style trouser suit and with her fair hair again in two short pigtails, drove us up into airy Bel Air in the Packard. We were not far from Kay's home (or relatively not far for this area) when we slipped down the drive. I caught a glimpse of a good British red-brick residence, softened by Virginia Creeper, and then we were in the car park, discreetly camouflaged by rhododendrons. From the back seat of the open car I caught the happy Beverly Hills sounds of gut against ball and distant splashing from the pool.

The three of us sauntered across the lawns and presently a superb figure came into view. At this time I had seen him only amid the smoke and confusion of the Beverly Hills Golf Club at that first party. His tread was measured and the welcoming smile revealed the most famous set of teeth in the world. Lob shoes (Brian divulged later, always bought by the dozen), single-breasted sports jacket, flannel bags, patterned silk scarf instead of the Guards' tie (it was Sunday).

Ronald Colman bent down slightly towards Joan and touched his lips against her cheek, then turned towards me. 'How very nice of you to come.' His hand grip had the right strength, the strength of a man whose swordplay was only equalled by Douglas Fairbanks's.

Next I glimpsed Ginger Rogers all too fleetingly, and Carole Landis's legs for quite a long time, and then – there was Maureen

O'Sullivan again. Our earlier meeting and drunken hand-holding had already slipped her memory – and why should it not? – but she turned her radiant Irish eyes upon me again and remarked admiringly, 'It must be wonderful to be alive after all that you have been through.' The good old RAF uniform could always be relied upon.

Cary Grant strolled by, cocktail in hand, wisecracking away to Joan with whom he had co-starred in *Suspicion*, directed by Hitchcock. The other British chaps were there, too – Ian Hunter, Basil Rathbone, sleuth-like as always, Nigel Bruce puffing away on his pipe, and C. Aubrey Smith repeated (he always did) his invitation to me to play cricket.

All but about eight of us drifted away, and we, the élite, settled around a luncheon table on the patio. My impression of this table was the number of monogrammed 'R.C.' objects there were – place settings, table napkins, glasses, even the matchboxes, ashtrays and individual cigarettes, all with the flowery initials 'R.C.'

The conversation ran along smoothly enough, like the crêpes suzettes, until, in a brief pause, I heard Benita laughingly announce that because of the war she had stowed away several sacks of sugar.

'Benita,' broke in her handsome husband. 'Hoarding! This is terrible!' There was a theatrical frown upon his face and he was measuring his words as in that tense scene in *Prisoner of Zenda*. 'What would happen to my reputation if this were known? This sort of thing gets around, you know, and though I flatter myself I am without enemies, there are many malicious tongues in Hollywood.'

The conversation picked up after about a minute, and so did my spirits when I overheard Joan saying, 'Did you know Ginger's having another party this evening?'

By early May we were nearing the end of our course, with over 200 hours in our logbooks. Only some fourteen of us had been sent home as failures, and on a sunny, warm afternoon the survivors paraded for the wings ceremony, and then strutted off cockily on a few days' leave. It was my twentieth birthday on Saturday, and I headed for 703 North Rodeo Drive in the car of an instructor with a notable reputation for speed.

The last rites of the indulgent life in Hollywood and Beverly Hills were notably up to scratch. There was tennis and a farewell party at the Nigel Bruces', terminating with a crushing good luck handshake and 'We're all proud of you.' There were more drinks at Ginger's milkbar, and this time my wings were authentic. Kay Francis dropped a tear for me, and Joan and Brian gave up their entire weekend to amusing me.

British forces had just quit Burma, American forces had surrendered to the Japanese in the Philippines, Rommel was advancing again in North Africa, two German battle-cruisers had run the gauntlet up-Channel, and the Germans were winning the Battle of Kharkov. But, while it was rumoured there might one day be a shortage of tyres and razor blades, all was well and happy in Hollywood and the war was making everyone richer than ever. Benny Goodman had signed on young Peggy Lee ('and I am madly in love with her,' I wrote to Charlotte), Frank Sinatra had the bobbysoxers swooning at the Hollywood Palladium, Aimée Semple Macpherson had her congregations crying at her mighty Temple, new stars sanctified their footprints in wet cement outside Grauman's Chinese Theatre. Best of all, the nightclubs along the Sunset Strip were throbbing with life as never before, and Brian and Joan proposed a last teenage night crawl on Friday, followed by a second birthday night crawl on Saturday.

The names come back through a haze of highballs and fifty years – A Bit of Hungary, Mocambos, Slapsie Maxie's, Little Troc and a Chinese place with intermittent simulated rainstorms on the roof. We failed to dig out Ginger – 'such a head, darling' – but managed to assemble quite a cast for the birthday night, including swashbuckling Louis Hayward and petite wife Ida Lupino, Ilona Massey, Claire Trevor, a general with decorations like a page of a stamp album, and several pretty young extras imported (I supposed) for the general and me. Time after time the flashbulbs popped, and later Joan sent me cuttings showing me dancing cheek to cheek with her, and Claire Trevor. Claire was about as tight as I was. 'Oh, how I love you!' she whispered in my ear. 'Oh, me too – how I love you!' A newcomer called Lena Horne was singing 'Embraceable You', and we did so.

At the end, Claire and I broke apart and burst into giggles. 'I am also very happily married,' she told me (as if I did not know) as we steered an uncertain course through the cigarette smoke and near-darkness back to our table, 'have children I adore, and shall love forever my darling husband.'

'What's the big joke?' Joan demanded with a tiny touch of

asperity. She packed up the remains of the birthday cake she had ordered for me, introduced me to Deanna Durbin at the next table, and told Brian it was time we all went home. 'And off we went,' I wrote later, 'in the purring Packard, down the Sunset Strip at sunrise.'

Before I blacked out at 703 North Rodeo Drive, I pieced together bits of a long day and night. Above all, I recalled tennis with Ronald Colman in the morning, and the last handshake after it. 'Good luck, young lad,' he said, and I knew from his voice that he meant it. 'Mind you shoot down a lot of those Germans, eh?'

'I'll do my best, sir,' I replied stoutly, resisting the powerful urge to salute.

There was a last flash of teeth. 'Good show!'

And so it had been.

The real world of May 1942 was a mere five days and nights away by train. At Moncton again, suddenly no longer were we either pioneers at a half-finished transit camp, nor the darlings of California hospitality. We might be sergeants, with our wings up, but there were hundreds of those around as well as lowlier new arrivals, stunned and apprehensive, or failed airmen, defiant or defensive, waiting for a passage home to General Duties. Royal Canadian Air Force police were much in evidence, the locals were weary of the sight of us, and the huge camp, already seven months old, was as service-worn as Wilmslow.

As a troopship, *The Duchess of York* sounded more promising than *Louis Pasteur*, and so it proved. We shared cabins with North Africa veterans, near-black from the desert sun, returning for treatment or for compassionate reasons. We dodged a few U-boats, formed a convoy, picked up an escort and were safely home in early summer sun in eight days. And then a few days leave.

'My *goodness*!' exclaimed Charlotte's mother. 'My dear boy!' exclaimed Charlotte. And neighbours were summoned to witness the kitbag-full of tins of butter and meat, bacon and mixed fruit, silk stockings and rarities unseen for nearly three years. I had tipped them onto the cottage lawn at Bushey.

I was said to be brown from the California desert sun, and to have acquired an American accent, which I stoutly denied. Charlotte said she was going to join the Navy as a WRNS. 'Oh no!' I appealed to her. 'Not the services.'

'But I'll be conscripted soon. Working for a literary agent is *not* a reserved occupation,' she pointed out reasonably enough.

'Then for God's sake let's get married – that'll settle everything,' I implored her.

Her mother intervened and declared (kindly) that the idea was ridiculous. 'You're only just twenty with no money, and Charlotte was eighteen only three weeks ago, and she's got no money either. You're both far too young – and marriage is for life.'

I resisted pointing out that she had left her husband after a few months, thinking it would not advance my cause. Instead I took the train to Brighton, with a share of my prized loot. Here I was made to feel like some conquering hero rather than an amazingly lucky son who had tasted the good life in a tinsel fairyland.

Forty-eight hours later I was on my way to Norfolk.

'Are you going to be fighting?' my mother asked.

I reassured her. 'Not yet. I've got to do a conversion course first – to get used to flying in England. I haven't tried it yet but the gen is that it's very, very different.'

And so it was. An arbitrarily chosen dozen or so of us were sent to a place called Watton. It was my first taste of a wartime airfield, and the impression it made was at once chilling, ominous and exciting. There were Saturday night hops, ENSA concerts and film shows. Darts and shove halfpenny were played in the messes and down at the dispersals, and seduction of WAAFs was commonplace on and off camp in any odd place available. But there was no light touch in relationships or behaviour. Sentiment and refinement, to say nothing of intellectualism, were totally absent, discipline strict, hygiene minimal, except for the handing out of free condoms from the guardhouse in the evenings. I was thought exceedingly eccentric to walk the half mile or more to the nearest tap to wash last thing at night, and mildly dotty to produce my portable typewriter in the evenings.

Watton was about as far removed from the only other institutions I knew, Frensham Heights and the Polaris Flight Academy, as could be. But then its function was rather different, too. Wartime flying was the sole function of Watton and hundreds more airfields like it. The gaunt hangars housed aircraft in for repair and service.

One tall tower identified the parachute store, another tower was for controlling the flying, a third the water for this self-subsisting community. The messes, the stores, the armoury, the isolated bomb and ammunition store, the MT (motor transport) block housing petrol bowsers, ambulances, 15 cwt and 30 cwt trucks, the accommodation huts, all were plain and functional, their dark camouflage adding to the general depressing effect of the whole station. Even the dispersal huts scattered about the perimeter of the airfield, each with its flight of aircraft huddled in their blast bays, hinted at purposeful action rather than the romance of flight.

The other memorable characteristic of Watton and all other RAF stations was its restlessness. Something was happening every hour of the day and night. The sound of engines, testing or flying, was always in the air, trucks, bicycles, staff cars and bowsers always on the move, the kitchens cooking night-flying suppers at 3 a.m. and early breakfasts at 5 a.m.

Heavy bombing by the Germans was in abeyance at this time but there were plenty of intruders around at night, their favourite activity shooting down planes landing or taking off. The sirens moaned out when an intruder was spotted in close proximity, searchlights fingered the sky, and from time to time the Bofors opened up with their distinctive rapid crack-crack-crack.

Watton was an all-grass airfield given up entirely to advanced training and conversion training for pilots like us who had been trained abroad in sunnier climes. And just as well, too. The shock of flying below low cloud and through cloud up into the sun, posed entirely new problems and was very bewildering. So was navigation. No more dead straight roads and unlimited visibility. At first, with map on lap and glanced at every few seconds, only 'the iron beam' – the railway lines – were useful guides, and there were so many of them in East Anglia fifty years ago that you could easily be led to Norwich instead of Lowestoft. The first lot of 8th Air Force Americans were arriving at this time, and they were even more stupefied than we were, most of them never having seen a winding road or a small irregularly shaped field in their lives.

The planes were quite a handful, too: Miles Master IIs which had been given an oversize 850 horsepower radial engine to bring performance nearer to that of a Hurricane. After the well-mannered Harvard they were a great disappointment. So were the instructors, half of them resting from a tour on ops, the others recently qualified chaps who had opted for training school. At the Polaris Flight

Academy neither language nor behaviour was very refined, but all the instructors flew like angels.

For the first weeks I had a Canadian, Flight-Sergeant Mara, whose language made Mr Gordon's seem affectedly refined. I became very weary of this, and one afternoon after doing a dead-engine landing in a small field with his expletives in my ears all the way down, I rounded on him, telling him in equally lurid terms what a hopeless bloody instructor he was. He did not apologise but became much more temperate in language and manner, even praising me once or twice.

For the last two weeks of the course I was assigned a breezy, pink-faced pilot officer I shall call Lundin. He had been a couple of courses ahead of me in California, had chosen to be an instructor and had only just completed his training. He affected not to recognise me as he called out the terse information that I would be under him and that we were going low-flying. I followed him out to the ugly beast and climbed into the forward cockpit but was not given time to tighten my straps. When I plugged in the intercom our Miles Master II was already on the move, so decisive, so self-confident and in a hurry was this young man. 'I'll take it,' he snapped as if he had not done so since 'Chocks away!'

The legal low-flying zone was some distance away but Lundin was not prepared to waste time climbing and we never rose above fifty feet. I liked his swanky style as he banked steeply to port and starboard, skimming the treetops of Thetford Forest with wingtips. What luck getting such a skilful fellow with the joystick!

Then I felt a slight jolt as we brushed our belly against a pine top. That was really going it! I waited for brave Pilot Officer Lundin to pull up marginally. But that was not to be. Racing along at full throttle there was another, louder bump followed instantly by silence. It is amazing how quiet a plane is with a dead engine, and this big radial was dead all right.

Rather too late, Lundin pulled up the nose, the momentum giving us time – but not much – to look for some comfortable place to put down. It did not exist, just forest for as far as the eye could see.

'Looks as if we've had our engine,' Lundin remarked, in case the fact had escaped my notice. Then, as we lost height rapidly, in a rather more fussed voice, 'Turn off the fuel, for God's sake!' I had already done so.

I had time, but only just, to consider that this was rather a waste after all that time and expense of learning to fly, and mournfully, that I had little chance now of equalling Captain Ball's score of forty-four downed Huns.

8

Picking Up
the Pieces

The face of the girl looking down anxiously at me exceeded by far the beauty of Ginger, Joan, Olivia, Kay or Claire, of recent memory. 'Is there anything you would like?' Her voice matched the wonder of her face. Under ordinary circumstances I would have responded to this question quite promptly, but I was unable to utter a word owing to the deformity of my lips and teeth.

But *she* knew. In a trice she was fumbling in my pockets where she found a packet of uncrushed cigarettes, one of which she lit and placed in what was left of my mouth. Then she put her cool hand on my forehead, not so much to soothe, I realised later, as to staunch the flow of blood. For that moment in the no man's land between life and death, she was my whole world. Then she faded from view, and blackness embraced me again.

Our wretchedly abused machine had torn through a number of trees and, amazingly, ended upside down with the cockpit resting laterally across a forest drainage ditch. Nor did it catch fire, perhaps thanks to my only active contribution. In the front cockpit I had taken the brunt of the damage, especially as there was a lethal gunsight bracket in line with my face and my straps were not tight enough to hold me from hitting it.

Single-handed, this angel of mercy had in turn and at great risk from fire, dragged us from the wreckage and had laid us out some distance clear on the bank of the ditch by the time stretcher parties arrived. The ambulance journey was long and bumpy, rough enough to bring me back painfully to consciousness. Lundin opened his eyes and grinned. 'Wizard prang!' he exclaimed. And then, a few minutes later, 'Don't forget now – the engine packed up.' As he was to confirm later, his story was that the engine suddenly failed while I was at the controls, but he then took over, skilfully saving our lives. There was, after all, no way of telling whether those branches got into the engine before or after the crash. I hated committing perjury, and should not have done so, but I figured muzzily that no one would take the word of a green sergeant against a commissioned officer instructor. (Lundin, suffering only concussion, was soon back on flying. At his next crash, he killed his student; and then, I was told, he killed himself. What a waste indeed!)

When I had recovered consciousness again, I was aware of the sound of ball on bat and for a moment was back in the pavilion at school. Cricket was being played. I could see the bowler putting his all into a seamer, and a cheer arose as the batsman struck out stoutly. All the same, the scene was a bit awry, the pitch being the aisle of a hospital ward and the batsman possessing only one arm. A medical trolley acted as the wicket. Above the cries of encouragement came the sound of 'Music While You Work' on the loud-speaker above my head. Softly, and only just audibly, came a groan from the next bed. Sister entered, cheerfully halted the cricket and covered with a sheet the face of my neighbour. Then she came to my bed.

'How are you, sergeant?'

To my surprise, after an effort I could talk, or ridiculously utter, 'OK.'

'What hurts most?'

'My back.' And to my embarrassment I began to cry.

Sister touched a part of my face that was not bandaged and that made me cry more. So she produced a needle and I returned to the merciful darkness and silence for which I longed.

There was someone else in the next bed when I came back to that world of pain which I thought had gone away. He was groaning and being very sick. Ely RAF Hospital had a steady turnover of mostly bomber command crews. Over 500 bombers were lost in that month, and many more returned with wounded crews, most of whom ended up at Ely.

Charlotte turned up on my third day in this ward. I saw her walking up the aisle, examining every face. She seemed to be about to give up when she came back to my bed, only half-believing it was me. When she did, she was admirably matter-of-fact, and realising that I was capable of almost no speech, chatted away about this and that. Mirrors were forbidden in the ward, but I got hold of one later and saw with a considerable shock that I was quite unidentifiable.

Later, I learned that I had broken both knees, rupturing the ligaments in one of them; ruptured many back muscles; cracked my forehead, bent and twisted sideways my Huguenot nose, lost some teeth, and cut about my legs, especially shins. But I was young and fit, and healed quickly. When Charlotte came again, I was in a wheelchair in hospital blue. Two weeks later she had a letter for me from Brian who had been cabled, and was very severe with me. 'Didn't I warn you about low flying,' he admonished me. 'It is an extremely dangerous practice.' I ruefully pondered over Beverly Hills's remoteness from war, as I was to do many times later as I skimmed over enemy soil at fifty feet.

I was discharged in the middle of September and was given generous sick leave. My parents were for the time being living on my brother's farm, and I could not yet face the journey. In London I immediately became aware of two things, first that I was weaker than I had expected, and liable to pass out and be sick at any time, and second that, as in Hollywood a year earlier, I was again a 'hero' under false pretences. I was helped on and off buses, people stood aside for me in crowded restaurants, while in Keith Prowse's record shop a fabulously famous and alluring singer held my hand while trying out the new Duke Ellington and suggested I came home with her 'for a rest'. But the only rest I wanted was at that cottage in Bushey and the caring comfort of Charlotte and her mother. So Captain Ball remained as distant as ever.

But not for long. As another wartime winter closed round the nation, Alamein was fought and won, the Germans failed to relieve Stalingrad and the Americans landed in North Africa, I was sent to Scotland to learn to fly Hurricane fighters.

'Annan? Sod of a place,' I was told. 'Perched on a muddy hill, with fucking mountains all round, mostly hidden by cloud. Rain most of the time, bloody cold, bloody cheerless.' So that was the gen. I took a train through the night, lying on my kitbag in the corridor along with several hundred more servicemen and women.

My gen was ace. There were Nissen huts scattered haphazardly around in the Scottish mud, each with a small coke stove and a fuel ration good for a couple of hours a day. Stealing coke was a serious court-martial offence, but it happened almost every night. I arrived in rain and mist but flying was proceeding as if this was southern California. What was more, the airfield was set below everything else, as it were in a saucer, adding to the difficulties of landing. Clearly, RAF Annan had been laid out by some lunatic who had never seen an aeroplane, let alone flown one.

However, there were strong redeeming features about this OTU (Operational Training Unit). First, a very cheerful spirit prevailed, the place was well run, and – unlike Watton – the instructors were keen and efficient. The Wing-Commander Flying was Denis David, a Battle of Britain survivor with gongs galore and a cheerful demeanour.

Poor Martin Rivers had ended his flying career here, and when I looked up the crash details I saw that, like so many before and after him, he had flown into a mountain in dirty weather. Four of my lot went the same way, making a 25% casualty rate on the three-months-long course. That was about average.

'Have a good look at one in the hangar,' my instructor told me on the first day. Warrant Officer Chapman, an amiable Irish veteran, was a very different fellow to Mara or Lundin, capable and patient. There were half a dozen Hurricanes being serviced in the hangar and with their engine panels stripped, revealing the V12 Rolls-Royce Merlin which complemented the Hurricane and gave this machine its performance.

I climbed up into the cockpit and sat down for the first time in the real thing, a single-seat fighter capable of about 320 m.p.h. and armed with eight .303 Browning machine-guns. I tried, but failed, not to feel impressed as I contemplated the array of instruments, the throttle and pitch controls on the left, the spade stick between my legs with its brake grip and gun button set 'safe' at the top. I memorised the position of all the controls, hoping to find them by touch and trying to accustom myself to the cramped cockpit and the absence of dual seat and controls. Here, in this seat and from first take-off to first landing, you were on your own.

Besides some fifty Hurricanes, Annan had a few Miles Master Mark Is, the more docile version, for checking out pupils. Then, suitably on Trafalgar Day – 21st October – I was ordered off. 'Don't try and do too much first time,' Chapman told me. 'Just take it easy until you feel at home with the kite.' He stood on the wing root, leaning over the cockpit, pointing out again the cockpit drill before starting the engine. With cockpit hood open, I indicated

'Chocks away', released the brake and taxied gingerly out to the head of the runway when given the green light from the control tower.

I wrote recently:

> The power after training machines was heady, one's back pressing hard against the seat as the 1,000 horsepower sent the aircraft racing down the runway, and then into a climb so steep and swift that it was hard to credit the truth of the instrument figures. Though I later flew faster machines, nothing could equal the joy of handling the utterly predictable and vice-free responsiveness of the Hurricane. But its most enduring memory is the song of the Merlin, deep-noted without harshness, accompanied by an unobtrusive and steady pulsation.*

After a shaky take-off, warm relations led swiftly into a total love affair with the Hurricane. Ailerons and rudder responded to just the right pressure. Such was the confidence she inspired, night flying over blacked-out Britain held no terrors, though what our American instructors would have made of moonless, 10/10th cloud flying I could not imagine.

Flying the Hurricane at night was a heady, full-blooded experience which did much to flush away my boyhood timorousness and helped to build up the sort of self-confidence I would soon be needing. It was a magical business to take this husky machine, exhausts glowing a reassuring blue, up, up to 20,000 feet. On a moonlit night the serrated coast of south-west Scotland, the deep cut of the Solway Firth, the bulge of the Lake District ending at Morecambe Bay, all clearly marked the frontier of black land against the mauve of the sea. The fells of Cumberland shimmered white, the lakes were black and sinister below the peaks.

One moonlight night, in an ecstasy of power and joy, I dived my Hurricane vertically towards these mountains from a great height, pulling up low over the Scafell range where I had once stood so proudly as the highest human in England, with throttle wide open. I held the machine upside down at the top of a loop, looking down possessively at this black and white living map. For a moment I owned all the peaks and I was so buoyant with pride that the

---

* *The Battle of Britain: the Jubilee History* by Denis Richards and Richard Hough (1989), p. 38

straps hardly had to hold me. Then I put down the nose again and skimmed Bassenthwaite Lake flat out, weaving from shoreline to shoreline, and so home to bed.

Then there was live firing, with the eight guns chattering away and the scent of cordite filtering into the cockpit, proving what a steady gun platform the Hurricane was. We fired at towed canvas drogues, improving from 4% to over 11% hits, and at ground targets in a dive.

We flew in loose finger-four formation on dummy patrols, our instructors trying to jump us out of the sun – usually succeeding at first, the proof of our being shot down confirmed by the cine-film. We flew at zero level over the sea to the Isle of Man, assumed to be the French coast, the anti-aircraft gunners using dummy ammunition. Once, on the banks of the Solway Firth, our Army friends used live ammunition, we hoped by mistake, and the puffs of exploding shells all about us was somewhat disconcerting.

And goodness how we worked! My logbook shows seventeen flights by day and by night in the first eight days of December, mostly in filthy weather. Although much stronger than I had been a month earlier, I found this immensely taxing, with my left leg especially aching from tight formation flying. In our Nissen at night, with schools of noisy poker going on about me, I crashed into a deep sleep and had to be shaken awake at dawn.

There were also moments of pure joy, especially over the Lake District fells. My brother Philip had married a local girl, Peggy Stephens, and they were honeymooning in the Langdale Valley. I pinpointed their hotel, naughtily flew low over it, and in rare winter sunshine performed a series of aerobatics, giving them all I knew. Then old show-off flew home.

What with time spent in hospital and the pressure of the flying at Annan, there was little time to form friendships, and I often wished I had not become separated from Allan Palmer. But in the last week of the course we were sent in small numbers to a satellite airfield at Longtown near Carlisle for intensive air-to-air gunnery and dummy dogfighting. I was paired up with an engaging fellow called Johnny Hadow, a pilot officer of, as near as could be, the same flying standard as me. The weather was good during the last days of 1942, and he and I flew twice a day, taking off on the grass in formation, climbing together, first one then the other leading, broke into aerobatics, began dogfighting at our maximum comfortable height of 20,000 feet, dodging in and out of cloud. Once or twice we threw back our canopies and discarded our helmets, letting the slipstream tear through our hair and making faces and laughing unheard through sheer exuberance. This was flying at its most joyous and irresponsible, something we suspected, rightly, that we would never again experience.

On the ground, Johnny Hadow and I played chess and talked flying between moves. Like dogfighting we won about an equal number of times, and before we left, while warned that we were both over-confident, were passed out as 'above average' and joint top of the course. I never saw or heard from him again. With some two million people in the RAF at that time, most on the move several times a year, this was typical of service friendships. I wonder if he survived. I hope so.

I had given up romantic thoughts of getting onto night fighters. These were all twin-engine machines by now, full of radar and radar operator while something called GCI homed you onto the target. *Not* romantic by my reckoning though many pilots loved this electronic stalking of the foe. No, it would be Captain Ball and a single-engine fighter squadron. And so it came to be.

There was a new shape and a new sound in the sky. A section of four fighters passed a thousand feet above me as I stood on the open wooden platform of Hutton Cranswick railway station, waiting for transport. The engine note of these big machines was harsher than a Hurricane's Merlin – harsher, deeper, lacking the sweet pulse of the Rolls-Royce engine. The fuselage was similar to a Hurricane's, though bigger, the wings thick and canted with four cannon projecting aggressively from the leading edge, the nose heavy-jawed from an enormous cowled air intake.

One by one these machines lowered undercarriage and flaps and turned on the final approach, looking head-on like crouching beasts about to spring. I was so transfixed by this sight that I did not at first hear the female voice, 'Wake up, Serge?' She was a WAAF MT driver awaiting my attention, my luggage and me.

'Sorry.'

'You for 195?' she enquired, hurling my kitbag, parachute bag and suitcase into the back.

'That's right.'

'Poor sod.'

Now did not seem to be the time for enquiring the reason, though my imagination played over several possible explanations.

'Who else is here?'

'Poles. Spit Vs.'

A WAAF of few words. But she got me there, with some sang-froid, and I went off to report to the adjutant.

The Hawker Typhoon was Sydney Camm's successor to the Hurricane, 100 m.p.h. faster, the 20 mm cannon giving this masculine beast more than double the firepower of eight machine-guns. It was still firmly on the secret list but word had got round Fighter Command that it had experienced many early troubles, little hiccoughs like the tail falling off in a dive and the asphyxiation of the pilot from leaking fumes, or perhaps the two together, which seemed unfair.

The first had been corrected by riveting steel fish-plates aft round the fuselage, the second by making oxygen masks compulsory wear at all times, typical wartime makeshift made necessary because no other RAF fighter could catch the tip-and-run raiders of that time. 195 Squadron had only just been formed and was working up to operational state before being sent south where the action was more intense than in this part of mid-Yorkshire.

Frank Jensen, Flight-Lieutenant, AFC, sought me out after lunch. 'I'll take you down to the dispersal and show you the tits.' Jensen was a peacetime Auxiliary, highly experienced, friendly and an extremely able pilot and Flight Commander. He brought along, too, in his staff car a contemporary of mine who also had trained at the Polaris Flight Academy of now distant memory, Johnny Webster. He had been at school at Stowe, and like me, had not put in for a commission, preferring the egalitarianism of the sergeants' mess. We were initiated into the daunting secrets of the Typhoon together and became friends.

The machine we were to examine was being run up, panels removed, and emitting a cacophonous row. 'I don't really believe it can get off the ground,' Webster said sceptically. 'I mean it must weigh five tons.'

'Seven,' corrected our Flight Commander, and ordered the engine to be switched off. 'Just look at that and you'll see why it works – some of the time.'

The engine was an enormous 24-cylinder Napier Sabre, the cylinders arranged in H-form, with sleeve valves and two-stage super-charger. 'It takes a ten-year intensive course to learn how to service it,' he added sardonically. 'We've only had them a few weeks and

ABOVE The wedding of my parents, Margaret May Esilman ('Meg') and George Stanley Hough, Southport, 10th June 1911. 'My bouquet was all lilies of the valley, and tulle streamers . . . Reception when we got home, then cut cake, had photos taken . . . beautiful sunshine all the time.'

BELOW Meg and George in late middle age. They were married for fifty-nine years and 'never a cross word between us'.

My mother was thirty-five, my father forty-one, when
I was born 15th May 1922. I was one year old in the
bath, about seven in the jersey. My father, 'a positive
agnostic', did not think it in the least odd to send me
to Lourdes Convent, Preston Park, Brighton at this age.

I enjoyed bicycling from home in Brighton across
Sussex and Surrey to Frensham Heights School.
It was a wonderfully happy place, presided over
by Paul Roberts (below), the best progressive school
headmaster of his time, loved by all.

At nineteen the unpredictable tides of service life swept me onto the shores of southern California and movieland. Here I learned to fly between long weekends with the kind Hollywood stars, an unusual way of spending seven months of the war. The Ronald Colman–Benita Hume hospitality for lunch and tennis was especially warm, while Olivia de Havilland decorated the garden of my principal host and hostess, Brian Aherne and his new young wife, Joan Fontaine.

Sunday morning bath for Joan Fontaine's Nicky. Brian Aherne was gardening, and soon Charles Boyer, Nigel Bruce, Herbert Marshall, Reggie Gardiner and their wives turned up for Pimms by the pool. So did George Sanders, with girls.

Back home, life became more robust with Hurricanes and Typhoons, chasing
tip-and-run raiders and dive-bombing. This, on my second tour of ops, was the
latest version of the Typhoon. No longer did the tail fall off, nor the monster
24-cylinder engine fail so often, nor asphyxiate the pilot with its fumes.
(photo: Imperial War Museum)

ABOVE With Lord Mountbatten, who asked me to write his family's history, which I followed with biographies of both him and his wife, Edwina.

BELOW The first three girls, Sandy (b. 1947), Sarah (b. 1944) and Deborah (b. 1948). *(photo: Louis Klemantaski)*

ABOVE The last daughter, Bryony (b. 1960) with Harry, one of a succession of Border Collies.

BELOW Grandson Jack Garland, Sarah's youngest, with my present wife, Judy.

they can be sods. They're also bloody fast – make rings round the FW190. Sink like a stone if you have to ditch.'

After this, Jensen cheered up, and also cheered us up, a little, extolling the virtues of the Tiffy. 'Bloody strong, takes terrific punishment, and, oh boy, those cannon can drill a hole in a battleship.' He considered this claim and with a smile corrected himself: 'Well, let's say a heavy cruiser.'

Our CO, Don 'Butch' Taylor, could surely have commanded only a Typhoon squadron. From his broken nose to his crouching stance he was a human embodiment of this machine. He was bouncy, on the go the whole time, flew much faster than anyone else regardless of fuel economy and liked driving his V8 Ford staff car, which could get across the airfield almost as fast as his taking-off Typhoon.

So, here was my first operational – or nearly operational – fighter squadron, and on the whole I liked what I saw. I also liked the Poles with their Spitfire Vs who shared the airfield. They were very elegant and stylish, with impeccably tailored uniforms, wings high upon left shoulder, even their flying boots clean at all times. They had flown in peacetime at home and were highly skilful pilots, irresistible killers in the air and entirely without discipline, or English – the one allying with the other. They used to fly down south for the day sometimes, in order to be nearer the enemy, for whom they held a contempt and hatred right off the scale of any measure. On my first evening at Hutton Cranswick, a section of four returned at dusk, and the word soon got round that they had snatched a pair of Me109s. It was as usual a case of overkill, all four banging away even when they were on fire and about to enter the sea. Still, from the enemy's view, that was better than being riddled as you floated down under your parachute, which was the only alternative.

Evening celebrations and vodka drinking were frequent anyway, but if there was real cause – like that night – the Poles were heroic. By 8 p.m. they were fighting good-naturedly but violently among themselves, breaking up the furniture, squirting the mess fire extinguishers, singing patriotic songs round the piano, until midnight. The following morning they might be a touch subdued, bowing gravely towards us, but their batmen had done wonders with their uniforms.

That same morning, without more ado, Jensen sent me off on circuits-and-bumps. 'Don't let it intimidate you. It's only a grown-up Hurricane – a bit more torque at take-off, and don't let it run away with you.'

You almost needed a ladder just to enter the cockpit and then you were so high off the ground you might already be airborne. The canopy did not slide. Someone had devised a hood hinged on the port side, with winding windows on both sides, just like a car, but for emergencies there was a toggle to pull to rid yourself of the whole contraption. It was appropriate that you did not swing the prop (as if anyone could), nor set the engine in motion electrically, like the Hurricane, but it, literally, exploded into life.

The Koffman, below right, had six large cartridges which you activated by pulling a piece of wire. An airman stood by on the ground, according to safety regulations, extinguisher aimed at the exhaust stubs, for not only was the Sabre a devil to start but it occasionally celebrated by catching fire. If you exploded fruitlessly four of your cartridges, as I did this first time, an eager genius of an engine fitter would leap onto the port wing and juggle the throttle and mixture controls with a timing and touch which always worked.

Then I eased away the Typhoon and I could already feel the beat of eager fire, like an odds-on stallion at the start. As we gathered speed, with rudder trim set full port and left leg putting full weight on the rudder pedal, still the torque from the 2,400 h.p. engine edged the Typhoon towards the right runway edge. Fortunately, this same power, two and a half times that of a Merlin, got the seven tons off the ground quickly, and then things were better. A slight sinking as you closed your 15 degrees of flap, a double clunk as the wheels hid themselves into the wings, rad. flap up, close the windows – and then you could get on with the flying.

I did not fully appreciate the power until I was allowed out of the circuit the next time. It was a revelation, especially in the climb. Nothing, you felt, could possibly get near you – and you might (not too fancifully) even outpace the flak. I did a few formal banks and turns, tested the dive speed, found it nervously breathtaking, like the proverbial stone, climbed a few thousand feet, avoided Hull's balloon barrage and went out to sea a few miles. I was about to reverse course when the Sabre decided that it had had enough for the day and expired, all twenty-four cylinders. I fiddled in fair frenzy with the fuel cock, from main tanks to nose tanks, for I had started out with 154 gallons and had been flying for only forty minutes. Magnetos off and on again, fiddle with mixture and throttle. There was not really much else to do except keep your head and decide whether to bail out or stay with it. The coast looked a long way away. It did not deserve such loyalty, but I decided to stay with my Tiffy.

Luckily, there was a rare east wind that day, and though the seven tons was losing height with alarming speed, I thought we might just make it. In the event I was able to skim over Mable-thorpe towards some nice soft flat fenland, unfortunately crossed by some biggish drainage ditches. I pulled the canopy toggle and away it all went, turned off the fuel, tightened my belt (I was not going to be caught a second time) and listened to the silence, which was quite as profound as in that wretched Master II a few months ago.

Without flaps and with wheels up the stalling speed was well over 100 m.p.h. and there was a lot of weight and momentum as well as wind behind me. Mud sprayed up on both sides, a bank set me airborne again, and like a bad steeplechaser at Becher's I went through the next hedge as if it did not exist, over another ditch and on and on, bumping and tossing about.

'Just when I thought I'd never stop,' I wrote to Charlotte, 'a final jar, followed by eerie silence except for a drip of escaping oil and petrol and the hiss of a very hot engine half in water. At a safe distance I sat on a bank.' My long-suffering nose was bruised again and my newly mended back muscles had taken a beating but otherwise I was all right. I lit a cigarette and contemplated the ruin.

9

Coming of Age

We used to read about shot-down Battle of Britain pilots being cosseted by housewives and given cups of tea, or helped into the golf clubhouse for a stiffy or two. 'Jolly good show, old man.' Reality in this case was more negative. In fact, I don't believe anyone saw my little prang; certainly no living being nor habitation was in sight. So I had to trudge off in search of help, giving DN 306 a last resentful glance and tracing back the long scored trail of mud and metal fragments she had inflicted on the landscape.

A little village called Maltby-le-Marsh eventually hove into view, and then the village policeman – they had them in those days. I duly reported the accident, the pencil came out, was licked and details were diligently taken down. 'Would you go and guard it, please, it's still on the secret list.' And off he went, scarcely attempting to conceal his excitement at helping the war effort.

The village also had a post office and post-mistress, a dear stout figure who wound the handle of her telephone, put me through to Hutton Cranswick, and produced the inevitable cup of tea. Then the schoolmistress, on hearing the exciting news, let the school out for the rest of the day and the whole village became en fête. With somewhat shaky hand, I signed a dozen autographs, and the boys and girls ran off to get as near to the wreck as the bobby would permit.

I believe that that Sabre, like a frisky horse, had been showing me who was master round here, and had scented that I was a sprog pilot. After this, Sabre engines sometimes coughed and spluttered, once several times and for too long for comfort, they sometimes ejected so much oil onto the screen that you couldn't see where you were going, but they never let me down completely for the next two and a half years of our relationship.

The CO assembled us on a murky February afternoon, the wind whistling across the Yorkshire flatlands. He surveyed us with an expression of distaste. Especially by contrast with our Polish allies, we were a scruffy crowd, partly because there was hardly ever any hot water and shaving was to be avoided, and partly because it was so cold we piled on the jerseys for indoors as well as outside, and partly because we were an undisciplined, filthy, useless crowd of layabouts. Anyway, that is what 'Butch' Taylor declared now. He was a funny chap, taking no interest in us for days on end, knowing that we were lounging about, drinking too much, playing poker or darts when there was no flying – as there was not for much of the time. Then he would order us, through his flight commanders, to run round the perimeter track – say three miles – twice in the pouring rain.

'I'm not having you putting on a rotten show at our new station.'

This woke us up. 'New station, sir?'

'Yes, from tomorrow we're fully operational.' He waited for this to sink in. Only one or two of 195 had been on ops before, and I was fairly certain that I was not the only one suddenly viewing life from an entirely new perspective. On the first morning of the war, when the air raid sirens had moaned their message of warning, everyone who heard them had, in some degree or other, experienced the disquieting feeling that someone somewhere was intent on hurting or killing you. That is, after all, what war is all about. Now, that *frisson* was renewed, rather more strongly. But, of course, on no account must the smallest hint be revealed that you were anything else but thrilled at the news of going into combat. Not shooting a line, mind, but deeply pleased to the point of a little cheer or two.

'Can you tell us where we're going, sir?'

'You'll know soon enough. But it's tomorrow and the Adj will fill you in.'

'May I take the Moth, sir?' I pleaded.

The CO, like everyone else, thought my love for the squadron Tiger Moth was evidence of, at the best, eccentricity. 'You're mad!' he exclaimed. This meant OK and I smiled like the Cheshire cat. This dainty little machine was used for odd jobs and errands and

I flew it whenever I could, sometimes ferrying people around. In my view, it was flying as it used to be and ought still to be. Speed was all very well, but to float about the sky at fifty feet, waving and blowing kisses to the Land Girls on their tractors and taking a close look at an interesting manor house, was my idea of heaven. No one on the ground minded the Moth. It was quieter than a motor bike while low-flying Tiffies made everyone jump, aborted the lambs and dried up the cows.

The only member of 195 who shared my love for the Moth was our Intelligence Officer, Pilot Officer 'Spy' Pugh, a tall, shy man, much liked and much teased, who I would take up whenever opportunity occurred. When, the next day, we learned that we were going west, not south, to help defend Liverpool, the Spy asked if he could come with me. It was blowing a westerly gale when we saw off the squadron, then, wrapped up in everything we could lay our hands on, we puttered off in the Moth.

To offset some of the effect of the headwind, I flew as low as I safely could and the Spy, in the cockpit ahead of me, was entranced, his head turning from side to side, missing nothing. As we climbed up above the road over the Pennines, we spotted a large Army convoy, with many troops in open trucks. We just managed to keep up with them as they laboured up the pass, the men waving and encouraging us to put on speed. We had no more, the gale being stronger than ever up here. As soon as they mounted the summit and began to descend we were left hopelessly behind and we could see them laughing and mocking us.

We eventually made it to the west coast, having to refuel and taking nearly three hours in all. Our destination was Woodvale, an airfield just south of Southport. There was no danger of daylight bombing of Liverpool nearby but the Germans were always seeking news of convoy arrivals and departures for their U-boats, and we were supposed to intercept their high-flying recce machines. As the Typhoon was less and less effective above 20,000 feet, this seemed a fairly futile exercise. During the few weeks we were there I was scrambled just once to try to catch a high-flying photo-recce enemy over Liverpool. I actually persuaded my Tiffy to 26,000 feet before giving up the chase.

We were happy below 12,000 feet, happiest of all right down on the deck, chasing tip-and-runners or attacking ground targets with our cannon. And this is what we practised most days in this delightful spot among the sandhills and golf clubs of the north-west English coast.

During that late spring of 1943 we were constantly hearing of the cross-Channel shipping strikes and anti tip-and-run patrols, 'rhubards' and 'lagoons', which were keeping our fellow Tiffy squadrons busy down south. The combat reports were circulated, and I kept seeing familiar names from Polaris Flight Academy days. Johnny Baldwin had shot down three Me109s in one day with 609 Squadron, and there were other successes, and inevitable losses. I remember one morning someone on our flight breaking in when I was reading a report from 183 Squadron. 'What the hell's the matter with you?' he demanded. My eyes were fixed on the name Sergeant Allan Palmer, missing on a low-level attack near Fécamp. I learned later that the flak had got him.

'An old chum of mine, that's all.' A year ago we had been living it up in Beverly Hills. His mother wrote to Joan Fontaine where he had sometimes been a guest with me, and Joan later told me she had written several times trying to comfort her. He was an only child.

When our time came at last it was with the suddenness of so many wartime moves. Either someone in the hierarchy of Fighter Command had recognised belatedly that we were being wasted up here in the north, or it was the clamour from 12 Group, which had become so loud that it had at last been heard. The fact was that the tip-and-runners from Holland and Belgium were making life a misery for the eastern coastal towns and harbours. All they had to catch them were Spitfire Vs and they were simply not fast enough.

We were given twenty-four hours to pack and for the ground crews to have serviceable as many Tiffies as possible. As always, they did wonders, and for the first time we were about to put fourteen aircraft into the air. I let someone else have the Moth; I wanted to be with the squadron this time. Butch Taylor led us with great panache, forming up over Southport, and then doing a very low beat-up of the seafront hotels where lived the very rich Liverpool folk, all too familiar to us, safe from the bombing, mean with their drinks and disdainful of servicemen and women.

'Goodbye you lot of scrimshankers!' Butch called out over the R/T as we skimmed the roof of the Prince of Wales Hotel. We enjoyed that.

May 13th was a clear day, and the flight south-east was a revelation of the impact on the countryside of the RAF and, more recently, of the American Air Force. The Midlands, Lincolnshire and Norfolk were spotted with hundreds of airfields, the circuit of one often brushing the circuit of its neighbour. All the bombers that were pounding Germany day and night were identifiable below, the dark Lancasters, Stirlings and Halifaxes of Bomber Command, and the medium bombers of 2 Group, scattered about their airfields or in their blast bays, and the American B17 Flying Fortresses and B24 Liberators on fields which had only just been completed. Fresh score marks told of many more fields under construction. Scarcely three years earlier, Hitler had boasted that no enemy bomber would ever darken the skies of Germany, but Germany was bombed almost every night of this month, five times by more than 500 aircraft. Nevertheless, German bombers and fighter-bombers were still knocking our towns about, too, and killing people, and now it was to be our business to help correct this situation along the Norfolk and Suffolk coasts.

Butch Taylor took us once round our new airfield, and ordered us to land successively in pairs, 'And I'll castrate the man who makes a balls of it.' No bad show, thanks. We did quite nicely, I thought, and after landing we followed the machines ahead along the perimeter track to our respective flight dispersals. The ground crew had only recently arrived, but B Flight's 'Flight' (the Flight-Sergeant in charge) had his erks out to guide us in.

'What's it like, Charlie?' I asked my fitter.

'In the middle of bloody nowhere, Sarge.'

'We'll miss the Southport pubs.'

'We bloody will.'

RAF Ludham was a satellite of the big sector station, Coltishall, and the nearest airfield to Germany. It was therefore best situated for convoy protection on our side and convoy attacks on the enemy. It was also handy for damaged returning bombers which could just make it to the coast and for others short on fuel. It was a standard wartime-built airfield, the buildings well scattered to minimise bomb damage, a WAAF section, airmen's, sergeants' and officers' messes, concrete paths full of bicyclists. No one walked if they could bike, and no one biked if they could cadge a lift in a truck.

The area was, in fact, by no means publess, and you could bicycle to any one of a dozen in the evening, including the marvellous Horning Arms on the river. This had received a direct hit earlier in the war, killing a lot of airmen and WAAFs but had now been repaired and was a very popular rendezvous. But there was none of that for the time being. Group had told us we had twenty-four hours to settle in and familiarise ourselves with the area.

Jensen said, 'We're doing a standing patrol of two aircraft, ninety minutes each, throughout the daylight hours. God knows how the troops are going to keep us serviced, but those are the orders. Two more on instant readiness.'

A faint groan from one of us was answered sharply, 'Yes, you're going to work for once. No more of the soft life. And you're all to get in a sector recce. Today.'

Navigating your way round this part of Norfolk was not too bad. The Broads were a great help and so were the Norwich balloons, while from the shape of the coastline you could nearly always identify your whereabouts. Further inland there were airfields everywhere so that a dead engine above, say, 5,000 feet was not the hazard it might have been, and was up in Yorkshire.

The next day was my twenty-first birthday and with a promptitude not much known today, the GPO had forwarded from Woodvale all our mail in twenty-four hours. A cake from my mother did not last out the day – did not last until teatime, and there were presents from the rest of the family, from Charlotte and kind cousins and the Coxes.

The CO was known to be making the patrol roster for the second half of the day. I knocked on his door.

'Well?' He was cross.

'Could I have an early one, please, sir?'

'Why?'

'It's my twenty-first birthday and I'm going to have a party.'

No congratulations, no acknowledgement. He bent back to his task and I let myself out. When the roster went up mid-morning, I saw I was on the last patrol which, with double British Summer Time and the patrol finishing at 10.30, ruled out any possible celebrations. I wondered what I had done wrong and why Butch Taylor himself had chosen to lead me on this patrol.

We met down at the dispersal half an hour before take-off. The only communication was a shout from him before we went out, 'Keep your eyes open.' He was in his own DMT for his initials, and I had DN 389 – JE-F, a plane I had often flown before. The sun had already set but there was still plenty of light in the sky.

We met the pair we were relieving just north of Great Yarmouth and waggled wings in greeting and proceeded on our way. The blackout was particularly strict along this vulnerable stretch of coast and there was not a glimmer of light from houses to be seen as darkness began to close about us.

Up and down, up and down, we went, Great Yarmouth to Southwold at 1,000 feet, turn and back again. We were on every radar screen and the anti-aircraft gunners could see us in silhouette against a moonless dusk sky. The only sound was faint static over the radio, not even the most distant voice. I suddenly realised that willy-nilly I had become a night fighter pilot after all as I turned my head one way and then the other. 'Ceaseless vigil', as Biggles would have recorded it. It was obviously far too late for a tip-and-run raid. No fighter-bomber could find its target. But, remember what the Boss had said, 'Keep your eyes open.' I did my best, goggles raised for better vision, gun button on 'fire'.

They came in under the radar at 9.56 p.m. precisely, about twenty-five of them in rough line astern, their arrival heralded by an outpouring of inarticulate cries from our controller and a twinkling of lights as if Lowestoft had reverted to its peacetime rôle of holiday resort. The coastal guns were putting up a terrific fire but the brilliance, moving with the speed of the planes southwards down the coast, made it all the more difficult to spot them. I thought I caught a glimpse of them between Great Yarmouth and Lowestoft and tried to alert the CO but the ether was filled with several voices, none, it seemed, quite under control.

We had both opened up to full throttle and revs with speed up to 350 and plenty more to come. More flashes now from the Lowestoft guns and the bright yellow burst of bombs. Suddenly there was no sign of the CO. Was he attacking them over land, equally despairing as I was of communicating by radio? Certainly he must have seen the illuminated proof of the enemy's presence.

I remembered later, to my surprise, that I was fairly cool now that the long-awaited contact had been made. I had the benefit of height, of greater speed, of heavier armament, and of surprise. What a gift! And the time to catch them was when they turned out to sea again when their silhouette would be visible against the lighter ocean.

The first of the enemy were beating up Southwold, with sickening bomb flashes from the centre of this pretty little village, and then turning to port, and racing in loose line-ahead over the water – like a swarm of frightened fish, and appearing to be quite uncatchable.

I turned east, kept well above them, confident that I would not be visible, waited until what I thought must be the last one to leave the coast, and then went down, at the same time turning on my reflector sight – something I should have had on all the patrol. I tried to adjust it to full low intensity, but it was either off or full blinding on. I knew the rheostat had gone and I had, in effect, nothing to aim with.

Press on regardless, as the half-comic-half-serious expression went. So I did, selected the last in the line – they were all Me109Fs – throttled back and opened fire first with full bright sight and then none at all, firing at the water behind my target, and then pulling up my aim. To my astonishment, I began hitting him, bits flashed past me and he began jigging up and down evasively.

I thought I might as well go on hosing away, in the belief that I could as blindly hit the 109 just ahead of him as my primary target. Then there was a splash and I saw my 109 hit the water, and a much bigger splash as he went in after a single bounce. I just had time to pull up over the spray and then continued to fire my ammunition into the dim mass of fighters ahead.

It must have been a second or two after that when I noticed a lot more splashing going on where I was not aiming, and in any case I had now used up my ammunition. Also my Tiffy did not feel quite right. In fact it felt uneasily lopsided. To my outrage, someone was firing at *me*. I did not believe it could be the enemy. I mean to say, this was *my* show. Obviously the CO had misidentified me. So I made a sharp climbing turn to the right, at the same time flashing 'Q', the letter of the day, on my belly lamp.

When I had a chance to look back – something I should have done all along – I saw that it was indeed the enemy, a Me109F, uncomfortably close and with intermittent sparkles from its wing cannon. I steepened my angle of climb, 'went through the gate' into emergency boost and he slipped away, completely outperformed. I did not always love the Sabre, especially not on 23rd January at Maltby-le-Marsh. But I owed my life to her that evening.

The 109 and I went our respective ways, and I pondered on several subjects like what a lost opportunity to get at least three of them, what had happened to my CO, and more immediately, what had happened to my Tiffy. There was a very substantial hole in my left wing, the metal sticking up like a fixed aileron, and there were odd draughts as if there might be more holes in the fuselage. I had to use full opposite stick to keep her more or less straight, my arms were already aching, and I was still a long way out to sea.

I crossed in again north of Southwold, where fires were burning and the anti-aircraft gunners had a brief go at me, and then called up base to tell the controller that I would probably have to make a belly landing if I made it home, so blood wagon and crash wagon please. This was crisply acknowledged and it was nice to hear a calm voice again. They put on runway lights for me, bless them. Wheels came down all right but no flaps. I cut the throttle as early as I dared and almost clipped the trees in my anxiety to get down. I landed very fast, ready for the ground-spin if one of the tyres was blown. It was not, but both tyres became hot and smelly as I applied brake as early as I dared and came to a halt twenty feet or so from the end of the runway.

The crash wagon followed me closely along the perimeter track back to A Flight dispersal where aircrew and ground crew and a body of WAAFs had assembled, the gen having got around swiftly. When I opened the window and shouted the news, there was a quite considerable cheer. First day of proper ops and we had broken our duck. I was not at all sure about my legs as I stood up, and I was quite glad not to have to walk back to the dispersal, as I was carried shoulder high.

Butch Taylor said resentfully, 'Why didn't you call me? I didn't see a bloody thing.' But he had the grace to congratulate and thank me, and then Group was on the phone to do the same and for the only time in my life I was the centre of all admiring attention. Frank Jensen seized a torch and we all went out to examine my poor old battered Tiffy. My adversary had shot well in the near-darkness, scoring six 20 mm cannon strikes, one of them about two feet behind my head, and nineteen machine-gun hits – 'No, here's another!' someone called out in the dark.

Jensen took me back to the sergeants' mess where I was given first a telephone to send a telegram to Charlotte and my parents, and then a *jug* of beer and ordered to drink it. Happy Birthday was sung, we all – officers and sergeants alike – got fairly drunk before I went to bed even more blearily than I had exactly twelve months earlier after I had lived it up on the Sunset Strip instead of the North Sea.

All night long I did not close my eyes, watching the summer dawn slowly light up the sky and reminding myself how lucky I was to see the sun again at twenty-one years and one day old. At the same time, I repeatedly reflected that I was making a bit of a song-and-dance about an episode that had occurred time and time again during the Battle of Britain and since. Not at all Captain Ballish. I think it was Bunny Oury who told me the next day that Y (listening in) service had reported the loss of two 109s, one flown by the CO, and as the guns made no claim it seemed possible that my wild hosing had caused a second 109 to go in. I will never know for sure, but I certainly made no formal claim and just one swastika was painted under the cockpit of my new Tiffy, G for Georgina. But I *was* promoted on the same day to Flight-Sergeant, and that glinting crown above my three stripes gave me ridiculous satisfaction.

The standing patrols continued for several weeks, but as expected the wear and tear on the aircraft became too great for the ground crews to cope with. We were given some Hurricanes to keep our hand in while instead of the taxing patrols we were reduced to instant readiness at the end of the runway, strapped into the cockpit and ready to go in thirty seconds. It was very hot and very boring and I used to read, relying on my fitter to alert me to the red warning Very light if it should be fired. It was, one afternoon, and I started up at first cartridge, hurled my copy of *Horizon* into the slipstream and was soon in the air. We were given a course to steer and went hell for leather out to sea. After following several vectors we spotted something just below cloud. But our 'hostile' turned out to be a drifting balloon and we took it in turns to fire at it until it exploded and the remains drifted down to the sea. We said nothing on the R/T and when we got back, and were seen to have fired our guns, we answered excited questions, 'Yes, sent her down in flames. Wizard prang . . .'

My number one on this scramble was Pilot Officer 'Wig' (for his ample hair) Monk. We got on well, were of that rare breed, readers, and off duty went for long bike trips around the Norfolk countryside. By July, Group decided we had finally discouraged the Luftwaffe from attempting any more tip-and-run raids, and we went over to the offensive.

To the Dutch coast and back was 250 miles, and we became familiar with that stretch of sea from twenty feet or so above the waves. Sometimes a trawler or MTB would flash past, and if the Royal Navy had time to shoot at us, they did, their principle being that anything in the air was hostile. Otherwise it was the seemingly timeless unrolling of wave-tops and troughs, a mesmerising carpet of white and blue-grey. The purpose of these operations was to rendezvous with torpedo bombers and protect them when they attacked German shore-hugging convoys, or reconnaissance, or simply provoking a response from the German fighters at Schipol. Although we were 125 miles from home, they were oddly reluctant to come up.

A recently published book shows a facetious sign outside a dispersal hut advertising the numerous functions offered by 'Butch's Bastards' or '195th Pursuit', including 'Rhubarbs', 'Coastal Patrols', 'Lagoons (Sleepy)', 'Night Intruders', etc. The days were long, time off short. The summer of 1943 has always signified in my memory the essence of flying warfare. Over the North Sea and its coastlines we witnessed violence and death, death of friends and enemies. To kill and destroy was all, and yet it was such a beautiful summer, and the holidaymakers still swarmed in their boats on the Broads all around us.

Soon after the surviving RAF bombers returned to their bases, the deep groan of the American 8th Air Force day bombers began to fill the air. It might take them as long as one hour to climb and form up in their defensive groups above us, hundreds of them, etching the sky with geometric patterns of contrails, before setting off to the hell of the Ruhr or Schweinfurt. Their fighters would follow them later, to give them protective escort for a while before having to return and leave their 'big friends' to their fate.

Late in the afternoon, the mauled formations of Flying Fortresses and Liberators could be seen coming in low from the east, some on two or three engines. There was little we could do to help them. Our range was even less than their own Thunderbolts and Lightnings. But I do remember one afternoon being scrambled and sent out 100 miles to guide and talk back one of these savagely mauled Fortresses. I found this straggler without much difficulty and came close alongside. There were gaping wounds in the fuselage and both pilots and several gunners were dead. The navigator was flying her on two engines and the bomber was steadily losing height. I guided him over the coast and gave him a course to his airfield but had to leave him because I was running out of fuel. I waved and wished him luck but never discovered if he made it.

Most nights, the German intruders came over, ready like birds of prey to speed down and pick off a vulnerable victim the second runway lights were momentarily switched on. Searchlights ranged the sky and the airfield guns banged away. At breakfast, in the way news of disaster and triumph flashed from airfield to airfield, we heard of perhaps a landing Lancaster being blown up at Mildenhall, or a searchlight-coned Ju88 shot down not far from Coltishall.

Our own offensive work inevitably led to casualties. The Luftwaffe never caught us, and its fighters were rarely seen. It was the flak that was the devil. Dear old 'Wig' was one of the first victims. Two more from A Flight went missing a few days later. The most poignant loss was Wimpey Jones, a cheerful, amusing and sweet-natured fellow who went off, amidst the usual raucous chaffing, to marry. Within a few days of his return, aglow with happiness, flak shot him into the sea near an enemy convoy. His widow never remarried, but she bore Wimpey a son. All this low flying led to a number of accidents, too. Flight-Sergeant MacMillan spun in doing a tight turn too close to the ground. Sergeant Jones caught his wing on a wave-top and splashed in over the Dogger Bank in the middle of the North Sea, where it is notoriously shallow.

Because we were going to miss Sergeant Jones, a jolly Australian, we had a fairly drunken party in the sergeants' mess in his honour. He turned up in the middle of it. He had found himself sitting, feeling quite well, on the seabed, and had bailed out in reverse, floating to the surface quite quickly. Now he was in the same state of inebriation as us, after being served rum by the Navy in an MTB all the way back to Great Yarmouth.

'Do you mind if I get married, sir?' I asked my Flight Commander.

We had just returned from some op and it was an unexpected subject to raise at this time, or any time that summer.

'What for?'

'Well, the usual reasons, I suppose. I mean you're married.'

Frank Jensen was indeed married, and earlier had given Wimpey Jones permission. He tactfully did not refer to this precedent but said he would have a word with the (unmarried) CO. It seemed silly to go on *not* being married when we both wanted to and there was a moderate chance of my never knowing what it was like if we did not. We did not actually talk like this; it was more a mutual understanding and Charlotte's mother probably felt the same when she gave her consent.

I got ten days' leave and so did Charlotte, who was now at the Admiralty as a cipher Wren. So we married in Bushey Parish Church on 17th July 1943. I had borrowed a two-seater Morris 8 tourer from my cousin Raymond Cooper who was away in Burma, and we went off happily in this on empty roads to the Lake District. People were very nice to RAF pilots, especially if they had a bit of ribbon up, and a petrol coupon, winkled out of the RAF, usually produced double its value.

We stayed at a hotel in the Borrowdale Valley which was evidently popular with middle-aged seniorish Army officers with not much to do and their dowdy middle-class wives. The RAF was rarely popular with the Army after Dunkirk, where they thought they had been let down after their own defeat, and the Battle of Britain when they thought public adulation had gone too far at the RAF's victory. On top of that, I had a car which we used every day, and a young blonde bride who seemed *happy* and unsubdued by their disapproval.

We climbed the fells, supplemented our meagre sandwiches with bilberries, boated on Derwentwater and swam in the freezing becks. The war suddenly became distant, and then ceased to happen altogether. We hardly ever saw a plane, and on the fellsides heard only the buzzards and curlews and the tumbling ghylls, and smelt only the bracken and heather.

There was a new ugly word in the air when I returned to Ludham. It was Bombs. There had for long been rumours that we might be losing the purity of our function. We were all pathetically conscious and proud of being *fighter* pilots, successors to those heroes of the RFC in the First World War, and Stanford-Tuck, Denis David, Duggy Bader *et al* of the Battle of Britain. We had all undone our top button as we stepped from our first Hurricane, wore silk scarves, frequently beat up the mess and generally behaved in the hell-for-leather wild way expected of us. I believe it helped a great deal, and in 195 Squadron we had only one case of a pilot who had to be sent away for suffering too frequently from 'engine trouble' halfway to the action. (Much later I saw him at 11 Group HQ, mightily promoted in admin and mightily pleased with himself.)

But now, it seemed, we were going to become fighter-bomber pilots. Fitters were fitting bomb racks under our wings, and in no time we were practising dive-bombing a circular target, coming down from about 8,000 to about 1,500 feet, using the gunsight, and pressing the bomb tit. There was much grumbling but our rôle in the coming assault on Europe had been decided: it was to be close support for the Army, rocketing, bombing and strafing battlefield targets at short notice, beating up enemy road convoys and tank concentrations and that sort of interesting but slightly dodgy sort of activity.

Meanwhile we continued through the rest of the summer crossing and recrossing the North Sea until that stretch of Dutch coastline around IJmuiden and Texel became as familiar as Southwold and Great Yarmouth, if more hostile. There were several scrambles, all proving fruitless, and a high-level medium bomber escort which brought up some twenty enemy fighters which sheered off when they saw us.

In the midst of all this, my mother and father decided to have a short holiday nearby. It was as well it was short for it was not very satisfactory, and I knew they would have preferred to be at my brother's farm. I was flying or on standby much of the time and there was little for them to do. Although the guest house was almost within Ludham's circuit, my father evinced no curiosity in what I was doing. On their first night I had dinner with them and my mother greeted me, 'You look peaky, dear.'

'Nothing that a good walk won't cure,' said Father. 'Too much drink and hanging about doing nothing,' he added with a somewhat censorious laugh.

To mention that I had in fact been up since 3.30 a.m., and had patrolled on reconnaissance between Egmond and Texel being hit by intense flak that morning, seemed under the circumstances of my father's confused pacifism to be in poor taste. I longed to talk to my mother about it all, opening my heart, but I suspected – probably wrongly on later reflection – that she would feel such confiding would suggest disloyalty to my father.

Relief of a rather bizarre nature arrived at the same guest house in the form of the delightful, easy-going Mrs Frank Jensen. She got on famously with Meg and George and eased the embarrassment. We all five had dinner together, and in my junior capacity it was just like eating with the headmaster and his wife while they reported on my progress.

'You had better be off,' my Flight Commander told me soon after 8 p.m. 'You're on early standby again,' he added but it might just as well have been 'We want you bright for the house match tomorrow.'

My guilt about my lack of communication with my father and the simultaneous duty to see my parents as often as possible was a distraction I could do without just then, and it was an unmitigated relief when they left to help Phil with his harvest. I wished I knew why they had come.

The squadron moved to an airfield called Matlaske in north Norfolk at the end of July. We messed in a beautiful manor house and swam in the lake on hot evenings, and practised more dive-bombing. 'What about a live target?' Jensen muttered almost as an aside after one session. I said I didn't mind if I did. 'It's full moon tomorrow,' he added as if air warfare was now embracing astrology.

This puzzled me and I asked about the moon's relevance. 'It's a *night* rhubarb,' he explained, meaning a one-man beat-up.

'Oh,' was all there seemed to be to say.

So in the afternoon I took H-Harry, my new mount, down to Manston in Kent, the nearest airfield to enemy soil, and an armourer or two clipped a pair of 250-pounders to the underwing racks.

On these night rhubarbs, with two 500-pounders next time, you hoped to find a target worthy of your bombs early on, thus making you more nimble for strafing later. You did need to be quick sometimes, too, because this area was stiff with gun sites and blue or yellow searchlights which picked you up by radar with worrying speed, and then the light tracer flak would come arching up, always accurately. It looked lazy and unlethal at first in its trajectory, and then seemed to accelerate unnaturally quickly before passing you by – if it did.

Those big, fat, black French trains made the best target. Once I bombed the locomotive first and then in the course of two or three cannon attacks set the trucks burning from end to end. Canal bridges were less satisfactory, and the occasional dimly lit car made a tricky target in the dark. St-Omer airfield offered great opportunities as it was one of the biggest in northern France. I chanced upon it one night and wished I had not, the defences being in proportion to its size. It was best to leave the French and Belgian coasts flat out and as tight to the ground as you could, and with luck the gunners could get their sights on you only when you were halfway home, four minutes or so.

This night-time free-lancing was dropped in November 1943 and I never did it again. On the 10th of that month the entire squadron was gathered together for a briefing. There was, for once, an air of solemnity in B Flight's dispersal, with the CO and the Spy standing behind a table on which there were maps, not of the Dutch coast this time but of the Pas de Calais, and high-level photographs.

The Spy had gained greatly in authority since those early weeks of the year and was not often teased. This time, however, his opening words were greeted with guffaws.

'These are Noball sites,' he announced, and Butch Taylor told us to shut up. 'They are secret weapon sites of some description,' the Spy continued gamely. 'We're not quite sure but we do know they are dangerous and going to get top priority.' All that could be seen were narrow white slits in the chalk soil of north-east France, dozens of them, with the faint signs of spoil tips and a number of carefully camouflaged buildings.

The CO added that we were going down at once to Manston to get bombed-up and operate with 3 Squadron Tiffies. 'Take a toothbrush,' he added.

We had a drink in 3 Squadron's mess, and at mid-day on 10th November twenty of us formed up, climbed to 8,000 feet and nipped across the Channel. The heavy flak came up before we reached the white cliffs on the other side and continued with an intensity none of us had ever experienced before all the way to the target area. This was not difficult to find. Several hundred medium bombers had dropped their loads that morning, and the landscape about the white slits was deeply pockmarked with craters.

There could be no doubt about the priority rating the enemy was giving to the protection of this area. We flew through a cloud of black puffs, each with its evil scarlet-yellow centre, hearing and feeling the rattle of splinters against our machines, and were rocked by the explosions. There were larger yellow clouds, too, later identified as phosphorous flak, and I saw one of 3 Squadron go straight into one and fail to come out again. He was one of their flight commanders, a fellow called Walmsley we learned later.

Butch Taylor was not going to hang around. 'Right, going down now!' he bellowed over the radio, turning onto his back and as he did so, revealing his two 500-pounders. We all followed in quick succession, dropping like meteors, releasing at about 2,000 feet and using our speed, by now edging towards 500 m.p.h., to go through the light and heavy flak.

Evasion and getting clear was an indecorous, every-man-for-himself business. I had never jinked so hard in my life, skidding left-right-left-right again, and, as at night, pulling up halfway across the Channel.

The mess before lunch was full of exclamatory chatter over pints of bitter. Walmsley had been a popular flight commander, and we expressed our sympathy as well as we could. 'There's another go after lunch,' a small, dark Australian replied ominously. And it was true. H-Harry had been almost inevitably hit before, and was hit again on the repeat show, but not very seriously, and we all returned safely. I recall lying on the grass in the late afternoon sun beside my hot Tiffy, using my 'chute and dinghy as a pillow, contemplating life and death,* and for the first time feeling rather veteran at twenty-one.

Later in the month, we moved down to Tangmere in West Sussex and took the longer journey across the Channel to the Cherbourg peninsula, where the same scene and the same strength of flak met us. Again my Tiffy was hit, and the engine coughed, lost power and coughed again several times. I fell behind and was given an escort, and even began searching Guernsey from 5,000 feet for a large enough field to accommodate a crash-landing.

This was one of my last ops with 195. I had been commissioned in the autumn, and after nearly twelve months it was decreed that I, and several others, were to go on rest. A great deal had happened in 1943, and on the domestic front, Charlotte had been discharged, pregnant, from the WRNS. For the first time for three years I had Christmas at Bushey, and very nice it was, too.

* Some 3,000 aircrew in all were killed attacking the sites of Hitler's first secret weapon launch sites.

10

The Secret Weapon

Woodlands, Harrow Road, Middlesex, was a soft posting all right after the hurly-burly of Norfolk and Essex. Bentley Priory, just up the road, had a fancy mess, accommodation was superior, the West End was forty minutes away by bus or tube and working hours not onerous. It could not have been more convenient for me as the Bushey cottage was within walking distance and I got permission to sleep out and thereby led a relaxed domestic life, with weekends off, just like peacetime. Meanwhile, I was one of a dozen or so 'resting' pilots learning about radar.

Charlotte was now heavily pregnant and I blessed my luck at being able to share these last weeks with her. On the evening of the day the Woodlands course finished and I would have been sent elsewhere, Charlotte went into labour at home. It was a lengthy business, and in 1944 no doctor or midwife could countenance the presence of the father, nor would I have expected to be there. I even had to sleep elsewhere, but on Easter Sunday morning, 9th April, Charlotte gave birth to a baby girl. She was five hours old when I was allowed to see her, all puckered up like a last year's walnut, though soon, of course, Sarah was the most beautiful baby in the world.

After some GCI (Ground Control Interception) experience elsewhere, I was given a posting to RAF Beachy Head which, because of its commanding position over 500 feet above the Channel, was full of the latest electronic gear for spotting the enemy. Behind a mass of security barbed wire was one constantly rotating radar aerial, and nearby a Nissen hut, the ops room for this T16 radar. Here we sat for four-hour shifts through day and night watching the signals from the aerial reproduced as an illuminated rotating arm on a dark screen. On this screen was marked the coastlines of France and Belgium and southern England. Anything located in the air was seen by the radar operator as a smudge, or blip, left behind by the white arm. Progress was noted by tracing on the screen each blip and thus, by simple calculation, giving its speed and course, while another screen indicated the height.

All this electronic gear has become many times more sophisticated since the CHs and CHLs had contributed so greatly to the victory over the Luftwaffe in 1940. This new T16 had the tremendous advantage of seeing so low and distantly that it could pick up a German aircraft almost as soon as it was airborne from its French base. At this time, in late May 1944, the Luftwaffe was much too preoccupied with Russian offensives in the east to give trouble to us, except in the form of snap raids and photo-reconnaissance ops. What we were concerned with was the imminence of D-Day, and the opening of the secret weapon attack, which seemed likely to coincide.

The bombing offensive against the Noball targets had continued at enormous cost to Bomber Command. Thousands of tons of bombs had followed our puny contribution last November, but still intelligence from France suggested that the attack would soon come.

There were about six officer controllers on the T16, WAAF and RAF, a jolly party billeted out in Eastbourne at a mournful Plymouth Brethren hotel, where grave, abstemious, civilian permanents did not blend easily with the light-hearted and not always totally sober boys and girls in blue. Squadron-Leader Bill Igoe was our boss, a renowned controller from the Battle of Britain, and within his minute command he had two more professionals besides ex-pilots like me, who still had a lot to learn.

There was a tremendous state of tension all along the south coast of England at that time. The remaining civil population was severely restricted in their movements, and a special pass was needed to visit the area. Tanks, armoured cars, trucks, amphibious vehicles and guns were tucked away in vast numbers along the road verges and in fields close to points of embarkation. The first wave of some 150,000 troops, American, Canadian, British and their allies, were camped out or billeted in the coastal towns. Every day and night the bombers went out to cut communications to prevent the rapid movement of German divisions after the invasion, and our T16 screen was never empty of plots.

I came on duty at 6 a.m. on 6th June and was greeted by Bill Igoe who turned his attention briefly from the screen. 'Take a look at this – the balloon's really gone up!' Clear across the Channel in a thick band from the Portsmouth to Portland area and further west to the Cherbourg peninsula and the Normandy coast, was blanked out by the bright light of 'window', millions of strips of foil dropped by aircraft to defeat any enemy radar attempt to locate ships or planes.

'So, this is it,' I replied. Unprofound, but what else? Outside the High Command, no one understood that when the invasion of Europe took place, the allies would strike with such superiority in numbers and quantity of material, with almost total control of the air, that it could scarcely fail. But we, in this cliff-top Nissen hut, were as excited but profoundly anxious as everyone else. The 'window' drifted away, and for the rest of the watch we saw the follow-up in the air to the first landings.

The next day, Bill Igoe gathered us all together up at Beachy Head. 'We're watching for the Hun secret weapon. It's coming any time now. You'll recognise it when it does – very, very fast, dead straight course, no pilot, just a lot of TNT. Code word is "DIVER".'

Later, I asked him why it was that all our bombing had failed to prevent the enemy from setting up this counter-offensive to the D-Day landings. 'Most of the big launching sites you saw last year were wiped out,' he told me. 'But the Hun extemporised mobile launching sites that could be tucked into clearings in the woods, heavily camouflaged.'

And so it was. Exactly seven days after the allied troops stepped ashore in France, the first pilotless planes, the flying bombs, buzz-bombs or doodlebugs as everyone called them, came over. They were easy to identify, from their launching locality, their speed of climb, and the way they crossed the Channel towards us, the blips at every sweep of the aerial marking their high speed.

The response was clear. 'DIVER! DIVER! DIVER!' we called Sector, followed by their position, height and course. At first there was little co-ordination and fighter pilots scrambled as the news came in, from us or the CHL stations, of approaching flying bombs, in Spitfires, Typhoons, Mustangs, Thunderbolts and the new refined Typhoon, the Tempest. The sky was full of machines milling about, and though there were some successes, it was clear to everyone that urgent reorganisation was needed, and the order went out that only the Tempest V wing at Newchurch on Dungeness, one or two squadrons of Mustangs with specially uprated engines, and a handful of the fastest Spitfire XIVs were to tackle this new enemy. At night, twin-engine Mosquitoes and our first jets, Meteors, were drawn into the battle.

At Beachy Head our main responsibility was the wing of Tempests, which were faster than any other fighter at that time and could catch the doodlebug comfortably. With two of us on the tube we could handle a number of these fighters, and worked up a special understanding relationship with 'Bee' Beamont, their exceptionally skilful Wing-Commander.

As the numbers increased, by day and by night and in all weathers, we and the fighter pilots and above all the maintenance staff became busier and busier. 'Bee's' pilots were doing five and sometimes six missions a day. They were not always successful, for the doodlebug made a very small as well as very fast (around 380 m.p.h.) target and if you cut the range down to 200 yards or so the effect of exploding the 2,000 pounds of high explosive could throw you out of control or simply incinerate your aircraft.

The Poles with their Mustangs did not take much notice of us or anyone else and went free-lancing on their own. What they enjoyed most was to follow the doodlebugs coming over the Beachy Head cliffs and send them down by nudging their wing with one of their wing tips, and thus upsetting the gyro just as they approached. They 'scored' two direct hits on the cliff just below us, shaking the ground and sending vast quantities of chalk into the sea. They thought this was the greatest joke and cackled over the R/T before making for home.

This 'war of the robots' was an alarming and uncanny business. The doodlebugs, at around 2–3,000 feet, with their stubby wings and flames from their simple pulse-jet engine trailing from the rear, became a too-familiar sight over London and south-east England, and when their gyro ceased at the pre-set time, the ensuing silence followed by the cracking explosion often caused the destruction of a dozen houses and many deaths. They and the later V2 rockets were the most wanton of all civilian killing weapons, and when amateur historians and censorious liberals still today deplore our bombing of German cities, it is worth remembering that the enemy reckoned on sending over 3,000 a month, or 36,000 (which they had ready) in the year.

Thanks to the earlier bombing of the launching sites and the fighter, anti-aircraft gun and balloon defences, only 2,242 flying bombs got through to London, almost their sole target. These killed over 9,000 and severely wounded 50,000 people. If Hitler's aim had been fulfilled and, say, 30,000 had got through, some 120,000 Londoners might have died – three or four times as many as were killed in the notorious Dresden raid.

From our little Nissen hut, it was tempting to regard the whole doodlebug business as something of a competitive game, and we threw a 500 shot-down celebratory party at Bexhill for Beamont's pilots. But a few days later, I had to travel to London on some official business and was appalled by the sight of the south London suburbs where the flimsy houses (23,000 in all) had been flattened and many times more grotesquely damaged. Because of the blast effect of the instantaneous fuse, almost every tree and shrub had lost its leaves, leading to a freak false spring of bright green in October that year when it was all over.

It was a sobering experience, and it was difficult not to accept personally the blame for every flying bomb that got through, and certainly no cause for the party of celebration. The guns, trying to cope with the flying bombs that got past the fighters, had not had much success so far, but by superhuman efforts, General Pile, the C-in-C, had taken delivery of tens of thousands of British-designed, American-manufactured proximity fuses as well as super-refined predictors.

The decision was now made to transfer every one of the thousands of anti-aircraft guns of all calibres from the outskirts of London, down to the coast. By an amazing piece of organisation, this was accomplished in seventy-two hours, and – to their fury and ours – the Tempest pilots and the rest were allowed to operate only out in the Channel or some distance inland.

But the results from the gunsite behind Eastbourne, for example, when they had settled in, were amazing to witness. Night and day and in all weathers they shot down almost every doodlebug within their range, the explosions like some Western Front offensive, pitting the farmland with craters over many acres. Soon, the guns worked up to an 82% success ratio, and although they never shot down in total as many as our fighters, this rate of attrition turned the tide. Then, across the water, the armies advancing from Normandy overran the launching sites, and the Battle of the Robots was virtually over.

*   *   *

RAF wives and children now began to join us in Eastbourne, and our Plymouth Brethren hotel assumed, for the permanents, a more domestic and agreeable air. A stretch of beach was opened to the public for the first time since 1940 and all of a sudden wartime austerity and anxiety gave way to summer holiday sunny serenity. Charlotte arrived with our five-months-old baby Sarah and, for a brief week or two, it was as if the war was over.

But it was not to be. Brussels fell, Antwerp fell, then suddenly, as Bill Igoe put it, 'The bloody Hun's put the shutters down.' It was an awful anti-climax. The armies in the west had ground to a halt. The Rhine was not yet crossed, the Panzers were digging in, and British airborne forces were soundly beaten at the Arnheim 'bridge too far'.

I said to Charlotte one day, 'I think I'd better get back into the real business again.'

'You mean flying?' And I said yes, and she did not say anything, which was nice of her.

I quickly learned that it was out of the question. There was now a great surplus of pilots. But while stationed at Bentley Priory I had played billiards with an officer, of no high rank but enormous influence in postings. We had become rather friendly, and it now seemed the time to put this friendship to the test. I darted up to Fighter Command HQ. It was not difficult to allow myself to be beaten on the billiards table, and then we went to the bar.

'I want to get back onto flying, Chris.'

'Impossible,' he said, draining his glass and holding it up to the light to make sure none was left.

'Operational flying.'

'Don't be daft. Out of the question.'

I signalled the barman. 'Typhoons. But I would compromise with Tempests.'

Less critically now, Chris held up his glass again. 'Do you know,' he asked, 'there are *several thousand* fully trained pilots that Second TAF can draw on.' He explained there were sergeant-pilots cleaning lavatories and eating their hearts out in transit camps . . .

I broke in with a brief line-shoot about my experience. The barman was filling Chris's glass without prompting, knowing what was going on. Chris warned of bombs and rockets – no real fighter pilots left. 'Ah, ta very much, perhaps I will . . .'

Pride forbade my postings flight-lieutenant from giving me what

I wanted at once. For a few weeks I stooged about in old Spitfires and Hurricanes, exercising my combined flying and radar knowledge for the benefit of new young trainee controllers. But on 1 January 1945 I was despatched to Aston Down and was soon studying the familiar lines of my old friend and enemy, the Tiffy.

He had been smoothed out since I had last flown him. The complicated and awkward car-type door had been replaced with a one-piece sliding hood, giving better all-round visibility, the radio whip aerial replaced by a streamlined mast, the prop was four-bladed and the Sabre had been uprated. To feel the kick of the engine and the tug of the torque was like resuming the challenge with an old bruiser in the ring instead of those namby-pamby sparring partners, the Spit and Hurri, I had been flying in December. This Tiffy took me up to 20,000 feet in less than the time taken to smoke a cigarette. It was a crystal-clear winter's day and southern England lay below as a map, from Beachy Head in the east to the north Cornish coast.

I felt drunk from the adrenalin-stirring sense of power the massive engine, the four projecting cannon and the primitive masculinity the Tiffy always induced in me. I did a very slow roll, sank at least 2,000 feet from the sheer weight of the beast, looped once or twice, found no one to play with and went home. Over the following days I practised with bombs and tried rockets for the first time. The rails seriously flawed the performance, I thought, but they certainly packed a punch, each of the eight rockets having the explosive power of a six-inch naval shell.

In a day or two I was packed off to a Tiffy squadron at Antwerp, travelling by boat and train. I was thankful for this experience. It had been tantalising only to read of the advance from Normandy, the liberation of Paris, the siege of Calais and other Channel ports, the December German offensive in the Ardennes, the British-Canadian advance to Nijmegen and the liberation of half of Holland. From the train window, and later from a 30 cwt truck, I could see the devastating trail, the flattened villages, the knocked-out tanks in the ditches, the massive detritus of modern war. It could as well have been the last year of the First World War rather than the last year of the Last Great War – anyway in pre-nuclear conditions. I spent a night in a transit camp and the flash of gunfire lit up the sky and the rumble of artillery continued through the night.

197 Squadron was quartered in half-destroyed suburban houses

outside Antwerp. There were holes in the roofs and gaps in the walls, while the last remnants of an extinguished domestic life – one or two smashed pictures on the walls, a three-legged sofa downstairs, a chest of drawers with a single child's sock in one drawer in my 'bedroom' – all added to the poignancy. It was bitterly cold and when not on standby we pilots spent most of our time collecting firewood, sawing up the less needed floorboards, the banisters, anything that would burn in the open grates.

Outside in the streets, Belgian citizens showed in their faces and their walk the price of more than four years of German occupation. Women in black and their children picked over the railway tracks for an unlikely lump of coal which had escaped so many eyes before. Antwerp itself had a haunted air. Liberation had brought only temporary relief and, ironically, had led to more deaths than under the Germans. Here was a key port for supplying the allied armies in their final assault on the Fatherland, and the Germans threw at it all the weapons they had – which were the doodlebugs that could no longer reach London, and their V2 rockets. In proportion to the size and population of the two cities, Antwerp suffered much worse than London and more than 4,000 people, including allied servicemen, were killed by nearly 6,000 missiles which landed within the greater Antwerp area. We were discouraged from going into the city at all, and it was hardly an attraction anyway, with nothing in the shops or restaurants, and the wretched people sunk in disillusionment.

Instead we took the train to Brussels on the occasional day off, and that was a different scene indeed, a city undamaged and doing a roaring trade in nightclubs, restaurants and brothels, and of course the black market. Even the bookshops were doing good business, and I added modestly to it.

There were a lot of good people on 197 Squadron, which had been formed at the same time as my old 195. They had been hard at it since before D-Day. They had not suffered undue casualties but there was evidence that some of the pilots needed a rest. In fact the CO left soon after I arrived, combat fatigued and drinking heavily. There was a pair of Rhodesian identical twins, inseparable in the air and on the ground, a jolly Siamese, a more serious Belgian, Philippe, who was hot at bridge, a particularly nice farmer's boy, Bob Gibbings, several Australians, always good company, and the new CO, Ken Harding, made a fine leader.

Shaving and the occasional wash in cold water were the sole

concessions to hygiene at Antwerp. I soon learned that baths or showers had been rare all the way from Normandy, and for days on end, in the bitter cold, clothes were only added to, never removed, like those peasants in the higher reaches of the Bolivian Andes. No one seemed to mind much, and everyone looked forward to an hour or more in the only warm place, a Tiffy's cockpit.

On my first op I looked somewhat askance at my machine. 'What sort of bombs are *those*?' I asked, for they were disproportionately large.

The armourer patted one and answered in a matter-of-fact voice, 'The usual, sir. Thousand-pounders.'

We had begun, way back in the summer of '43, daringly with 100-pounders, then went to 250s. Would she take off? She did, without much trouble. So we doubled the weight again. That really was daring, and before I left 195 I *landed* with two 500s after an abortive night mission because I could not bear the waste. But two 1,000-pounders – almost a ton! About the same load as the early American Flying Fortress bombers.

But the Tiffy did not seem to mind. The take-off *was* long, and she wallowed about a bit, but we went up to 8,000 feet without trouble, going north into occupied Holland, where we dropped sixteen of them on a bridge, and what a mess they made! Unfortunately, perhaps because of the speed of the dive or only because I had a cold, I burst my left eardrum, which was never to be quite the same again.

We soon moved out of Antwerp, to no one's sorrow, and advanced in company with the British and Canadian armies, from airstrip to airstrip, bombing and strafing the German front line, especially in the bloody battle for the Reichswald forest, SS headquarters, ammunition dumps, and towns like Winnekendonk, Calpar and Kappeln which were giving the troops trouble. We cut railway lines, strafed transport convoys at zero feet and once used incendiaries to set alight, spectacularly, an enormous fuel dump.

All these ops were carried out in the undramatic, matter-of-fact style of real veterans, and it was wonderful to be part of such a well-knit team, and at last feel genuinely Captain Ballish. Flak was invariably awful still (would they never run out of ammunition?) but we were skilful at evasion after these many months, and although we were all hit from time to time, few were shot down. Bob Gibbings and Tommy Clift were both forced out of their Tiffies one afternoon, but they survived as POWs. The worst casualty was one of the Rhodesians, killed in a bombing attack near Emden. His brother scarcely spoke another word, utterly shattered at this loss.

At an airstrip at Mill in Holland, Harding told us the Rhine was to be crossed the next day, and that our job was to suppress the flak, ranging about individually at low altitude, to protect the gliders and paratroops who would be dropping in great strength. For many of us this was the most interesting day of the war. Before take-off I sat on the wing, legs dangling between the protruding cannon, and lit a cigarette. The armourers were mucking about with the two fat bombs under the wings. Two of them were talking luridly about the Dutch girls they had taken out the night before.

We knew all the erks by name and our relationship with them was entirely democratic. One of them pulled himself up by the gun barrels and took a light from the end of my cigarette. Within a few feet of us in my plane were hundreds of rounds of high explosive shell, 1,000 pounds of anti-personnel (AP) bombs and two hundred or so gallons of high octane fuel. Back at Coltishall we should both have been court-martialled.

'They're doing the fucking Rhine today, eh?'

'That's right. Quite a party.'

'You're doing the trenches, are you, with the APs?'

'Gunposts, Jim. And it's time to go.' We stubbed our fags out on the wing and he slid off and ran to a passing bomb trolley jumping on board to save the walk.

Three hardstandings away the CO's prop was already turning and he was shouting at Red Mason who was late at his aircraft and still lumbering out with his 'chute banging against his buttocks.

The Mustangs which shared our strip had already gone. They were to meet the gliders and give them fighter escort. One of them had just come back early, in trouble, and had flipped upside down on landing with unpleasant results. About a hundred erks had run out and cleared the wreckage away for us.

We taxied out quickly and took off in pairs into a clear sky, formed up briefly and then broke up again as we neared our operating area. There was no difficulty in finding it. The night-long bombardment, and the fires it had started, had filled the air with slow-drifting smoke which combined with the early morning mist near to the river to make visibility very poor.

I dropped down low over the fields to the east of the Rhine, wondering how the glider trains would manage in these conditions. But I suddenly saw that some of them were already arriving, wallowing aerial armadas that seemed to fill the sky.

To port and starboard, above and below, released gliders were floating nose well down, fast towards their landing areas. Some were being fired at and badly hit. One right under me turned over on touchdown and spilt out everyone.

On my port side a Dakota plummeted out of control and on fire and went into a wood. It was impossible to tell if the parachutes were the crew or paratroops who were falling by plan in small scattered groups from other Dakotas.

I weaved about at our favourite height of fifty to 250 feet, fussed because I couldn't find a flak post while all this damage was being done and so many were dying. The Germans were master camouflagers and there was so much drifting smoke and mist that I began to feel helpless and as if trapped in some frustrated dream sequence. Above all I was angry.

Another Tiffy crossed in front of my nose. I caught a glimpse of the 197 letters OV on his side and noted that his bombs had gone. I turned sharp to starboard in the direction he had come from and saw a glint of muzzle flash among some trees. 20 mm tracer like a fireman's hose came up from a four-gun automatic battery, and I could just make out some figures moving among the trees and between barrels of heavy flak guns that were crashing away as hard as they could go.

I don't suppose that the short burst I gave them with my guns had much effect, but it had genuine feeling behind it and I was able to drop my two big APs in the area before skidding and skating my way out as fast as I could go. The flak didn't follow me. If they had any guns left they were after juicier targets.

The kaleidoscope of falling planes and men, gliders landing seemingly without plan if they were not shot out of the sky first, of smoke of every shade and hue, and sometimes the sharp blaze of flame from building or machine, all seen from the solitariness of a fighter's cockpit, left me stunned and anguished.

After another half hour of dodging about through the clouds of smoke, avoiding the Dakotas and gliders that were still pouring in, I shot off the rest of my ammunition at what I thought was a German gunpost, and then pulled up and out of the maelstrom.

Everyone else's impressions were similar to mine, and it was difficult to make any clear report on the results. Here, and no mistake, we had seen 'the blood-red blossom of war with a heart of fire'. And I thought I had witnessed, too, a terrible allied defeat. But we were all wrong. As we ate a scratch lunch down at the flight in the warm spring weather we were told that the British and American armies were across and well entrenched, with few casualties, and were already linking up with the airborne divisions.

The telephone rang in the squadron caravan and the CO came out a few minutes later. 'Come on, chaps, we're wanted for tank-busting now . . .'

At odd moments from time to time it passed through my mind that this second ops tour was coarsening me, and I recalled with wonder those fastidious doubts of school days. I suppose one way and another I had killed a number of the enemy on 195, but they were scarcely seen. Now they were all too evident, especially when strafing retreating enemy, mostly on horse-drawn vehicles for lack of anything else.

In a curious way I was somewhat reassured by something that happened to me on 7th April, two weeks or so after the Rhine crossing. Three of us went out with long-range tanks far to the north, in the Groningen area, to attack targets of opportunity, which really meant anything that moved on the roads, and this was certain to be enemy as civilians did not even have tyres for their bicycles.

We flew at 8,000 feet in clear weather, taking it in turn, the other two providing top cover in case one of the few Me262 jets around attempted to intervene. We dealt with a number of lorries, and then as we were due to return I saw a car speeding along a dead straight tree-lined road.

'You take that,' Hartley instructed, so down I went, very fast, to 200 feet, taking it from the rear. I suppose I had about two seconds' firing time, undershot, pulled up the nose, the cannon strikes dancing along the road like an hysterically fast fuse racing to its point of detonation. I just had time to make out several figures in the car, not one with the sense to keep a look-out.

My cine-camera was recording these officers alive, chatting, smoking perhaps. The next frame as my shells tore the car apart was all blood and fire. Then I felt a violent thud and the Tiffy was no longer under my control and half on its back at a hundred feet. I used all my strength to recover, but just as powerful in my mind was the age-old sense of guilt and acceptance of just retribution for my multiple murder. If I had died then, as I knew I was about to die, and deserved to die, I would have died with peace in my heart and with my brain registering that justice had indeed been done . . .

Leslie Hartley came alongside when by great effort I pulled the Tiffy up a few thousand feet. It was cold and draughty because I had jettisoned the hood and I was yawing about like a drunkard. 'What the hell have you done to yourself?' he asked.

'Flak.'

He moved in and I could see him study my tail. 'You *are* in a mess, aren't you? One of your wheels is down, too.'

I could manage about 200 m.p.h., and we flew back for forty minutes to Mill. Control ordered me to fly low over the watch tower. Johnny Baldwin, of all people, was our Group Captain, and I saw him come out with a pair of binoculars. He told me the wheel that was down was not locked. 'Do you want to bail out?' he asked. And when I decided that I preferred not to crack my unbroken record of remaining seated, he ordered me to the nearby strip at Volkel where there was grass alongside the metal-link runway – no sparks.

So, again I tightened straps, put down the other leg, which mercifully *did* lock, and glided down with a dead engine and fuel off. I ran along bumpily on the one wheel, stick hard over, for quite a distance, before everything collapsed under me and I went into a dusty series of ground loops. The crash wagon and ambulance were right beside me, and several airmen got to me before I could unstrap myself and get out. We then retreated fast, fearful of a blaze. But the poor old Tiffy just lay there, like a great dark beast that has met its match.

I had two successive cigarettes with the chaps, and an enormous draught of brandy, then someone drove me home. I never discovered whether it was really flak that had nearly done for me, or whether the wheel lock had given under the pressure of the pull-out and my hood had done all the damage to the tail. Both seemed equally unlikely but my suspicion was that it was the old enemy. On record, then, I had been forced to land once by a Me109 and once by flak, and recalling the circumstances of both events and what had happened in between I decided that I had fully exhausted all tanks, including long-range tanks, of my supply of luck. Inexplicably, God had forgiven me for my sins.

The following day I was off again on the same business, and this time there was no doubt that it was flak that hit me, if not so badly. Over the next couple of weeks, 197 was worked harder than ever on armed recce and pinpoint dive-bombing, and the only evidence that the war must be nearing its end was the dropping of surrender leaflets on a village west of Oldenburg which was holding out especially stubbornly.

We were operating from a field inside Germany now, under canvas, but not too austerely. The locals had long since fled their damaged, wide-open homes. We had a great veneered walnut radiogram in the officers' mess, fine carpets on the grass here and in our tents, and 'liberated' Mercedes took us around in style. But we flew in plain khaki battledress and carried little silk flags identifying ourselves as '*Ya Anglichánin*' (I am an Englishman), the Russians being near and liable to shoot on sight in the event of bailing out. The locals were not over-friendly, either, and who could blame them? I remember later, sight-seeing the ruins of Hanover, when the car broke down and curious, silent and hostile civilians gathered around. Two of us drew our Smith and Wessons and assumed a defiant stance while the third worked on, and cured, thank goodness, the engine fault.

My last op was the same old bombing and strafing raid on a small town, after which in effect my war came to an end. 'You're on sodding leave,' proclaimed my flight commander, waving a piece of paper. 'Lucky sod.' I picked up a Dakota to Nijmegen, where there was some delay, then on the way back in another Dakota, full of erks and kitbags, the co-pilot came back into the cabin. 'The fucking war's over. Just heard the Hun's suing for peace . . .'

The celebrating was instant and tumultuous. Kitbags were thrown and there was much dancing. The weather was rough any- way, and now this additional plunging about was making me air- sick. So here I was, the only pilot passenger, about to shame my calling.

'Come on, sir, the war's over – aren't you glad?' and the airman tried to pull me to my feet. Then he noticed the pallor of my complexion. 'Sorry, sir.'

Two days later, feeling quite well again, I was with Charlotte in the crowd before Buckingham Palace, champagne bottle in hand, shouting for the King.

11

An Occupation for Gentlemen

On the bus journey home from Uxbridge where I was discharged some twelve months later, various things went through my mind, like what the hell am I going to do now, that with capital resources of less than £400 I would shortly be responsible for *two* children as well as a wife, no degree, qualification nor skill in anything except flying single-engine machines of destruction at a time when all that was needed was construction, no roof except a borrowed part cottage of totally inadequate size, not even many thoughts or ambitions except, very firmly, like Jefferson, I had 'seen enough of one war never to wish to see another'.

We had been instructed to take full advantage of our demobilisation paid leave – in my case about four months – to settle back into a civilian existence. I thought I would have no trouble in obeying this last RAF order and dawdled about at home, playing with the baby, gardening rather lethargically and discussing with Charlotte what to do. We had bought a 1931 Standard 9 car at the end of the fighting which we had used in Cornwall where I had spent the last months of service, for visits to London and to my parents.

Charlotte agreed that I should do something with books, and we considered taking over Read the booksellers in Grasmere in the heart of the Lake District. Here one of her great-aunts had a primitive two-room cottage she would rent us. More seriously, we thought about the Red Lion Bookshop at Reigate, which was run by a friend of my father who was retiring. But we both felt the call of London, or at least its doorstep, and decided to try for a job in book publishing.

Meanwhile, I was becoming bored. Five years of being kept by the state seemed to have sapped any enterprise or initiative I might have had. I cannot believe that I can put the blame on flying ops. Many people, especially on Bomber Command, had had a rougher time than me, and they seemed to have slipped straight into well-paid jobs or applied, as I could have done, for a short course at a decent university and obtained a degree, meanwhile enjoying a generous allowance from the government.

I pulled myself together to the extent of applying for interviews with publishers between doing a part-time job as a delivery driver for the local Victoria Wine Company. The driving was for a time more fruitful than the interviewing, making me a number of friends among the housewives of north Watford while delivering a dozen Bass or Light Ale and sharing a cup of tea in the kitchen.

I began with Jonathan Cape. He had been a neighbour at Frensham and a Governor of the school, although the girls were more aware of this than the boys. I wrote to Paul Roberts, who wrote to Cape, who agreed to see me. In his elegant and palatial office in Bedford Square, I told him how much I admired his author, Ernest Hemingway, but this did not much impress him. 'We have nothing here,' he said. 'But I'll have a word with a friend of mine. His name is Philip Unwin, and his uncle is a great publisher called Sir Stanley Unwin.'

A week or two later I was offered an interview with the younger Unwin, and he was much nicer than Cape. He was a tall, fine-boned, pale-faced man who, I imagined, would not even have had to attend a medical board to be given exemption from military service. He talked a good deal about his uncle in an admiring tone, and said that he had mentioned my name to him. But they had no vacancies for young men without experience. On the other hand . . .

That is how I met C.J., a prominent figure in my early civilian life. Cyril J. Greenwood was the manager of a publishing house called John Lane The Bodley Head. It had gone bust in 1936 when John Lane's nephews, Allen and Richard Lane, had pulled out of the business without any notice, leaving behind many debts. These were mainly related to a subsidiary sixpenny paperback business they had set up with the financial backing of this established publishing house. After a short time the rest of the board lost confidence in this chancy offshoot enterprise and refused further financial support, whereupon the Lanes quit and set up business elsewhere, leaving behind all the production bills, and founding Penguin Books Ltd with a capital of £100.

Greenwood himself had begun a publishing business in the thirties, too, with a friend John Morris. This they called Boriswood, publishing mainly left-wing poets and indecent novels by James Hanley which got them into court a couple of times. Times were hard, and Boriswood went into liquidation along with several contemporaries at the same time as The Bodley Head. Stanley Unwin, aided and abetted by W. G. Taylor of Dent's and G. Wren Howard of Cape's, collared the lot and put C.J. in to run them under The Bodley Head name and colophon. This amalgam was housed in an old fruit-and-veg warehouse an apple's throw from the British Museum and even nearer to Unwin's hallowed premises of George Allen & Unwin Ltd in Museum Street.

It was to this unpromising old warehouse that I presented myself one morning in November 1946, as nervous and unconfident as I had been six years earlier with the RAF recruiting officer at Edgware. A diminutive ogress called Mrs Digby, acting as receptionist and C.J.'s secretary, greeted me and sent me up a wooden staircase to what I later learned was grandly called the Board Room, and thence after a few minutes to the office of C. J. Greenwood.

I took an immediate liking to this slip of a middle-aged man with a schoolboy's face, uptilted nose, sleek head of hair and a smile – and manner – of the utmost charm. Above his right eye was a dreadful old scar – from going through the window of a car, I later learned. 'Why do you want to get into publishing?' he asked me. 'There's absolutely no money in it, and it's mostly drudge anyway.'

I mumbled something or other and he told me what a small outfit he managed and how unimportant it was in the great world of publishing. Having explained what it was all about in the most succinct and informative manner, he led up to the fact that there was no vacancy now nor in the foreseeable future.

I must have shown my disappointment. He apologised again with absolute sincerity and regret. 'I really am most sorry.' I was just getting up when I identified the spines of books I knew well behind his head. 'Ah!' I exclaimed quite innocently. 'So you publish Rex Warner!'

It turned out to be a career-turning remark. With a great smile, C.J. declared, 'So you know Rex.' He sat down again. 'Where did you first meet him?'

'In the Latin room at school. He was a great favourite with us all and I love his books. He read aloud the opening chapter of *The Aerodrome* in manuscript to a few of us.'

Rex turned out not only to be a close personal friend of C.J. but about the only Boriswood author who had made the firm any money. We chatted on for ages and at the end, brought about by the entry of the ogress from downstairs with her dictation pad, C.J. offered me a job – a nebulous one starting on 1st January 1947 and paying £4 a week.

'Until then, why don't you find a job in a bookshop, just to get the feel of the trade?'

I returned to a hero's welcome. Charlotte was heavily pregnant, with our second daughter, Alexandra, 'Sandy', and it was just the news she needed. The next day I went to see another nice man who ran Truslove & Hanson, booksellers of Clifford Street, off Bond Street. It was a very smart place, busy with Christmas customers. I was told I was welcome to help out but I would not be paid. The invaluable experience will be your reward, said the manager, though he did give me a £10 bonus after Christmas.

It was quite useful, too, but surprisingly exhausting. The first lesson I learned was, even as a fit twenty-four-year-old, it took it out of you to be on your feet all day attending to the requirements of customers, who were mostly despotic and ill-mannered and cross if you did not have what they wanted. Books were rationed by publishers because of the paper shortage and we kept copies of the most wanted, like Veronica Wedgwood's *Velvet Studies*, Peter Scott's illustrated *Snow Goose* by Paul Gallico and the new Agatha Christie, under the counter. There was an even blacker market between the sales staff who chose obscure corners to conceal supplies for their favourite customers.

All this exercise, after an early start from Bushey, gave me an enormous appetite for lunch, and once a week I had a lovely change from Lyons at a very expensive local restaurant. These lunches were by invitation from the shop's number two, a spritely, rotund little man, dressed invariably in a black suit, white shirt and dark tie. He was very popular with the titled ladies who were finishing their Christmas shopping, to whom he was ingratiating but also firmly authoritative about what they should buy.

I supposed at the time that he must have been rewarded by these customers for how else could he afford a costly lunch daily. But, alas, six months later, after I had left, he was charged with putting his hand in the till and went down for quite a stretch in Parkhurst Prison.

We worked until late on Christmas Eve, and I returned for a few days before the New Year to help tidy up and stocktake. Then I became a publisher, on £4 a week plus £4 from my father.

The Bodley Head, like most publishers, had done well out of the war. The paper shortage was a handicap in some ways but also discouraged improvident overprinting and the taking on of marginally publishable books, especially fiction. C.J. had control of an impressive backlist, including the early C. S. Forester and Agatha Christie novels, some Max Beerbohm, G. K. Chesterton, C. S. Lewis and André Maurois titles, Joyce's *Ulysses* and Nehru's *Autobiography*. There was, for a while, the absolute certainty of selling out before publication every new book published, and this coincided with C.J.'s golden age of inspiration.

Now within the safety net of Sir Stanley Unwin, knighted in 1946 for his work for the book trade, with its old literary reputation and C.J. at the helm, agents sent along the work of the new generation of novelists. These authors then came to the office for a session with C.J. before lunch, mainly liquid. From my desk I could see them briefly coming up the wooden stairs before disappearing into the Board Room, and mightily impressed I was, too. Among them was the very young John Mortimer with his first novel, the craggy Howard Clewes, the portly John Pudney, the crashingly handsome Australian, James Aldridge, beefy Jack Lindsay and that old-timer poet and friend of C.J. from the '30s, Roy Campbell, hot from the South African veldt, in his wide-brimmed hat.

More than a counter against Campbell's right-wing views, were a number of old communist poet friends of C.J.'s, mostly from Boriswood, men like Montagu Slater, Edgell Rickword, Christopher Caudwell, and from America, Archibald MacLeish.

All these talented people appeared to me as a brief frame in a kaleidoscope of stairway film, and for months I never got near an author. Nor was I expecting to. C.J. had made clear the humbleness of my position and tasks. These were 'general assistant' and I cut out reviews, stuffed catalogues in envelopes and after a few months assessed copyright permissions. These were a steady source of income for the company. Anthologists, magazines, newspapers and the BBC often wanted to use extracts or poems or short stories

from the Bodley Head backlist. These included the short stories of
'Saki' (*The Open Window* dozens of times a year) and T. O. Beach-
croft, *Going Downhill on a Bicycle* by John Davidson, *For Johnny* by
John Pudney, extracts from *Ulysses* for some academic tome, Max
Beerbohm's *Works* and *More Works*, and something by Anatole
France, or Stephen Leacock.

Then after many months of service I was called into C.J.'s office
and *met* an author. C.J. had suddenly decided it was time I won
my spurs as an editor, and here in front of me was the once-
glimpsed James Aldridge. I was introduced and C.J. said, 'You'll
have read Jimmy's *Signed with their Honour*. I wonder if you would
like to go through his new novel which we're publishing?'

Signed with their Honour was about Gladiator pilots in Greece, and
perhaps that was what gave C.J. the idea I would like this new
book. There could have been another reason. This manuscript was
enormous, fully six inches thick, and titled *The Diplomat*. Whether
C.J. had read it all I gravely doubt, and he certainly had neither
time nor inclination to edit it.

'Of course I will.' I did not care if it was the Cairo telephone
directory. I would be working with this nice-looking Australian not
much older than myself, who, I learned, had been a war correspondent in the Mediterranean and the Middle East, and had married
an Egyptian of high intelligence and sublimely lovely appearance.

I began reading the MS on the way home in the train, old show-off
imagining the impression as an intellectual he must be making on
his tight-packed fellow passengers. It turned out to be an intricately
woven political novel, with strong communist leanings, set mainly
in Persia during the threatened Soviet invasion in 1946. No MS
before or since has had such minute and loving care lavished upon
it. For several weeks I worked on it page by page and intermittently
Jimmy would come into the office and patiently go over my every
suggestion. I cannot think, after this, how we became friends, but
so we did while disagreeing on almost everything from cars to
politics, people to planes.

He loved talking about planes and flying although he had never
been a pilot. But as he was a strong supporter of communism, and
decidedly anti-American, I did not divulge to him two flying non-
events in my life at this time, which did not matter as both were
abortive. Joan Fontaine arrived in this country in 1951 and came
out in an enormous limousine to see us, and her god-daughter
Sarah, now seven years old. She could not understand why we lived

in such evident penury in this little cottage and invited us to come and live in California. 'We need good test pilots at Lockheed,' she said. 'I can fix you up there. With your experience, you would be invaluable. *And* the money's good.'

Before I could reply to this offer, which rather intrigued me, Charlotte chipped in emphatically. 'Certainly not,' she said. 'We would never live in America.'

In that same year, the Korean war had become headline news. Day after day we read of setbacks to the United Nations' forces. On my twenty-ninth birthday, the North Koreans launched a massive offensive, and recalling an earlier, twenty-first, birthday I dropped in at Bentley Priory, Fighter Command HQ. Things had changed there a bit since then but reimbued with the spirit of Captain Ball VC I found the office where I could offer my services as a pilot. They were very grateful, and let me down gently, but it was made clear that I was far too old. Soon after, my old mate Johnny Baldwin went missing in Korea in a Sabre jet. I returned to the unexciting task of publishing books.

It was communal working at The Bodley Head, a sort of pioneer open-plan office brought about by the warehouse origins of our building. All the office staff were on the first, or attic, floor, at various levels and divided by whole or half partitions. In our unit there worked two old-timers, Frank Baker, and, rather younger, Len Lake, who between them produced the books and organised reprints, ordering paper and printing and binding, the target for the printers' narks who cruised the London publishing offices. Their world was one of calculations by hand, letters, written out to be typed, and immense ledgers. The telephone was for emergencies only.

The younger generation, all of us ex-service, was made up of Mike Legat, 'Wat' E. T. Tyler, both designers, and me the odd-job-man. I was extremely lucky with these two as fellow workers. Wat had been on minesweepers and still sometimes suffered from the nervous aftermath. He was very much the gentleman, partner to a stately Frenchwoman and with one small child. He was amusing company, with strong prejudices about class and race, and was inclined to drink whisky in the evening before catching his train. Mike Legat was also ex-Navy and equally good company and we became close friends. He was mad about amateur dramatics which he performed in church halls in south London with his wife.

While the older generation soldiered on, awaiting pensioned retirement, we three youngsters endured the discomfort of mutual penury, the eternal search for a rise and discreet plotting in search of better paid jobs. Wat was the first to go, as an ardent agnostic to a religious publishing company, to be greeted on his first morning (he recounted to Mike and me over a large whisky) with 'We're not in this business for our health, Mr Tyler'.

Then, to my disappointment but with my assistance, Mike made his way to a richer seam in the publishing business. An American company was starting a British branch, intending to break into the paperback game which was proving so profitable to Penguin and Pan Books. Helga Greene, the wife of Sir Hugh Greene (Graham's brother) had for some mysterious reason taken upon herself the task of finding staff to man the London office of what was to become Corgi Books. She summoned me to her flat and asked me if I would like to run the production. As I had done everything at The Bodley Head except production I said it might be better if she were to see Mike Legat. Mike liked the idea, especially the pay, and off he went.

Meanwhile, back at the warehouse, things began to go wrong. By 1949 you no longer rationed out your books. Suddenly you had to *sell* the things, and the gentlemanly element in publishing became a thing of the past. Not only did you have to fight for your share of the market, but author poaching became commonplace. Moreover, a new characteristic in C.J. manifested itself for the first time. Wonderful as he was at winkling out these new authors, nursing them along and ensuring that they got reviews, no sooner were they acclaimed and began to sell seriously, than C.J. lost interest in them. It was as if, once the struggle had been won, they could look after themselves.

The truth was that C.J. preferred brave failure and future promise to success. There was not much urgency in getting a reprint through when John Mortimer's or Howard Clewes's new novel sold out on publication, nor when Jocelyn Brooke's wonderfully clever and acclaimed *The Military Orchid* disappeared from the shops for months. The amiable, tall, tatty Jocelyn Brooke remained loyal and produced some more minor masterpieces without defecting before he died of drink. But most of the others strayed off to Macmillan or Michael Joseph, where money was available for decent advances and the sales teams made The Bodley Head's seem amateurish. As if to confirm this uncomfortable truth, I was made sales, advertising and publicity manager – yes, all three.

Profits, such as they were, lurched to a halt, awakening Sir Stanley Unwin to the truth – or near-truth – of what was going on. I did not care for Unwin. No one at The Bodley Head did. He was devious and a bully, egocentric and sharp-tongued, and worst of all mean and proud of it, retelling time and again tales to prove his parsimony. The book trade generally took the only way out with such a prominent monster and that was to make a lovable joke of his meanness. I shall not risk giving his memory even the smallest lift by recounting any of the stories that floated around during his lifetime. To me he was no more than patronising, but I somehow concealed my disgust and dislike for the man.

Just as John Lane had begun in the 1880s and 1890s publishing Aubrey Beardsley's most scabrous work, so in the 1930s his nephew Allen shamelessly put on the market such mildly pornographic works as *Sunlight and Shadow on the Female Form*. C.J. had discovered no reason against continuing the tradition and welcomed the work of the well-named John Everard from South Africa who contributed a number of colossally successful photographic volumes at high prices.

'You'll let me know when the new Everard comes in,' Unwin would remind me anxiously, several times. 'I would like to see it right away.' 'Right away' meant before the airbrush people got busy on the pubic hair. Unwin's morning visits were normally and mercifully brief, but not on Everard days.

Unwin regarded C.J. with a mixture of irritation, suspicion and contempt. Heaven knows why he appointed him, and then retained his services. Unwin's own list comprised Eastern mysticism, philosophy (represented by Bertrand Russell), biography, and almost anything of a heavy nature especially if the author was prepared to pay the production costs. Himself a liberal and a pillar of the Reform Club, he had no time for left-wing politics and left-wing intellectuals.

As the years passed and the profitability of The Bodley Head sank lower and lower, Unwin naturally took a deeper and more anxious interest in his wayward subsidiary, and he would point meaningfully to his own company's relative success with books like *The Kon-Tiki Story*, *Lord of the Rings* and *Queen Mary* by James Pope-Hennessy. C.J. now resorted to new sly tactics. Unwin insisted on seeing not only the orders received every morning but also the carbon of every letter despatched the previous day by every department. C.J. replied by censoring his own carbons by using a coloured paper for those which Unwin was not to see, and circulating them only among the senior staff. This resulted willy-nilly in the founding of a sort of grey unauthorised Bodley Head. C.J. even succeeded in commissioning for large advances and then publishing a whole disastrously unsuccessful series called 'New Developments' about the arts of the day, written by his indigent Hampstead communist friends. The correspondence, contracts, and even the final books themselves were all concealed from Unwin. But I was present when he found a copy of one of them by mischance, and it was difficult for me to suffer his ire while remaining loyal to C.J.

Oh dear, how poor C.J. suffered, daily, and how foolish he was! His cigarette smoking became more frantic, his lunchtime visits to Long's Wine Bar longer and longer, until sometimes there was no time for lunch at the Black Horse after half a dozen large amontillado sherries. He did not make much sense in the afternoons, but he was all the more amiable and this was the time to present your expenses chits.

By the early 1950s I was running the sales side more seriously in an effort to improve things, supervising the travellers, as they were then called, and covering some of the bigger accounts in London and the provinces. I had acquired an ancient open Rolls-Royce 20, with rear-wheel brakes only which hummed along at 50 m.p.h. at a pinch. Today, when it would be worth at least £100,000, this sounds wildly extravagant, but it cost me £300, most of my RAF gratuity. I used to tour the London stores in the car, often taking as a passenger our enormous dog, Garth. It was quite a good way of causing buyers to remember you, and I suspect Garth sold more Bodley Head books than I ever did.

The influence of a young family also conditioned my editorial interest. There had always been a good nucleus of a children's list, created largely by Allen Lane who bought some excellent books in America in the 1930s. Now, thanks to the guidance of Naomi Lewis, the leading children's book critic (then as now), and John Bell whom I had met at her flat and was running the top list at the Oxford University Press, I was able to specialise in that side at The Bodley Head.

Growth had been stifled during the paper rationing days by Unwin's insistence that approximately one quarter of the entire

Bodley Head quota was dedicated to his son David's children's stories, on which David ('Severn') also received a 20% royalty. A good deal of the remainder was reserved for the companion children's stories by M. E. Atkinson, the niece of G. Wren Howard, one of Unwin's fellow directors. But now we could expand and thankfully this coincided with the increased interest by public libraries in children's books so it became a profitable business and helped offset some of C.J.'s bigger bungles.

Charlotte was the first of us to contribute to the children's book world, and the ever-precarious family finances, by illustrating children's books, some for The Bodley Head but mostly for other publishers, which she toured zealously with her portfolio. When she completed her first picture book, *Jim Tiger*, which she wrote herself, she sold it triumphantly to Faber – and then she was away.

Her output increased, as did the quality of her work, both as an artist and author-artist of her own books. She began to earn enough to pay the school fees, and employ a daily nanny to look after the children.

I had never had much trouble making up stories as required by the children, who by 1948 now numbered three girls. The most recent, Debby, was born in 1948, and today she is widely known as the novelist Deborah Moggach. It may have been because my early attempts to write adult short stories during the war all failed that I was slow to get writing again, but it suddenly occurred to me that I might be able to produce a children's novel as publishable as some of those that I was already publishing. I bought an exercise book in the traditional manner, and sat down with a pen after supper and began writing.

I was surprised at how quickly I got on. I had always enjoyed science-fantasy, Verne in particular, and this first tale was decidedly derivative – derivative and partly autobiographical, as the two heroes were shot-down Tiffy pilots. I called it *The Perilous Descent* and sent it immediately to John Bell. He gave it an immensely careful and thoughtful reading and decided that it was not for him while telling me it would certainly find a publisher.

By this time I had completed a second MS, quite different, an historical yarn called *Peril on the Iron Road*. Travelling every day from Bushey to Euston along the tracks of the first mainline railway in the world, I had become interested in its construction by Robert Stephenson in the 1830s. I wrote an article about it and sent it to the newly founded *History Today*, edited by Alan Hodge and Peter

Quennell, a friend and neighbour today. To my astonishment they took this piece – my first ever published writing – illustrated it superbly and sent me a cheque for £50, well over £500 in today's money.

John Bell was nice about *Peril on the Iron Road*, too, but that was not enough for me now. So, in a fever of enterprise, I typed new title pages to both these MSS with the author's name changed to Bruce Carter and sent them both off to The Bodley Head's outside reader. He was Norman Denny, who lived in permanent and desperate penury in Devonshire, retaining a salary of £300 plus expenses from the firm. He was a nice, gentle, intelligent man who suffered from the misfortune of regarding himself as the new Balzac. Between reading MSS he wrote very long, very bad novels which C.J. felt obliged to publish. He also wrote children's stories as Norman Dale, and they were much better.

Norman would come lumbering and grumbling up to London once a month loaded down with (nearly always rejected) MSS, and stayed at the Savile Club where he was a proud and long-time member. He had the use of a desk in our office, upon which he would drop all his stuff with his reports, and C.J. and I would take appropriate action.

Norman rolled over to my desk. 'You sent me these two,' he began. 'One of them is quite good. I enjoyed it. Here's the report. Science fiction. I think you ought to publish it.' So did I.

'This is funny,' he continued. 'It's by the same bloke, though you wouldn't credit it if the same name wasn't on the title page. A very snobbish MS, I thought.'

I did not care what he thought though I never did understand what he meant. I thought it would be as well to suppress my real identity so I went along to see Paul Scott, then a young agent with Pearn, Pollinger and Higham. He thought it was a fine joke and threatened to squeeze me dry on terms. He looked at *Peril on the Iron Road*. 'I bet this is even better. You watch me sell it for you.'

Paul Scott was a friend for life and a marvellous agent. When he became a famous novelist there was no greater pleasure in life than to be in a pub with him and his editor, Roland Gant, of Heinemann.

The Perilous Descent was put through with loving care, with illustrations and colour jacket by my favourite *Mickey Mouse Weekly* strip artist, Tony Weare. I even got my own photograph on the back flap, distant enough in the cockpit of a Typhoon to be unrecognisable. The book sold well in America, too, and I felt a renewed tingle of restlessness in my 9 – 5 plus Saturday mornings job. Paul sold the railway book to Hamish Hamilton and my next story, *Speed Six!* about racing Bentley cars, struck a paper-thin seam of gold in the USA and sold well at home in hardback and Penguin's Puffin series.

The seeds of ambition, diminutive and wrinkled though they might be, were stirring belatedly in the early 1950s, and even show-ing signs of germinating. We had moved into a rather larger cottage next door in Bushey, a pretty place with three decent-size bedrooms and a large enough garden bordering on to fields. I became an evening 'balloonist' – writing comic strip balloons for *Mickey Mouse Weekly*, *Junior Express* and *Eagle*. We were not even comfortably off but did keep a bottle of gin in the cupboard for friends and we drove the Rolls-Royce up to the Lake District for a holiday. But I was increasingly discontented and wanted a complete change.

'I don't want to leave publishing altogether,' I told Charlotte. 'But if only I could get a part-time job with more time to write.'

She was suitably cautious. 'If you stick it out you may get C.J.'s job.'

She was right, for he was not at all well and there was no one else within the company and I knew every side of the business and could handle the odious Unwin. But I was loving the writing part of my life and was flushed with the American success. Moreover, I was becoming suspicious of what was going on behind the scenes at The Bodley Head without my knowledge. Several publishers had telephoned me, rather than C.J., to pick my brains about turnover and profit and that sort of thing. Several had invited me out to lunch. One of them, Max Reinhardt, took me to Rules and gently and courteously picked my brains. I did not tell him anything I should not have done, but I did want to know why all this interest?

'I think there may be a change of ownership. Didn't you know?'

I felt an awful fool answering him that I did not. He looked away in some embarrassment and we talked more generally of the trade.

That evening I declared to Charlotte in outrage, 'That devious bugger's selling the place over my head.'

'Has he told C.J.?'

'I don't know. I'll go and visit him and find out.'

C.J. had been in and out of hospital recently. He was very secre-tive about his condition, but whenever I saw him his cough seemed worse, he had succeeded in achieving the impossible by losing more weight, and was very depressed. It was some time before I discovered that he had cancer of the throat.

Neither of us held shares in the firm but the idea that Unwin should be negotiating the sale without divulging his intentions greatly angered us. 'Go and ask him straight tomorrow,' C.J. croaked. 'I don't see why he should get away with making fools of us.'

In C.J.'s absence I always sat with Unwin at 9.15 a.m. as he pored over orders, carbons and letters, tearing off the unused stamps for the return postage of MSS. 'My only source of untaxed income,' he would mutter with appalling repetition.

'Oh yes,' he admitted at once when I asked him. 'Greenwood doesn't seem to be able to make the place work, so if I can get the right price I'll sell.'

His cold eyes behind his bifocals gave me a brief incurious glance, before he returned his attention to the stack of orders.

'And the people who've worked here all their lives?' I asked with quite a lot of aggression in my voice.

'I'll see that they're looked after.'

That was enough. I was off. Hearing of my restlessness, two friends had suggested that there might be an opening for me where they worked. One was Max Martyn, an amiable and kind Long's Wine Bar habitué, where I was now quite often to be found before lunch. He produced Hamish Hamilton's books, which now included my modest *Peril on the Iron Road*. If I had a reputation for anything in publishing it was for building up The Bodley Head's children's list.

'Jamie's often spoken about developing the children's side. Let me have a word with him.'

I thanked him and added firmly, 'But not full time.'

Then kind Mike Legat told me that Corgi were going into children's paperbacks to compete with Penguin's Puffin series. What about it? Two brief interviews led to my agreeing, on a day-a-week consultation basis, to start lists for these two non-competing but highly successful imprints. Wednesday Hamish Hamilton, Friday Corgi Books. Five free days a week to write.

This may sound swiftly conducted and tidy, but there were things to clear up after eight and a half years at The Bodley Head. Authors had to be told, as tactfully as possible, and more important, I wanted to hear more specifically what would happen to the staff. I asked for and was given a special interview with Unwin. I told him what I intended to do and for the first time I had known him, he looked seriously put out.

'Well, this is a fine time to hand in your resignation, Hough. I suppose you've been plotting this for months.'

'No, for weeks. It's you who was plotting for months without telling me.'

He looked even more put out, stroking his little white goatee beard. Then he smiled puckishly, and I wished he had not. 'Perhaps you would consider staying if I put up your salary to £1,000 a year and put you on the Board of Directors? I don't think Greenwood's ever going to come back from all I hear. Most inconvenient.'

I was getting £750. Both Corgi and Hamish Hamilton were going to pay me £500. Not that, for even a split second, I would have reconsidered my decision. But first I still wanted to know about the staff. 'I can assure you,' he replied, with a fine show of openness, 'that no one will lose their job in the foreseeable future and the old-timers will continue until retirement and pension age.'

'Good, I'm relieved. But as far as I'm concerned, I'm afraid I've made up my mind.'

'You'll regret it.'

There was no goodbye or thanks or anything. I just left the room.

There was one member of the staff who knew already that I was going to leave. She was Judy Taylor, a dear friend of twenty-two, the adopted daughter of a woman who had been an infant school-teacher and had taught Charlotte many years earlier. Judy's mother, Gaye, had led a valiant, self-reliant and self-sacrificial life since she adopted her sister's infant at a few weeks old when the mother died. Without money or resources of any kind – the father refusing all help – she had brought up this child, paying for her schooling – even for a time at St Paul's.

Judy, returning from an *au pair* job in Canada and still only eighteen, and with no career in prospect, was offered a temporary job at The Bodley Head by me. This later became permanent, and she had been there for more than three years, learning every side of publishing, when I told her I was leaving. I think she was sorry, and I would miss her willing and cheerful presence, but my departure offered, in time, the chance to do more of what she did best – edit children's books.

'A publisher called Max Reinhardt is buying the place,' I told her. 'I think you will like him.'

My last Bodley Head duty was a sad one. I had seen poor C.J. through every stage of his decline and ever more frightful treatment. At Mount Vernon Hospital, in a public ward where everyone appeared to be in a terminal condition, he lay in silence but for the gentle whistle of his tracheotomy tube, a sheet-white little boy of a figure, just able to smile. Such a kind man, who had suffered so many misfortunes and offered so much generous friendship to so many people, deserved a less tormented end than this.

I told him the news about the old firm, and about my final meeting with Unwin, which raised a ghost of a smile. Then I touched his hand and left, crying.

12

Foundations for Free-lancing

In the summer of 1955, ten years after the end of the war, domestic and working life both assumed a sharply different shape. For one thing, I was at home for most of the time instead of taking the 8.20 train every morning and returning to Bushey around 7 p.m. It was a beautiful summer to celebrate my liberation from the treadmill. We had American friends staying with us. Paul and Carol 'Siggy' Kendall were both writers from Athens University, Ohio, Paul a historian and author of an immense and notable biography of Richard III, and Siggy had written two thrillers which I had bought from Harpers. They had a daughter of the same age as one of ours, and the whole *ménage à huit*, crammed into our cottage, was compatible in every way.

Siggy was a pretty brunette (today as pretty and grey in her late sixties) and Paul, conversely, was built like a gorilla. He possessed a fair imitation of a gorilla's face, too, and an eagerness and wit and modesty which made him exceedingly special. He was also a fanatical tennis player. We had the use of a court at the school (attended by all our girls) on the other side of the road. We made a special point of playing on Monday morning in order to flaunt my new freedom.

But before the children came home, it was also a *ménage* of immense industry. I had built on a glass extension at the back of the house, where I wrote, and the others sprawled about the house or garden according to the weather, scribbling or drawing away. Then it was croquet, sometimes by torchlight such was the competitive enthusiasm, and after supper and wine, interminable sessions of that form of charades, 'The Game'.

I cannot imagine what it was that instilled in me at around this time a deep fascination for motor racing. It was a time-consuming and sometimes expensive hobby, not shared with Charlotte, but which I naturally exploited in my writing and publishing. I had published a few motoring books at The Bodley Head, all of them profitable, and I had nudged the edge of the motor racing world at a golden age of British sports car and Grand Prix racing. Two of the sport's author-photographers were Louis Klemantaski and Michael Frostick, both bearded, the first of Russian birth with a sardonic manner and dry wit, the second amusing, improvident, impulsive and effervescent. Louis had driven at Brooklands before the war, winning as a prize an early Leica camera which he put to such good use that he became a professional high-speed photographer in war and peace. They both attended many of the big race meetings in England and on the Continent, and were well known figures in the pits and at hazardous viewing points around the circuits.

In this same summer of 1955 I said to my friend and neighbour David Higginbottom, 'Let's go to Le Mans and join Louis and Michael,' and so we did. Both of us had young families and not much money so we converted my Jowett Javelin, which I had exchanged for the rather slow Rolls, for sleeping and took a lot of food with us. On an impulse, before leaving, I telephoned the *Manchester Guardian*, asked for the newsdesk and got through to a man called J. R. L. Anderson.

'I notice you don't report motor racing except through the agencies,' commented the new full-of-initiative Hough. 'I'm off to Le Mans – shall I be your special correspondent?'

'Yes,' he said, 'what a good idea! We'll pay you, too, but not more than five guineas.'

That would help pay for the petrol so I agreed, and off we went. Louis was staying at a tremendously swagger hotel at Loué, full of drivers, managers and grand figures of the motoring world like Stirling Moss and the eminent Laurence Pomeroy whose weekly judgements in *The Motor* were followed by all. I parked my well-used Jowett among the Jags, Ferraris, Aston-Martins, Lancias and Mercs, and we met Louis in his spacious bedroom.

'I've booked you two places at a table for dinner,' he greeted us.

We thanked him, with a good swallow at the prospect of the cost, and made free use of his washing facilities. In the exquisite all-white dining room a table for eight awaited us after a stroll through the packed garden down to the river. Everyone was talking about the race. Listening, I felt like Adam in Evelyn Waugh's *Vile Bodies*:

> '. . . Changed the whole engine over after they'd been scruti-neered. Anyone else would have been disqualified . . .'
> '. . . just cruising round at fifty . . .'
> '. . . stung by a bee just as he was taking the corner, missed the tree by inches and landed up in the Town Hall. There was a Riley coming up behind, spun round twice, climbed the bank, turned right over and caught fire . . .'

And at the dinner table we both felt like first-formers mysteri-ously sitting with the prefects. I sat opposite the great Pomeroy, who suffered from a considerable limp, which I later learned stemmed from a crash with his father as a boy. M. Ricordeau, *le Patron*, had a similar limp, and there were numbers of scars among the diners, testifying to the hazards of their calling.

The burning question was, will Mike Hawthorn in his Jag be able to hold off the mass attack by the new Mercs, manned by World Champion Juan Manuel Fangio, Stirling Moss and a French driver? The general opinion favoured the German cars, which had sprung a surprise by fitting enormous air-brakes for slowing from 180 m.p.h. at the end of the long Mulsanne straight. 'Very surreal-ist!' commented a particularly scarred driver next to Louis. Forrest Lycett, an eight-litre Bentley man, agreed.

I hung on to Pomeroy's every word, none of which was directed anywhere near me. Nor did anyone except Louis take the slightest notice of us.

The *Manchester Guardian*'s fee had gone after the giant asparagus and *filet mignon*, and the dinner was so prolonged and rich that shortly after returning to our car, now parked in a field, with the intention of sleeping in it, David began to be sick, and sick again, and again. He was sick for the last time around dawn, quoting, 'If I should die, think only this of me: that there's some corner of a foreign field that is forever England.'

We joined the merry throng of 380,000 at lunchtime, for the 4 p.m. start. The main excitement would be around the pits, the winding hill after the start and the fast S-bend leading to a right-angle corner. Here there was every kind of stall and entertainment, including the inevitable naked lady in the snake-pit. The row of warming engines was cacophonous and rose to a pitch. Then the drivers switched off, crossed the road and lined up as if for a 100-metre sprint. When the flag fell they dashed back across the road to their cars, leapt in, restarted them and squealed off beneath a rising cloud of blue smoke.

David, Louis and I installed ourselves, with the passes we had been given by the authorities, on a bank well known to race-wise Louis. The opening two or three hours were breathtakingly exciting, with the lead constantly changing between the D-type Jaguars and the silver screaming Mercedes, with their air-brakes rising and closing like fishes' gills. Then the hero of the British crowd, Mike Hawthorn, managed to draw away.

It was still light when David and I decided to make for the pits to watch the refuelling. We were easing our way through the masses when a new sound reached our tortured ears – first a screaming whistle and a thud, and then, rising slowly in volume, all about us the soughing whisper of disaster, so often heard during the war, passing through the packed crowds. As we neared the scene of catastrophe we could hear the heartbreaking cries and groans.

It seemed that the least experienced of the Mercedes drivers, the Frenchman Pierre Levegh, had lost control when a refuelled car emerged from the pits, had skidded across the wide road and struck the safety bank. Here the crowds below the grandstand were thicker than anywhere else, and when the car exploded and disintegrated into a fireball, it had torn through the crowd at head level, killing over one hundred people and injuring hundreds more. The devastation was frightful and sickening.

The authorities decided that to halt the race would only add to the panic and so it continued at undiminished speed while an SOS went out to every nearby town for ambulances. I think we might have left, when it was possible to do so, if I did not have the responsibility of a report to telephone. In fact even at the end of the race the following afternoon, there was not a line out of Le Mans that was not being used in connection with the disaster and I never got through with my report on how Mike was in the lead when the Mercedes team withdrew out of respect to their dead driver and went on to a subdued victory.

This terrible affair did nothing to diminish my enthusiasm for the sport, and for some ten years I continued to cross the Channel and report Grands Prix and Le Mans for the *Manchester Guardian* and got front-page billing. I even got a rise, to eight guineas. Louis and Michael were my invariable companions, and a great deal of fun we had, too, at Monaco, Spa, Rheims, Clermont-Ferrand and other circuits. These were not the safest days of motor racing, and I often reported the death of some unfortunate British driver. At John Anderson's behest, I wrote obituaries of most of the top Grand Prix drivers. It was heartbreaking that so many of them were used so quickly.

My interest began to wane when the style and character of the drivers and cars began to change, the cars becoming mid-engine dinky cars covered in advertisements, the driver an unidentifiable dummy wrapped in asbestos, or so it seemed, and earning a king's ransom. Sponsorship money killed racing as far as I was concerned. At the last Grand Prix we attended all the cars travelled at the same speed, with almost no passing, the only bright event being the retirement of the entire first-ever Japanese Honda team.

One of the nicest and most interesting men in the motoring business was W. O. Bentley, whose cars had won Le Mans year after year in the 1920s. I first met him about a book I had been asked to write on the Tourist Trophy race at his Surrey cottage in retirement. After a couple of visits I persuaded him to let me write his autobiography – in fact to 'ghost' the book, my first effort in this activity. W.O. was an elderly, smallish brown nut of a man, modest and soft-spoken, who had been a railway apprentice engineer when he was smitten by the excitement of the motor world before the First World War. He had begun by importing French cars, tweaking them up and racing them. He then took to designing aero engines when they were in great war demand and his Bentley Rotary powered many a Camel fighter. Then in the 1920s his massive cars, and drivers of great colour and wealth, dominated the field of sports car racing. But the Bentley company became a victim of the slump and had to be sold out to Rolls-Royce.

I was very slow and inefficient at getting W.O.'s story out of this unforthcoming, quiet old man and it took ages to put the book together, but the story itself was so fascinating, and his following through the Bentley Drivers' Club so enthusiastic and admiring, that *W.O.*, as we called it, went to the top of the bestseller list. He was astonished and thrilled to bits.

While revelling in all this motoring writing, collaborating with Michael Frostick on a number of historical illustrated motoring books which sold on both sides of the Atlantic, I certainly did not wish to become known as a specialist in this narrow field, so I cast about for a broader historical subject to exploit.

In 1946 I had bought for 7s 6d *The Golden Jubilee Book of the Daily Mail* which turned out to be perhaps the best purchase I ever made. Thumbing through it ten years later, I paused at 1904 and the reproduction of a *Daily Mail* news column, eight times headlined thus: 'Ultimatum to Russia' 'Expires this Afternoon' 'Lord C. Beresford's Orders' 'To Turn Back the Russians' 'Channel Squadron Ready for Action' and so on. This marked the beginning of the tragi-comic voyage half round the world of a Russian fleet from the Baltic to the Far East where it was intended to defeat Admiral Togo and regain for Russia control of the seas in its war with Japan. It began badly when the Russians mistook British North Sea trawlers for Japanese torpedo boats and opened fire on them. They blundered on, stricken by insurrection and mutiny, coal shortage and refusal by a number of powers even to allow the massive fleet to anchor.

This subject appealed to me in a number of ways, and re-aroused my old pre-war interest in naval history. Now, in the summer of 1957, I bought a new typewriter and settled down to write about Admiral Rozhestvensky and the troubled voyage of his fleet and its annihilation at the Battle of Tsu-Shima.

I began writing *The Fleet that had to Die* at a damp, primitive cottage we had bought in the New Forest. It had a nice little garden and a paddock, albeit too small, behind. Our three girls, Sarah, Sandy and Debby, had in turn been struck by the pony plague, a common enough disease between the years of, say, eight to eighteen.

The seizure first struck in Bushey, a most unsuitable *venue* as almost the only good clear ride was along the verges of the Watford by-pass, itself littered with broken bottles while the cars whizzed by yards away. But as soon as we got possession of our little weekend cottage, all three ponies were shipped down there, where the riding was ideal and consumed virtually every weekend waking hour of the children. It consumed much of the week in Bushey too, in pantomime, with a lot of neighing and tossing of the head at school, the wearing of jodhpurs for the smell and traces of ponyhair, and the carrying of horsenuts in pockets for pretend feeding of ghost ponies.

In the New Forest, while the girls went whinnying and whickering off after breakfast, and Charlotte settled into gardening, I took myself to the dining table and my new typewriter.

For about two years my dual publishing consultancy arrangements prospered. The new children's paperbacks were called 'Scotties' and I had no trouble in obtaining licences from publishers for their best children's writers, like Captain W. E. Johns, Geoffrey Trease and David Severn. At this booming paperback age, we printed 60,000 and sold out on publication. Even the tough American proprietor was delighted.

The only trouble was that the art department, which was all important and all powerful, used the same top commercial artists as for their adult books. Avid readers of Corgi's Westerns, spy and detective stories, and their very popular fiction, mistook our Scotties for the real thing. But their lack of a rape or two, a shoot-out or the long lingering kiss caused disappointment. It took time, but certainly within two years the sales declined to the sort of figures Penguin's Puffins enjoyed, around ten to twenty thousand. This was a perfectly healthy figure but the Americans did not care for declining figures and I had to agree to close down the operation.

Mike Legat was most disappointed and embarrassed, but I really did not mind as the Hamish Hamilton one-day was proving not to be enough. As at The Bodley Head, I was not starting from scratch. Jamie Hamilton's partner, Roger Machell, bought the occasional promising book, like *Charlotte's Web* and Jamie himself had bought the first 'Dr Seuss' books and *Ferdinand the Bull* before the war.

The first thing I did was to tour the agents where I had a sympathetic reception because Hamish Hamilton was one of the most admired lists, and I had a small reputation for children's book publishing at The Bodley Head. I decided to start with short series books which could be written quickly, offering good terms and 'borrowing' established authors with the assurance that this would not disturb existing good relations with their publishers. The first series were called 'Reindeer', 'Antelope', and – for the very young – 'Gazelle' books, supported by a non-fiction series on specialised subjects called 'Look Books'.

We offered authors a £100 advance (£1,000 in today's money) for a text varying from 2,500 to 7,500 words, and any number of well-known writers contributed – Gerald Durrell on zoos, Rex

Warner on birds, Air Chief Marshal Sir John Slessor on aircraft, and stories by Rosemary Sutcliff, William Mayne, Dorothy Clewes and a host more. These books all needed artists to do the line drawings, and finding them, commissioning them and checking their artwork all took time. It also led usefully into a further broadening of the list.

A young man from south London called Raymond Briggs looked for and found his first commission from me, and this later led to his first picture book; the beautiful Krystyna Turska was another; and Michael Foreman brought us his superb colour artwork. The idea was to sell this work in America, and other foreign countries if possible, in order to increase the print run. We used to buy from America, too, where there was a great renaissance in picture book publishing and the libraries there were buying as if there were no tomorrow. *The Very Hungry Caterpillar* by Eric Carle was only one of dozens of books I bought and some were very successful.

One day a week became two and sometimes three, and I got a full-time assistant and a production manager to counter the threat of my reverting to full-time work. In all this Jamie Hamilton was totally supportive, and we saw plenty of one another outside the firm, too, playing tennis, and dining in each other's houses.

My introduction to his style of publishing took place in his large office where the weekly meeting was held. There were no more than five or six of us present, and Jamie presided informally, conducting business at a brisk pace. He was in his mid-fifties at this time, a dark, good-looking man with a full head of dark hair and a broken nose from rugby at Rugby. His hands were always well manicured, his shoes shined and his dark suits always up to scratch. His speech tended to be staccato, often waggish and always and visibly in a hurry to get on to the next thing – set of tennis, signing up a new author or deciding on a print run.

Even his best friends had to accept that Jamie Hamilton was the biggest snob and name-dropper in the country, and was quite shameless, even naïve, about it. Everyone he knew had to be the well-known best. In the case of Kathleen Ferrier, or Alan Moorehead, or Simenon, or Nancy Mitford and all his top friends and authors, that was easy. But in my case, for example, because he knew I was interested in motor racing and had just been to Le Mans, I was introduced at his dinner parties as Richard Hough, you know, the racing driver in his spare time, and then he would add absurdly, 'as fast as Stirling Moss'.

Jamie was not averse to first novelists but what he liked best was to buy fame, happily pinching authors from his competitors, the exact reverse of C.J. He did this partly by reading, or skimming, the newly published and well received books, and at once writing a fan letter by hand, each with a special little individual touch – 'I did especially admire how you . . .' It was surprising how many even mildly dissatisfied authors looked upon Jamie with a favourable eye for their next book as a result. With agents, and with authors face to face, he was much more positive in his approach, often acquiring books by offering over the odds. He seldom regretted it. He would go anywhere and pay almost anything for a book, like Truman Capote's *In Cold Blood*, or *The Catcher in the Rye*, he desperately wanted. He was awed by no one, but frightened of Nancy Mitford, partly because she might defect but mostly because of her manner, which was very lofty. He needed a day off on his return from Paris after discussing her new book.

He entertained lavishly and frequently, either at home (always black tie) or at White's or the Garrick. The great and the good associated with the arts all at one time or another dined at 43 Hamilton Terrace, where a maid and butler took the coats and hovered until the last brandy. His wife Yvonne, a charming, Italian contessa, was the perfect hostess and managed people like Princess Margaret with complete aplomb, while just able to sustain a cultural conversation with Cyril Connolly. Once, when dining Evelyn Waugh among others (with a view to making a bid for Waugh's next novel) in the summer of 1940, which was not a good time for Italians in England, drunken Waugh suddenly and loudly broke into ice-cream-vendor language. Jamie threw him out of the house, literally kicking him down the steps.

Although he was authentically a cultured man and read widely and attended the opera, I never heard him refer to 'reading' some obscure French work of criticism, say; it was always 'I have just been re-reading Racine's . . .'; and he never went to Covent Garden other than for a first night and in white tie.

I was greatly impressed by this first Wednesday meeting. Decisions were made, not all by Jamie, on whether or not to buy a book, on terms to be offered, on the print run of half a dozen books recently taken, who could be got onto television or the radio, how much we should spend on advertising, who would serialise it – the entire process of publishing, all decided in less than an hour, including exchanges of quips and anecdotes with his partner, who

had a rich and wicked sense of humour. This was personal publishing at its best, far, far away from corporative publishing today,
when form-filling, reporting, authorising, minuting, exhaustively
discussing, post-morteming and heaven knows what would take
weeks.

'What about the new Chandler, Jamie? 40,000 as before?'

'I think we can risk fifty, don't you, Roger?'

'Right. Full colour jacket?'

By chance, at this meeting the cream of the autumn list was
discussed, *Noblesse Oblige: U and Non-U* (50,000 and not enough), the
new Moorehead, Angela Thirkell, and Chandler and John Gunther
from the USA and half a dozen more.

I sat in awed silence, thinking of the hole-in-the-corner, ever inde-
cisive ways of dear old C.J., and Unwin's total dictatorship at his
place. The same spirit and speed prevailed at the twice-yearly sales
meetings when the travellers came to town to be briefed on the next
season. No one lasted for long on the road unless exceedingly effective, and they were all nice men, too, with excellent relations with the
sales manager. Everything was open. They were told the print-run
of all the books, and Jamie or the editor responsible commented on
the merits of their books, without overdoing it. It went like a precision
military operation, and when it was all over, there was a party.

I learned that the shape of these parties had been the same for
years. The double doors in Jamie's office were opened to embrace
the secretaries' quarters, in which a barrel of beer was installed,
and bottles of gin and whisky, tonic and soda were placed in the
main office. Rather thick cheese and ham sandwiches were provided with the barrel of beer, while canapés and smoked salmon
complemented the hard stuff.

The packers from the warehouse arrived, rather shyly, at the
office at about five, along with the travellers who had dodged back
briefly to their hotel to spruce up. The class divisions of the 1950s
arranged this large congregation tidily into three, the warehouse
packers about the beer, the middle management and secretaries
about the gin and whisky, and Jamie and Roger Machell at Jamie's
desk talking about last night's first night and the dinner party
Roger had given in his set in Albany the night before.

Like the good old English class system itself, there was some
movement: travellers exchanged dirty stories with the packers, the
girls giggled over g & ts with the male invoice clerks and Max
Martyn and I and, later, Christopher Sinclair-Stevenson, intruded

into the hierarchy. The further down the social scale the more drink was consumed, and long after Jamie and Roger had gone off to change into black ties for the evening's revels, the packers and travellers would be hard at it, and chaps slipped away to obscure corners of the office with girls. The travellers' parties typified the easy-going spirit of this successful publishing firm.

When I had completed *The Fleet that had to Die* I never thought for one moment of sending it elsewhere than to Jamie. He and Roger both liked it and offered good terms. Soon after, I saw a letter from Roger, scouting in New York, to Jamie telling of his successes and disappointments, ending, 'Isn't it good about Dick and the *New Yorker*'. What in God's name did *that* mean? I rang my new agents, Curtis Brown (Paul Scott had left his agency), and was told that not only had Viking taken the book there but William Shawn, the revered editor of the *New Yorker*, offered to run the book as a serial. The total sum involved was about ten times what I had earned in total from all my writing to date.

All this happened in the early months of 1958. Siggy and Paul Kendall were back in London and we celebrated and discussed our plans. First, we could now afford to buy a house in London. Then, we must be in America for publication of the book and the serial, and after New York, must come and stay in Athens, Ohio, and would I lecture to Paul's English class on creative writing – whatever that was.

There is nothing like some money in the bank to speed the processes. In no time at all, the American trip was arranged, the Viking people setting up a publicity programme and friends sending welcoming letters. Since demobilisation from the RAF we had been living from hand-to-mouth, and while we had our place in the New Forest, and the children at paying schools (thanks partly to the generosity of Helen and Aunty Bar), we had never enjoyed more than about £1,000 capital reserve. Now, the feeling of liberation from day to day fretting was an enchanting experience, though at the same time I recalled my father's oft quoted saying, 'A fool and his money are soon parted,' and did not – as was my almost spontaneous response to surprise money – go out and buy a new car.

Charlotte and I agreed that a London house came before anything else. She was a great house discoverer, diligent, wise yet swift. After only her third recce trip she came back with details of an early Victorian Georgian-style end-of-terrace house in St John's Wood. In 1958 this was a rather genteel, cultivated area, still the traditional locale for doctors (a healthy walk across Regent's Park to Harley Street and the hospitals), artists, musicians and writers. There were still plenty of them around. Elisabeth Schwarzkopf's mellifluous voice rang out across the ample gardens about us, Veronica Wedgwood, Philip Hope-Wallace and his sister lived almost opposite, and the publisher James Macgibbon and his wife Jean lived exactly opposite us, while Jamie Hamilton himself was only a short walk away.

To the dismay of my father and my bank manager we bought 25 St Ann's Terrace immediately for £5,900 cash and lived in it for the next twenty years. Now for the New World. Charlotte had been to New York recently *en route* to stay with the Kendalls but it was new to me, and its effect was as stunning and stirring as I had been told it would be. I have been back to New York countless times since but nothing can match the first time, the briskness of manners and mobility, the extremes of matter-of-factness and concern, the brash vulgarity contrasting with elegance. More than the shape of the absurd towering buildings it was the shape of the people that fascinated me. The polyglot mix had created a vast city of pinched gnomes of darkish hue, black striding giants, men and women with legs the girth of an ancient oak, graceful Levantines, small Hispanics, and, thick on the sidewalks, in the buses and elevators, more good-looking European-proportioned white men and women than you could ever count on the streets of London.

The people at Viking, our first point of call, were kind and gracious and very confidence-stirring. They gathered in the President's office and showed me yesterday's *Sunday Times* with a huge ad for *The Fleet* and an even bigger review by Nicholas Monsarrat. The *New Yorker*, fat and full of glossy Christmas ads, carried the first instalment of the serial, austerely re-titled 'The Difficult Journey', and I witnessed the first-ever purchase of the book from a stack in Scribners bookstore.

All this was very head-swelling and I tried not to let it be, having watched so many writers' conceit grow with their sales and become none the easier to work with. I had also, more sadly, seen the bubble burst with a swift decline in sales. Oh dear! So I went through the women's club talks and signing sessions with a modest, self-deprecating smile on my lips, though the smile was not easy to sustain as I increasingly discovered that, since Dylan

Thomas, the dry martinis were for the guests only. The dry martinis elsewhere were all right though, and right through the meal, too, in those pre-wine-drinking days in New York City.

Such kindness, such hospitality, so many lavish dinners! The two sisters of Jack Kahn, *New Yorker* staff writer, Joan and Olivia, looked after us time and again and for so many years and to this day. Then it was off to Ohio in an enormous train, just like 1941, with the whooeee of its whistle sounding out in the night, and the Kendall family at the station to greet us in the half-light of dawn.

Lord Beaverbrook, in Canada, had been reading the *New Yorker* serial and had cabled the nearly-new editor of the *Sunday Express*, John Junor, to buy the British serial rights. It was already running when we got home, presented more vividly and with pictures, and this began a serial relationship with this newspaper which lasted rewardingly for some eight years.

The naval writing continued throughout the 1960s – and to this day for that matter – and I acquired a modest reputation in this field, writing a naval history of the First World War for Oxford and the life of Admiral of the Fleet Lord Fisher for Philip Unwin (the nice one) of Allen & Unwin and an enormous heavily illustrated history of the modern battleship, called simply *Dreadnought*, for Macmillan in New York and Michael Joseph here. I found myself in New York once and sometimes twice a year on my own business and scouting for Hamish Hamilton, both for adult and children's books.

But by no means were all these books as successful as *The Fleet*. The *New Yorker* ran two more serials but the book sales did not always match those of that first book, and once or twice during the decade the financial worries came up again like old sores of a festering disease. In dire need of school fees cash I even accepted an offer to write *The BP Book of the Racing Campbells*, which took me into contact with that unfortunate fellow, Donald, shortly before he killed himself. I was paid £500 (£6,000 in 1992) outright, and as it sold fewer than 2,000 copies I was thankful.

We had a fourth child in 1960, yet another girl but a very sweet one, much adored in an aunt-like way by her much older sisters. We named her Bryony. These older girls were being educated all over the place – Millfield, Bedales, Francis Holland, Queen's College and Camden School for Girls in London, and later Roedean and Gordonstoun, all (except Camden) hideously expensive. I cannot imagine what else we spent money on except entertaining and a bit of travel, but it disappeared like Niagara and our joint earnings only seemed just to keep pace.

I suppose the purchase of a replacement country place accounted for some of this expenditure. We had been on one or two holidays in the Lake District since the war but every year the sense of deprival grew stronger, until in 1967 we determined to move from the forests of Hampshire to the fells of Lakeland. Charlotte made one of her lightning trips. She found some gems but on the second attempt came up with the ultimate house in the ultimate position. 'Town Foot Farmhouse' was the first, or last, house, in the straggling, ancient village of Troutbeck, tucked into the rock of the valley. It had views down towards Windermere one way, and up the valley to the high fells to the north, nearly always snow-capped in winter. It was a typical sixteenth-century stone dwelling, clad white, with an original inglenook gigantic fireplace, and characteristic rough oak partitioning between the rooms, and a shippon below for the cattle. The lav, a double-seater, was sensibly far from the house, and the water came out of the hillside. There was a ghyll running past the front door, a garden and orchard and five acres of sloping meadow for the ponies. The fact that it was 248 miles from St John's Wood mattered not at all. Here was the place for school holidays, half terms and occasional stolen weekends for years to come.

From here Debby married, at the village church, Tony Moggach, a publisher, just as Sarah had married her artist husband David Garland from the village church in the New Forest some years earlier. Then at the very end of this decidedly interesting if exhausting decade something unfortunate happened to start off the '70s. But before that, Charlotte and I went off to the sub-Antarctic.

13

The End Beyond the End

MR Shawn at the *New Yorker* had taken up my suggestion for a long historical piece on Cape Horn, and Norton in America, and Sir Robert Lusty of Hutchinson in London, had bought the book rights. Charlotte and I flew off first to Buenos Aires where we spent a couple of nights ensuring that we had the support of the Argentine Navy in Tierra del Fuego. The long-disputed possession of some of the islands down there might restrict our movements, as our prime host would be the Chilean Navy. It seemed all right. We were given introductions to the Naval Commandant at Ushuaia on the Beagle Channel, so we then flew on, over the Andes to Santiago. These were liberal, peaceful days in Chile. President Frei, a moderate, was in charge and trying to steer a middle course in this volatile strip of land west of the Andes, which were visible, rearing up, white-capped on the horizon from almost anywhere in the country. Santiago is an imposing city, sixty miles inland from its port, Valparaiso, and laid out by the Spaniards in the heyday of their colonial rule. The centre is as sophisticated as any city in the West, dominated by the two-mile-long wide Avenida Bernardo O'Higgins.

It was February 1969, the Royal Yacht with the Queen and Prince Philip had recently visited the country, Chilean Navy and Air Force armament orders were being negotiated as a consequence, and everyone was terribly pro-British. We visited the British Embassy several times, made contact with the British Council, but more importantly called on naval headquarters to make sure that wheels set in motion in London were still spinning here.

I was concerned with the natural life as well as the historical background of this fractured tip of the American continent, wanted

to see where the Spaniards had set up a township before understanding too late the inhospitable nature of the terrain (all died in
no time), where Darwin's *Beagle* had hove to, the island where
Gardiner and his fellow missionaries had all perished, Staten Island
where the Spaniards had set up surely the most secure jail in the
world, the coastline Drake managed to claw off before clearing the
islands for the Pacific, and a dozen more places mostly associated
with disaster – thus the title of the book, *The Blind Horn's Hate*, from
Kipling.

The Chileans are rightly proud of their Navy, which has always
been an efficient service, responsible for the longest coastline in
proportion to area anywhere in the world. They received us with
wonderful old-world courtesy, and perfect English, and told us
that in one week an armed tug would arrive at Punta Arenas
on the Magellan Straits with instructions to pick us up and
proceed on its duties. These were to call at a number of islands
to the south in order to replenish the unmanned navigation lights
of the area.

It was a spectacular 1,400-mile flight south over the Andes, with
the saw-tooth coastline on the right. I had never seen such a brutal,
wild seashore, with sometimes just the smallest strip of cultivation,
and some settlements supported by heaven-knew-what. I thought of
Admiral Cradock's squadron of doomed cruisers with their hungry
crews working its way up this coast in 1914, searching for the
more powerful German squadron, and Byron's grandfather as a
midshipman in the shipwrecked *Wager* 170 years earlier. What
awful desolation!

Our packed plane banked round the Magellan Strait and came
in on its final approach to Punta Arenas. It was blowing half a
gale, as it did for most of the time here. A taxi of wonderful age
battled against it, and the dust, along the only length of metalled
road in southern Chile to the Hotel Cabo de Hornos, Punta
Arenas's only skyscraper. From our sixth-floor room, we could see
the full extent of the town of rutted roads, single-storey, galvanised
roof dwellings laid out in the gridiron pattern, a few shops and
little factories, and the harbour, scattered with ancient wrecks.

This town had once been an important coaling station between
Atlantic and Pacific for the Royal Navy, and we were soon introduced to the British Club, down to five members now but full of
dusty reminders of the Imperial Age, with a grand leather visitors'
book, silver tankards, leather armchairs, two fine billiards tables,

and many brown photographs of RN ships' companies of the Edwardian era. Derek Walker, the British schoolmaster, wise in local affairs and the surrounding country, looked after us in this remote, very non-English-speaking town.

We had a meal in his house with his wife and children, and a German friend.

'I come here once a year for my skins,' explained our handsome German. 'Guanaco?' I asked, imagining guanaco coats, very stylish, being sold in the Hamburg fancy stores.

'*Nein, nein, nein* – for our sausages. Very strong intestines have the sheep.'

Derek explained that owing to the coarse nature of the grass of the southern pampas, the sheep developed extra tough intestines, ideal for German sausage. So this German had built a processing plant next to the abattoir and once a year he arrived to supervise the packing and despatching to Hamburg by sea of millions of fat sausage skins. There was only one other in the world.

Our host, after being told the Chilean Navy was going to be six days late, suggested we took a car up into the Chilean Lake District. He organised the whole thing, and even found an itinerant English boy, John Adgee, to go with us as interpreter.

We found this Andean Lake District, a full day's drive north of Punta Arenas over rough roads, a caricature of our own Lake District, the mountains many times higher, thick with snow in midsummer and precipitous beyond all reason, the rivers broad torrents, the flowers and flowering shrubs of the pampas near-tropical in size and colour. Grazing with the tough sheep were countless guanacos and rheas with their young. We stayed primitively at *estancias*, one on the frontier with the equally wild scrubland of Argentina.

Back at Punta Arenas, the Armada di Chile was in harbour in the form of our tugboat, *Lientur*, which looked rather shabby and very small for doubling the Horn. Also newly arrived was HMS *Endeavour*, the Royal Navy's Antarctic ship, spotlessly white, comfortably large and, as we discovered on the evening we were due to leave with our Chileans, hospitable. The charming, capable officers threw a small party for us, at which so much drink was consumed that the contrast when we climbed aboard our tug was softened. 'I think you might do better coming with us,' a lieutenant had remarked ominously.

Our quarters were a small cabin, with a basin, sea chest, and small table, and bunks. Quite orthodox, you might say, but all storage space was full with the unwashed property, we heard later, of an officer who had been put ashore sick. Where we would have been accommodated had he remained well, we never asked. Anyway, he had not been a very clean officer and no one had been inside the cabin since he left. But who were we to complain? We did, just a little, but were anxious not to appear namby-pamby at the outset of our voyage, and recalling it was entirely free, we shut up and pulled out one of our litre bottles of gin.

Later, rather drunk, we met the Captain and his two officers, and decided the personnel were better than the accommodation. Lieutenant Reinaldo Rivas González was a great conquistador of a fellow, dark, tall, crashingly handsome. I would have trusted myself anywhere with him. *And* he spoke good English. His two junior officers smiled away and offered us seating in the diminutive mess.

We steamed off south down the strait in the middle of the night, and at dawn I went up on deck to be faced with the breathtaking peaks of Mount Sarmiento, seemingly the product of a mad, giant wedding-cake baker. From the peak, crowned by a perpetual halo of mist against the blue of the sky, the jagged white shoulders fell away in all directions, each cradling a glacier. Every few minutes a chunk of ice fell into the waters below with a mighty splash, to join countless more icebergs.

For a week we steamed slowly through the empty channels between the Fuegian islands, accompanied by the rich bird life of the region – terns, boobies, gannets by the thousand, and great skuas which had so alarmed Magellan's men, and whose greed and daring slightly alarmed us, too. Condors, almost as big as the Tiger Moths I had once flown, floated threateningly high above us. Flightless ducks, noted by Darwin, thrust themselves out of our way with their abbreviated wings like Victorian paddle boats – thus their name, steamer.

The missionaries had wiped out the rugged, naked Fuegian population two or three generations ago, obliging them to wear clothes donated by kind Edwardian middle-class women instead of relying on seal oil, well rubbed in. They were all dead of pneumonia within ten years. So now none of the islands we landed on was inhabited, adding to the impression that we were in some lost world, and in truth some of the shore on the Pacific side was marked as a dotted uncertain line, *non explorado*. The forests were of towering

Antarctic beech, the previous generations rotting underfoot and the next generation of sprouting saplings growing between them. Not a mammal or insect was to be seen anywhere.

In the broad Beagle Channel, close to the disputed islands, we carried out firing practice with our three-inch gun, pock-marking the rock cliffs, the sound of the charge echoing away among the islands and sending a million sea-birds into a riot of terror. It was a gesture of warning to the Argentinians who occupied the northern shore. Years before, they had built the small town of Ushuaia, while on the southern shore lay the Chilean township of Puerto Williams, where we called for lunch with the Governor and his wife, and several of his officers. They welcomed us warmly as the only visitors for months. Being Chileans, a football match was played on the only bit of flat ground, while two Argentine torpedo boats made themselves evident as a counter to our earlier shooting.

'Ah, but we are great friends, in truth,' remarked the Governor, eyeing the 'enemy' boats tolerantly. 'Later today Governor Valdeas brings his wife and family for tea. It is just the politics.'

Later, we landed on the two islands to confirm Chilean possession, and ensured that the flag was still flying on one of the beaches. They did not seem to be worth all the fuss, but apparently it was to do with territorial waters and oil drilling, for they were at the mouth of the Beagle Channel.

Orange Bay, behind False Cape Horn, was our next destination, and our captain was for the first time eyeing the weather anxiously. He had been as charming and courteous as ever, but decidedly unforthcoming, perhaps because the uncertain weather called for flexibility. So far it had been brilliant and we were both brown in the face although sunbathing was out of the question because of the wind.

Early the following morning, a sense of urgency ran through our little boat, anchors were raised and we sped off at high revs through choppy seas round a headland and towards Drake Passage and the Antarctic. Six hours later, and far south of the Horn, we sighted some stumpy islets ahead. Our captain was looking very preoccupied and unapproachable, but I asked one of his subordinates what we were doing and where we were.

'We must leave some sheep on Diego Ramírez,' he said. This did not explain much but later he added, 'Two men live there. With a radio, and a light. They have been there more than one year, the weather too bad to take them off. Then we leave two in place.' Little

Lieutenant Carlos smiled and answered a call from his captain.

Captain Rivas had not always been enthusiastic about our going ashore, fearing we might get lost. But this time, we decided, we must somehow persuade him. Now that we were close to the islets, some of them mere rocks, the wildlife looked promising although there was no visible vegetation but high tussock grass. The sea was rising, there were dark clouds far to the west where Drake Channel becomes the Pacific. Our captain was in a hurry but when I asked him about going ashore, he nodded and smiled at Charlotte. 'You will be the first woman ever,' he said. 'It is called Boat Islet,' he added. None of the other islets appeared to have names.

We had anchored in the shelter of a ragged, high rock. Our two whalers were hoist out, the first loaded with sacks of coal, drums of fuel, cases of spirit to combat the cold, and hundreds of cans of food. Into the second boat were loaded our sheep, which had spent the journey from Punta Arenas forlornly huddled in a cage amidships. There was no room for humans other than by sitting on them, with their legs tied, and this we did, while four seamen rowed stoutly through the surf and up onto the beach. Then, hoisting sheep onto our backs, we waded ashore, soaked to our waist in the freezing water.

In the course of our half-mile row, we had caught glimpses of two men, the relieved meteorologists, waving their arms joyously, running down a track to the beach. They had emerged from a hut at the top, beside it a tall radio aerial and a navigation light of the kind which had become familiar to us.

What followed forms the opening page of this book; and later I wrote in the *New Yorker*:

> Higher up, the grass thinned out, and suddenly before us, spread out over half an acre, was a large albatross nesting area.
>
> Each nest was built up in geometrical conformity, a low column of mud, rotting vegetation, and old feathers, scooped out on top into a neat saucer. Every nest contained a single albatross chick, fluffy, grey-white and sitting bolt upright. From all sides they clacked their curved beaks and gazed at us in mindless, futile reproach. Soon they would acquire dignity. This was evident from the full-grown birds who strolled, nonchalant and monstrous, around their community, quite uninterested in us. These were the grey-headed albatross, with a wingspan of around nine feet, though it looked to be more when they stretched their wings.

... Their brown eyes are slits but have none of the predatory aspects of the great skuas; there is a grave elegance in the smooth configuration of the great head of soft white touched with grey. In flight they are the apotheosis of grace and power. At rest on the ground, much of their serenity survives. Only when they walk, with a hobbling gait, do they suddenly become grotesque caricatures, like Tenniel's Dodo, but on feet as wide-webbed as a penguin's.

The wind and spume whipped over the summit of our islet, which appeared so friendly and welcoming. A thousand guinea-pigs, bigger than we had ever seen, shared this little plateau with the albatrosses, scurrying in and out of their holes, and as we advanced further towards the leeward side of Boat Islet, we could see beneath us a steep cove, the slopes covered with countless little rockhopper penguins, doing what they were named for, but in a desultory sort of way for they were all moulting and miserable. They, too, took not the least interest in us as we picked our way among them, noting also the more cheerful Magellanic penguins standing proprietorially before their burrows.

I was changing a film when Charlotte called 'Look out!' and pointed upwards. Two red-backed hawks, of great size, 'Johnny Rook', the dreaded villain of so many mariners' tales, had been hovering above, and now one of them was diving towards me like an Antarctic Tiffy. I focused my camera on it, and the subsequent print revealed that it had filled the lens. Then we both covered our heads with our anorak hoods and squatted on the ground. Boat Islet's record of hospitality had been spoilt. Moreover, we had evidently overstayed our welcome. From the other side of the island, we heard the urgent sound of the *Lientur*'s siren.

'Oh Lord, we're going to be in trouble!' Charlotte exclaimed.

'If they bother to wait for us. Imagine being here for another ten months.'

Ten minutes later, panting and soaked, we were back on the beach where one of the whalers awaited us. As feared, back on board we got a piece of Captain Rivas's mind. We apologised profusely but he turned his back on us for a full minute on the bridge. Soon he relented, with a smile for Charlotte: 'Now we go to the Horn. And no going ashore.'

The sun had come out to match our conquistador's forgiving cheerfulness, but it was now distinctly choppy. We took seasick pills and stuck it out on the bridge, which was more than our captain could manage. 'He no allowed pills,' remarked the helmsman. 'He very seasick.' Absorbing this surprising news, we watched through the afternoon the flat, rugged triangle of Cape Horn looming up more and more clearly to the north-east.

This was the moment around which the whole trip had been built, and it was even more impressive than I had imagined it would be. I thought of the Portuguese and Spanish sailors, and then the Dutch and British, who had set eyes on it for the first time – Drake and Lieutenant Bligh in the foulest of weather, many more shipwrecked on its lethal shore, Lieutenant James Cook for the first time as if God had converted the waters into a millpond.

It was still only four hours since we had left the Diego Ramírez Islets astern. I later wrote in this piece for the *New Yorker* which I called 'The End Beyond the End':

> If geography were a tidy business, the Horn's grand, static rôle as a pivotal point of a continent would never have been jeopardised by that little string of islets, with a party of rockhopper penguins on the most southerly rock of them all, staring towards the Antarctic with unblinking red eyes.

14

The Sell-Out

When he was sixty-four, in 1965, Jamie Hamilton committed the misjudgement of selling his business. He claimed he had little private capital and was anxious about his old age, and also made the excuse that small private businesses could not keep pace with the new high cost of publishing, especially the big advances paid to top authors. (We had never had the least trouble in raising bank money for very hefty advances.) I had been a director for ten years or more, the children's book department was responsible for just under one half of the turnover and more than half of the profit. Max Martyn had been a director for much longer than me. But the only directors or senior staff who were given any hint of Jamie's intentions were his partner and the chief accountant, the excellent and much liked James Eastwell.

Jamie approached Lord Thomson's publishing group, which had already swallowed *The Times*, *The Sunday Times*, the whole Kemsley Group of newspapers and magazines, the *Illustrated London News* and various book publishers. Thomson and his board jumped at the opportunity and named a good price. Now there was only one possible impediment. Harpers in America had a stake in Hamish Hamilton Ltd. Jamie had begun in publishing, after a time in New York, as Harper's London representative, importing Harper books and then with their money starting to publish his own books as well in 1931. The proportion of the Harper financial stake was much lower by now but still substantial.

The ever loyal James Eastwell was despatched to New York to obtain the permission of the Harper boss, Cass Canfield, and his board to conclude the sale to Thomsons. Now Eastwell was very much an integral cog in the day-to-day business of Hamish Hamilton and all departments consulted him many times a week. Jamie let it be known that Eastwell had a bad attack of flu. On telephoning his home to enquire how he was and whether I could talk to him for a moment, his wife rather hesitantly told me he was not well enough. When he eventually came back to the office he looked not in the least convalescent, which was not surprising as he had enjoyed much New York sun.

Jamie then convened an extraordinary board meeting, and with his usual briskness told us the truth about Eastwell and of the sale and asked for our approval, outlining the benefits of having the strength, wealth and expertise of the giant Thomson Organisation behind us. We had none of the equity, all the shares had belonged to the Hamilton family and Harpers, and when Jamie asked for our authority we could do nothing but approve. The next day, or the day after, we were given cheques (in my case £2,200) for our contribution to the value of the company, from, mysteriously, Yvonne Hamilton.

This takeover led to great agitation in the trade, and many misgivings and some outrage among the directors and staff. The directors were further softened up with a lavish lunch with Lord Thomson and his senior management at which several speeches of praise at our past achievements were delivered. I sat next to Roy Thomson who talked to me throughout the meal and with scarcely a pause, about his deprived boyhood and rise to fame and untold wealth. Charlotte's mother, Helen, and my mother would have called him a common little man.

With this takeover, the firm lost its liveliness, spontaneity and spirit of enterprise. In spite of the independence we were promised, the Elm House lot soon began to take an interest in our day-to-day business, demanding figures and predictions – even, absurdly, prediction of turnover two years hence, though I gather it can be five years now. Forms arrived at 90 Great Russell Street, first in a flutter then by the van-load. The freehold premises housing our warehouse, manned by the best and nicest packers in London (Raymond Chandler when in London always visited them first and got drunk with them), was sold off. We were 'advised' to take on certain books we would never before have published. There were meetings with our fellow publishers in the group 'to rationalise the nature of our lists to avoid expensive overlapping'. There were meetings at Elm House, at first amiable, but less so as the figures did not improve as expected, then rather stern and frequent when they did not improve at all.

George Rainbird, who published heavily illustrated books and had sold out to Thomson's, too, was sent in as a troubleshooter. He suggested we put pictures in some of our old bestsellers and republish them. He also suggested we take on a volume of Churchill's paintings. We printed 20,000 and sold less than half. A military list was started by young Leo Cooper and showed considerable promise, but Jamie had it closed down and Leo removed the list and has prospered ever since.

At this time Eric Hiscock wrote a book about publishing and publishers called *Last Boat to Folly Bridge*. Hiscock was the nomadic guru of the trade, wandering from El Vino's to publishers' parties and clubs, forever with a glass of champagne, picking up gossip for his weekly column in *Smith's Trade News*. Jamie winkled an early copy out of those booksellers for the best people, and the only trade premises he would enter, G. Heywood Hill of Curzon Street, and was not pleased at what he read about the firm he had started. He was especially displeased with this: 'A children's book tail tends to wag the more adult dog. About 50% of the H.H. turnover stems from an actively growing tots booklist, a state of affairs that displeases the sober-minded, slightly egghead, certainly sophisticated Scot.'

Lawyers' letters flew and I was called down to Jamie's office and shown the book. 'Did you have anything to do with this, Dick?' he asked me. I had never seen him so angry. I told him that it was the first time I had seen it. He clearly did not believe me. Many years later I discovered it was the disgruntled Leo Cooper, a great friend of Eric, who had divulged this to him.

The matter blew over and shortly after this incident I proposed to Jamie that, in an effort to improve our fortunes, we might start a list of sponsored books under a different imprint. 'But you can't run anything like that *and* look after the children's books,' he told me. He obviously did not care for the idea of having anything so vulgar associated with his imprint. I said my new assistant, Julia MacRae, could look after the day-to-day running of the children's list which we could form into a subsidiary company with her and the production man as directors under my managing directorship. We could also form the sponsored books into a separate company, if that would please him.

Jamie and the rest of the board agreed to this and I telephoned my old friend James Leasor and asked him if he would like to be a part-time publisher. Jimmy was an accomplished writer and I had published a life of Lord Nuffield by him at The Bodley Head and *The Millionth Chance* about the R101 airship disaster recently at Hamish Hamilton. I had hoped Jamie would publish a series of thrillers he was embarking upon but he would not and the 'Jason Love' books sold in hundreds of thousands elsewhere. I judged Jimmy had the right entrepreneurial flair for what I had in mind, Jamie saw him and agreed, and we were in business. By happy chance, Julia MacRae gave us the idea for our first book. *The Weight-Watchers' Cook Book*, published on behalf of the highly successful American company of that name, which was now all the rage here, sold more than any other new hardback book in any category for the year, over 150,000 copies. It seemed a good start for what Jamie had named, to please Lord Thomson, Elm Tree Books, after the street in which his subsidiaries were housed.

It was 1970, and what with one thing and another, my own writing was seriously suffering while the fortunes of the general list at Hamish Hamilton were still not prospering. Thomsons decided that there must be a new managing director, and, through Jamie himself, I was asked to take on the task. The prospect was tempting, and Charlotte was in favour of my saying yes. But the fly was that Jamie would remain, in his own office, as President – still in effective control. I refused as gracefully as I could and Jamie asked me instead to go out into the publishing world and find one.

I lunched a number of potential candidates, all of whom have prospered wonderfully since, and any of whom might have come but for the presence and overriding control by Jamie, who was admired in the trade but not popular. It was, after all, a great challenge to pull round an ailing imprint of one-time great eminence. I reported my failure first to Thomsons, then to Jamie, who did not seem very put out, though he was by now at his wits' end. Even his dear, suave partner, Roger Machell, usually so cheerful, was beginning to lose hope of a recovery, and confided in me his disappointment that I would not take on the job. Max Martyn and Jimmy Leasor were both pressing me, too, but rather than do so I was beginning to think seriously of distancing myself from what was rapidly becoming a dog's dinner prepared in the Thomsons' insanitary kitchen.

Then in the late summer of this wretched year of 1970 a most extraordinary series of events occurred which to this day I am unable to understand. One Friday I was summoned to the presence of a senior Thomson man who asked me to come in early on Monday and occupy Jamie's desk. When he arrived I was to inform him that I had taken over as managing director. I refused to do so, as politely as I could.

The following week I was summoned again, this time to Jamie's office where he sat securely behind his desk as usual but surrounded by the rest of his directors, and George Rainbird, the Thomson man, to me all friends or friendly acquaintances, and was told that my services were no longer required.

What happened between these meetings I shall never know, but I am not now, twenty years later, prepared to speculate. But such innocence did clearly suggest that I would have been a rotten managing director.

Outside 90 Great Russell Street, the world looked more wholesome and the air smelt better. I bicycled down to the Garrick Club, ever the venue for consolation or celebration, had a couple of drinks, telephoned Charlotte and walked slowly round St James's Park. It was a nice day to contemplate a change in my status and fortunes, no longer a director of three companies let alone MD of a distinguished publishing house. The more I thought about it, the lighter the burden I felt on my shoulders and – oh boy! – I was totally free of any business commitments ever again if I chose.

At the same time, at forty-eight years and with three children at school or college, and two houses, and two cars, I had now only my typewriter on which to live.

15

A Royal Tour

My father George was becoming old and infirm. He had sold the house he had built when I was a little boy. I was sorry about that, especially as it went for a song, and they had moved back across Cornwall Gardens to the twin of the house in which I had been born. He had his workshop upstairs where he turned out useful things like bookcases for the family, but that was now his only hobby and exercise. By his eighties he had had to give up his bowls and could only just walk to the letterbox at the end of the road.

I don't think I had ever really understood my father, or he me. My brother he found accessible and compatible. They would walk round Phil's farm together, chatting away about crops and things. I wished sometimes I had a farm to walk round, but, while the processes of my mind were certainly no more complex nor deep than my brother's, George obviously did not care to relate to them. Like pacifism, my writing had an early cut-off point and he had no wish to cross the line into unknown territory. It was not so much that he was muddled, but he was nervous of becoming muddled and, as a non-swimmer, finding himself in deep waters.

Poor Meg had a severe stroke at about seventy, paralysing her right side. They both took it all with typical fortitude, and I really think she was rewarded for all that silent praying throughout her marriage by being granted a considerable recovery, though she could walk only short distances and with a stick, and her speech was always slightly impaired. We would all go down to Brighton on Sundays as often as we could and take them out for lunch. Sometimes my father paid and then I had to send one of the children back with a ten-shilling note to supplement my father's invariable 6d tip, unchanged since Edwardian days. Meg would giggle behind her hand and ask, 'Is it Sarah's turn this time?'

By 1969 when we returned from South America and visited Meg and George with our photographs, they were past going to a hotel and we brought lunch with us. George had loved sea travel and distant places as much as Meg had hated them. He had had scant opportunity for it while working in the bank, but the moment he retired in 1935 he booked himself passages to all sorts of distant parts – South Africa, Australia and New Zealand, and South America.

When I said, 'There, that's us at the prow, doubling Cape Horn,' he was fascinated.

'You're doing what Bligh failed to do in the *Bounty*,' he remarked. 'But then, the weather was better.'

He knew all about the *Bounty* voyage, had been to Pitcairn Island en route to New Zealand, and on return took us all to the Charles Laughton film. He was, rather surprisingly, of the Bligh-the-flogger school, as depicted by Charles Laughton.

'My next book's going to be about Bligh and the mutiny,' I told him.

With the Cape Horn book and the *New Yorker* piece out of the way, I got down seriously to the *Mutiny* research. I had been consumed by the romance and the conflicts of this episode ever since my father had brought back photographs of Pitcairn, one of the most remote and beautiful islands in the Pacific, in 1936. In the midst of all this, while I was working in London in the Naval Library, and in Cockermouth and Carlisle, on Fletcher Christian the leading mutineer, my father died in his ninetieth year. My mother telephoned early one morning. He had been in bed for a week and was losing his strength.

I had a fast Volvo at the time, and drove through south London at indecent speed, and then through the Weald of Sussex and over the South Downs which had been so close to his heart. My mother was sitting at the window, a frail, grey figure, when I arrived, and I could see that it must be all over.

'He went half an hour ago, dear. I think he was in pain,' she told me. 'His last words were, "Oh Meg, I didn't think it would be like this."'

I made a pot of tea and telephoned Charlotte. Phil had said he would come as soon as he could.

'Go and look at Daddy, he looks so beautiful,' begged my mother.

Goodness knows, I had seen more than enough of violent death but never an old man quietly on his deathbed. The undertaker had not yet come with his cosmetics, and the expression of pain on his white face greatly shocked me. But to Meg he had always been beautiful and so she had seen him in death.

Later in that year of 1970, I planned a trip to the South Seas. I had some time ago reached the conclusion that, if humanly possible, you must go to places that feature in your writing. It had helped me tremendously to walk the shore of Gardiner Island where he and his unfortunate missionaries had died of exposure and starvation, the shore of the Magellan Straits where Pedro Sarmiento had founded his ludicrous and disastrous colony, and so on. Now I determined somehow to see for myself Matavai Bay, Tahiti, where Bligh had spent too long collecting his breadfruit plants; Tofua, where the mutiny had been stoked up; Pitcairn where the mixed community of evading mutineers and a handful of Polynesians had shot or hacked one another to death; the Fijian islands which Bligh had first charted from his open boat; and the narrow passage through the Great Barrier Reef which had offered him respite from the appalling rigours of his open boat voyage after the mutiny.

All this could be done by paying fare money, and I was much supported by an adequate advance from Sir Robert Lusty of Hutchinson. Pitcairn was the difficulty. There was no airstrip, only the island's whalers could make the tricky landing, and on the rare occasions when ships hove to in Bounty Bay, no one ever went ashore.

I told my old friend Tom Pocock of my dilemma. Tom, once the youngest war correspondent, had also been Naval Correspondent of *The Times* and was then the Travel Editor of the London *Evening Standard*. He knew all the tricks of finding out and getting about. He at once fixed a lunch with the Royal Navy's PRO, who proved not only charming in himself but fruitful to a breathtaking degree.

'Well, it just so happens,' he said over the coffee, 'that there is a party going to Pitcairn in February. It's just possible I could find a berth for you. But you would have to be very discreet indeed. I'll let you know if there is any chance.' This seemed to call for another brandy, and we talked more about the mutiny. When asked for my theory on its origins, I said I had discussed this with several naval historians and there was, I believed, some suggestion of a homosexual relationship between Bligh and Christian, who were perhaps too close friends for their own good.

There was a sharp intake of breath from my PRO new naval friend. 'May I suggest you don't breathe a word of this on *this* voyage,' he begged feelingly.

Tom soon smelt out who this party consisted of. 'It's the Royal Yacht, with some of the royal family,' he divulged. 'Don't know who yet. They're going all over the place but a visit to Pitcairn is on the itinerary.'

A few days later, I was willingly press-ganged by the Admiralty and given details. 'Get yourself to Panama by 2nd February, and with luck there'll be a berth for you in the RFA [Royal Fleet Auxiliary] ship *Blue Rover*. You'll be sailing with the *Britannia* across the Pacific.' My friend turned over some papers, and pulled one out. 'Let's see. First stop Galapagos Islands. Then miles south to Easter. About two days there, then – very slowly I see – to Pitcairn for two more days . . .'

I thanked this kind – and, my goodness, useful – officer, who advised as we shook hands, 'Travel light if I were you – but take a black tie just in case.'

The *Blue Rover*, bursting with fuel oil for the *Britannia* and its own needs for the long voyage, and other supplies, docked at Panama opposite the *Britannia*, Prince Philip's standard flying and floodlit at night, by contrast with our practical workhorse. The word soon got round that our charge had on board Prince Philip, Lord Mountbatten, his daughter, Lady Brabourne and her husband, who had something to do with films, Princess Alexandra and Angus Ogilvy, and Lord Zuckerman, for his connection with the Darwin Institute at the Galapagos Islands. I did not expect to have anything to do with any of them, and assumed I would be with the *Blue Rover*'s officers and the all-Maltese crew.

And what about them? I surveyed them anxiously in the *Blue Rover*'s bar at 4 a.m. soon after the ship's arrival. The number one, David Lynch, took charge of me, showed me my 'cabin', in fact the ship's hospital which I was to share with Pat, an engineer from the factory that made the diesel engines which were playing up. Then back to the bar to meet the other officers, a cheerful company of fourteen, and the plump, relaxed Captain Brace, who was never last to the bar, which reminded me of Ronald Colman's, all beams and hanging pewter mugs. They wore white shoes, long white socks, white shorts and short-sleeved (except for dinner) shirts with epaulettes. Bob the purser looked promising company, tall, willowy, body-proud, I discovered later, talkative, especially on his mother and old people, an energetic hypochondriac who had strained his ankle at deck tennis already. There was a smiling rather-pleased-with-himself Indian; and Jerry, Chief Engineer, jutting teeth, good, wholesome capable chap who told me his Vera did not want any more kids, so he was going to have this vasectomy thing.

I slept most of the next day. Dinner at 6 p.m. revealed much about the social mores of the RFA, as against RAF officers' mess style and manners. The mess table sparkled with silver, and white linen tablecloth, and there were menus with embossed heading for all five courses, wine and *filet* of steak and all the trimmings, ably supported by the Daddy's Sauce bottle, which went round and round the table, like the port later. Afterwards, three of us retired to the Captain's cabin and killed a bottle of brandy, and *then* went to a film in the lounge. It was called *Carry on Cowboy* with Sid James, and as it was shot at Frensham Ponds, and I was heavily jetlagged anyway, I felt decidedly disorientated when I retired to my bunk in the hospital, surrounded by all the tools of the surgeons' trade.

A day before we left, the *Britannia* slipped her moorings and glided without fuss – just one short farewell blast on her siren – from her pier under the bridge and out into the ocean at sunrise. Then it was our turn, an event of no importance to the officers, let alone our happy Maltese, but for me it was a moment of profound emotion as for the first time the *Blue Rover*'s stem dug into the Pacific. After a day or two we caught up the Royal Yacht, which reduced revs at night to diminish the vibration in the royal quarters aft.

It was grey, the sea dead and with scarcely any bird life *en route* to our first islands. This made the arrival at the Galapagos, sunny and bang on the equator, all the more strange and moving. Suddenly the sea was full of dolphins and seals, the air with boobies and terns, frigates and diving brown pelicans, swarms of flying fish rising and falling amidst the spray of their making. Sharks' fins flicked up, danced through the water, half turned, showing a little of their dark body, then suddenly flashing off in a flurry of spray.

Once these islands had been nothing but fresh volcanic rock; now the larger ones were green and afforested high up, where it sometimes rained. Here at Isla Santa Cruz and the other islands was the home of a unique range of wildlife, from giant centuries-old tortoises, giant land and sea iguanas unique to this archipelago, birds that used tools, birds that cannot fly, birds that seek your hair for nest-making, penguins that should live in the Antarctic and flamingoes that should be in equatorial Africa. And all without fear of man because they had no cause for it.

The *Britannia* anchored in Academy Bay on the south-east coast, a glorious but anachronistic sight in this remote and primitive place. Almost at once a launch was lowered and sped across the water between us. An officer appeared on our deck and handed David Lynch two envelopes, and then was gone again.

David called me over. 'One of these is for you,' he declared, improbably. With a national mail strike in England, who would be writing to me from these tropical islands? It was a *very* stiff envelope, too, and the contents were sparse and formal. Beneath the Duke of Edinburgh's coat of arms was an invitation 'to dinner on-board HM Yacht Britannia. Dress: Dinner jacket . . .' Lucky I had taken the PRO's advice and brought mine.

The other envelope was for Captain Brace, and after he had got over a brief phase of rather pompous assumed non-interest in the engagement, we had a good giggle together. He had learned that the dinner was in honour of the hierarchy of Ecuador, in whose waters we now lay. The next day, an extremely rusty, very old and very small Ecuadorean destroyer arrived in the bay, no doubt the escort for the State Yacht, and our hearts went out to the crew for there could be no air-conditioning in that vessel and it was stiflingly hot.

I was on deck the next evening at 7.30 awaiting passage to the dinner. Brace appeared beside me, dressed in rather tight but impressive mess gear, his face a red light in the darkness. We had both stiffened our courage with a couple of stiffies. A single light detached itself from the galaxy of the *Britannia* and sped towards us. We descended into the royal launch and then into the cabin aft, all mahogany and white linen. The temperature was well over 100°F and Brace mopped his face ceaselessly while I stripped off my dinner jacket.

Flag Officer Royal Yachts – or FORY – Rear-Admiral R. J. Trowbridge greeted us at the head of the gangway, a fearsome fellow in full fig, red face, jutting jaw, with other officers, including Commander William Willett RN, OBE, MVO, DSC, Prince Philip's private secretary. Willett, who was to be my minder over the following weeks, and then a friend until his premature death in

1976, was a cool, quiet, sardonic man with a world-weary sense of humour and a patience that was often sorely stretched. He now led us to the ship's library, which sported many prints of bloody sea engagements rather than books, and a selection of tired six-day-old newspapers neatly laid out on a mahogany table.

'We're using this as a holding station,' Willett informed Brace and me, and then turned his attention to the guests of honour who suddenly poured in behind us, the men all tall, dark and menacing in their fancy dress, brigands one and all, their mistresses gowned and décolletée, scented and bejewelled, lustrous dark eyes flashing for the main chance, and with an aroma that much more than cancelled out the emanations from the brigands themselves.

Among them, Willett introduced me to the Chief of the Army, a vast mulatto-Prussian, close-cropped bullet head, black eyes presaging revolution, medals dangling, sword and long, long spurs clinking. Close by were the Chief of Police, the Marshal of the Ecuador Air Force, the Supreme Admiral of the Navy, all equally tall and fearsome. In the midst of them and their ladies was a Chaplinesque figure, a small, inoffensive fellow in white tie and tails. '*Il Presidente.*' ''ow do you do', 'so glad'. Either he had something we did not know about, or the bullets surely would soon be whistling in the streets.

Sheepdog Willett herded us into the yacht's main lounge and lined us up to be introduced to our host. When my time came, and I gave the appropriate nod, he asked me, rather severely I thought, 'There's been quite a bit written on Captain Cook already, hasn't there?' It was an inappropriate moment to deny or argue, so I allowed the non sequitur to pass, and passed on myself – to Lord Mountbatten as it happened. He could out-medal anyone there and looked very amused by the proceedings, until the Army chief backed up behind him, shining spurs glinting menacingly. Like every good soldier, Lord Mountbatten had eyes in the back of his head. 'Whoops!' he exclaimed and edged closer to me in search of protection. Mountbatten was better-informed about why I was here than his nephew and buttonholed in turn the Admiral and the yacht's Commander to emphasise my need to land on Pitcairn as early in the visit as possible. He was about to tap Prince Philip on the arm, too, but by now he was deeply involved in conversation with easily the most beguiling of the señoritas.

The champagne was going down quite nicely all round. I asked Solly Zuckerman if he was enjoying the trip. 'Yes,' he said, 'soon

I'll start my memoirs.' 'Who will be your publisher?' I asked automatically. 'Oh, I think George Weidenfeld. He paid me quite a nice lot of money for my bits and pieces. Jamie Hamilton made a bid, but I think he's a bit past it now.' I neither denied nor confirmed, but did wonder, rather discreditably, what Jamie, who so loved the grand glitter, would think if he could see me now.

We drifted into the vast dining saloon. The table was decorated with a veritable hedge of flowers down the centre, and two silver model galleons. I was on Willett's left – he of the tense expression, flat voice, and roving eye for breaches of protocol and execution of his plans – who was at the head. On my left a dusky, plumpish señorita (were there *any* señoras?). We mouthed at one another from time to time: her teeth were more predatory than mine.

Willett had his difficulties. 'What with the language and other problems, I thought we'd better fill in with a film afterwards.' Prince Philip, it seemed, had no sense of time, and Willett's life was one long struggle with timetables. He told me that yesterday during a buffet lunch on shore which followed the presentation to the village of football equipment, Philip overheard someone answering another's enquiry about the island's products: 'No, no coffee,' meaning we do not produce coffee beans. Prince Philip at once walked away in dudgeon, for he likes his coffee after a meal, and again Willett's timetable was wrecked.

After a superb dinner well washed down with riesling, vintage champagne, claret and port, dextrously dealt with by a dozen stewards, and soothed by the Royal Marines band playing softly behind a blue curtain, we headed back to the lounge. The señoritas were giggling a good deal by now, and brandy and coronas awaited us. In twenty minutes we were back again in the dining saloon, now a cinema, *il Presidente*, Mountbatten and Prince Philip in deep armchairs at the front. It was a deplorable Dean Martin comedy-thriller, a silent movie really, for we could hear nothing above the inebriated Spanish chatter.

Finally, Willett nudged us back again to the lounge, where the dogged stewards were serving whisky and squash. I talked to Princess Alexandra and Angus Ogilvy, who expressed keen interest in the *Bounty* mutiny and Pitcairn. I tried to persuade them to continue with the *Britannia* rather than fly home from Easter Island as they had planned. But I learned later that there were some difficult things to deal with in the City.

First Prince Philip, then Trowbridge and others, bade us good night. Willett said he hoped we would not mind sharing the launch with some of the Ecuadoreans, who were already tumbling down the gangway to the well-lit pontoon below. It was sheer Marx Brothers pandemonium on board with some twenty-four in the space for scarcely twelve. The three smart yachtsmen were tight-lipped and stoic in face of the giggles and fallings about and screams, sabres in the clutch lever, bosoms entangled in the steering wheel, as we made our choppy way across the bay.

Where *was* the Presidential Yacht, Brace and I wondered? We seemed to be heading for the rusting, unlit destroyer. 'My God, that *is* the Presidential Yacht!' exclaimed Brace, who was sitting half on my lap. And he was right. We came alongside, someone appeared on deck and switched on a single naked bulb hanging from a flex at the top of the gangway. What must it be like in there? The combined stench of fuel oil, chickens, urine and sweat! One or two of the señoritas were laughingly trying to hijack us, pulling at our arms. Our crew were heroes, saving several of them from falling in, and backing away in the half light immediately they could. A few minutes later, Brace and I collapsed in his cool cabin, jackets off for a nightcap and last laugh. 'If that's what they have to put up with, I'd double the royal family's wages,' Brace remarked.

We had only one tantalising day ashore, to be shown round the Darwin Institute where they were attempting to nurse giant turtles through their early, vulnerable years, amongst many other activities. Then, in ferocious heat, three of us walked along the shore, sampling the wonders of this archipelago – the tall, white cranes snatching at lizards, the brown pelicans crashing, wings folded, into the sea for fish, the giant land iguanas languidly chewing out the heart of yellow cactus flowers, the equally huge black sea iguanas basking on the sharp rock before wobbling off in alligator stride for the cool of the surf. None of them took the slightest notice of us.

We RAS'd (replenish at sea) every other day while cruising slowly south. It was a pleasant distraction in an uneventful voyage, with the two vessels closing to within hailing distance. A shot was fired from the *Blue Rover*, carrying a line over the *Britannia*'s forecastle, then hauling in the telephone line and the hose end, like a great red-tipped pencil which was inserted into the tank orifice. When the oil was pumped, at 250 gallons an hour, the hose swelled out, and the hierarchy of the *Britannia*, the women in bright afternoon dresses, waved to us, dropping a curtsy when Prince Philip appeared, but he was soon bored and disappeared again. The Royal Marines' band contributed a festive note. Fine adjustments of the helm kept the distance apart steady. A lone dolphin played at the stern of the Royal Yacht, ignoring us and perhaps recognising superior class. A dozen empty beer casks swung across; no wonder the yachtsmen had pot bellies.

I fell into a simple daily routine, walking the helicopter flight deck for two hours a day, playing deck tennis – not easy as my left, ligament-less knee had developed arthritis – sleeping, writing, eating, drinking, washing in the laundry and learning to iron. I wrote a long log of our activities for eventual despatch to the school that had adopted the ship, and played chess and bridge or watched a film in the evening. All very peaceful. It was fine all the way and I got very brown, and the *Blue Rover* rolled gently and with singular consistency. The telex told us of strikes and misery at home. On the correct day we solemnly changed our British money to decimal coinage.

The Chilean island of Easter, the most isolated in the world, came into sight at dawn on 18th February. I went up on deck in pyjamas, watching in awe as the sun came up, twice its normal size, touching with red the stark coastline of this mysterious island. We crept slowly down the west coast, as if fearful of the giant statues staring out to sea from the shoreline, and, indeed, once intended to deter strangers. But we were actually echo-sounding. Many of the hills behind were steep and cone-shaped, a semi-circular scar in the cliff marking the site of an old volcano. There was little sign of vegetation although many horses roamed the stark landscape.

There were two items of good news for me, made known as we dropped anchor off Hangaroa, the island's one village. First I was to transfer to the *Britannia* when we re-embarked, and second that a signal had been sent to the High Commissioner in New Zealand (responsible for Pitcairn) asking that accommodation should be arranged for me there so that I could be ashore for the night. Meanwhile, there was Easter Island to be explored and I was asked to rendezvous with a party of twenty officers from the *Britannia* and *Blue Rover* at the quayside.

I studied the yacht's officers keenly. I had seen them only formally on the banquet evening; now, off duty, they were wearing light holiday clothes and laughing and teasing like a bunch of amiable schoolboys. What's more, they appeared to be charges of 'matron' in the form of one of Prince Philip's highly attractive private secretaries, one Tanya Tolstoy, the only one among them all who spoke fluent Spanish and could interpret for our guide.

Among these eager, enquiring officers was the *Britannia*'s chief executive officer, Commander 'Dickie' Bird, Lieutenant-Commander Ronald Snow, the 'quack', and the sons of several Second World War admirals, including Dudley Pound's boy, Martin. Off we went in our mini-bus, crashing over rocks and potholes, our guide telling us about the long civil war between the slaves of the island, the 'short ears', and their one-time masters, the 'long ears'. It had lasted for several hundred years, reducing the population from about 8,000 to a few hundred.

High up on the southern end of the island we looked over the lip of a giant crater 1,400 feet down to pools and marshes, and then made our way, chatter, chatter, chatter, into a maze of caves and underground galleries, the last retreat of the 'long ears'. Their identification was clear from the weird carvings on the rock depicting themselves in Picasso-like whorls with enormous ears.

We re-embarked in our bus in time to avoid the worst of a dark storm which matched the doom-laden nature of the chambers, and drove through driving rain down the mountainside and along sodden tracks to the other end of the island. We passed countless statues, many said to have been toppled to celebrate the victory of the 'short ears'. After a very rough climb up the side of another volcano, we were shown the quarry where the forty-feet-high, seventy-ton statues had been carved out of solid rock by the slaves. They had then been moved, no one knows how for sure, as many as eight miles. No wonder there had been a rebellion! Many of the statues were uncompleted and many more were lifted vertically to stare out to sea from their place of creation, heavy-browed, heavy-lipped and malevolent.

At dusk I was back on board the *Blue Rover* packing and having a last quick drink with Brace, and David and the rest. 'Don't get above yourself,' 'Mind, now, you bow to all those grandees or you'll be walking the plank.' That sort of thing. Then a launch came for

me, and for the second time I slipped across the water to the noble
and graceful *Britannia*.

To say the least, the contrast between life on the ocean wave aboard
the *Britannia* and the *Blue Rover* was marked, and surprising. It was
all very well for the royal family and their guests, beyond the
broad mahogany doors where the thick pile carpet began. Elsewhere, it was hot and cramped for the 250 officers, petty officers
and yachtsmen, the last of these accommodated in hammocks not
much further separated than those of the *Louis Pasteur*, and the only
RN ship still so equipped. She had been designed in King Edward
VIII's reign, when the lower deck was not much molly-coddled.

For the officers the wardroom, with bar, and the dining saloon,
were spacious and comfortable, but the cabins were cramped, and
once again mine was full of an absent sick officer's gear. After the
extremely warm welcome and the drinks that went with it (and
what a nice civilised lot they were!) it was the sense of claustro-
phobia that I remember most. The men had the use of the forecastle, which they used mainly for a special and lethal form of
hockey, often cheered on by the royal party above, while the officers
had only a small sundeck – much too small for a long voyage like
this. Its size was further limited by the royal luggage which clut-
tered the upper deck – gleaming boats of all kinds, Princess Anne's
pet yacht, Prince Charles's new four-seat luxury launch picked up
in the Bahamas, Prince Philip's new catamaran, among them.

Breakfast the first day was easy: a silent meal. I pretended to read
a December copy of the *Illustrated London News*. Table napkin rings,
and my own pigeonhole. Table napkins were fresh at every meal on
the *Blue Rover*, where there was also a great deal more room and more
effective air-conditioning. Dickie Bird buttonholed me on the way
out. 'A couple of things – you're asked to lunch with Prince Philip.
Can you manage that? Just a small lunch, and I expect they'll give
you an hour's solid grilling about the mutiny.' I swallowed and
nodded simultaneously. 'Then, I wonder if you'd mind giving the
men a talk this afternoon? It's good for them to know something
about where they're going to next . . . Good, good, very kind of you.
I'll have a microphone rigged. And you might like a blackboard.'

A steward collected me at 12.45, and we passed through those
mahogany doors. Willett drifted in to join me in the lounge. 'Care
for a drink?' He regarded me quizzically when I asked for a vodka

and tonic. 'What a curious drink!' And he poured nearly enough to cover the base of the glass before filling the tonic to the brim. Even the single cube of ice was midget. Like this, it was indeed curious.

'Sorry about the delay,' Willett said in his flat voice. 'They've suddenly decided to go for a swim.' Even lunch for Hough presented timing complications. Then Prince Philip came down the wide main staircase, loose and easy, not jaunty or brisk, certainly not slack, in white shorts and sandals. Flat tummy, fairly brown, nose peeling slightly, creases from his eyes and mouth. He mixed himself a similar drowned drink and popped in a similar single cube of ice.

The Brabournes came in and had nothing at all to drink, and we all sat down, Prince Philip asking me if I had found anything new about the mutiny. 'It's the men, their relationship,' I uttered lamely, 'that's what I'm chiefly interested in.' My audience had the gleam of relentless interrogation in their eyes.

Prince Philip led us past the wide stairs towards the dining saloon, Willett indicating with one finger that I should follow his master. I sat on my host's right, with Lady Brabourne on my right, Mountbatten opposite me. I noted with reassurance three exquisite cut glasses before me, then heard a voice in my ear, 'Water or beer, sir?' We ate Easter Island corn-on-the-cob, undercooked and leaving razor spikes between my teeth. No one else cared: all the other cobs were neatly stripped in no time. (Later, the cook told me, 'Yes, that was a boob. Should've used the frozen ones.') Then tiny cutlets, and cheese, but I scarcely had a chance to eat as the barrage of questions continued.

'What an extraordinary fellow!' Prince Philip said of Bligh. 'His own worst enemy. Such a waste.' He mentioned the name of someone he knew with the same failing. 'I did everything I could to help him and yet he had this unconscious suicide streak. It's something I don't understand. Do you think Bligh was a homosexual?'

I laughed. 'Sir, before I left for this trip I was warned not on any account to mention this suspicion of mine.'

This was considered to be an enormous joke, and things eased. Prince Philip said, 'It probably happened that happily married men like Bligh had heterosexual lives, perhaps only occasional bouts of homosexuality far from home . . .'

Mountbatten broke in, rather late for him I discovered later. They began to argue about their estimates of the horse population of Easter Island, which enabled me to eat a mouthful. Then Willett gave Prince Philip his four-page close-typed account of events at that island which would be sent to the Queen. He made marginal notes. 'No, *not* that,' he said emphatically several times. Mountbatten argued several conclusions, too, and then everyone joined in. Prince Philip listened, head raised, blue eyes flashing from speaker to speaker, half smiling. Once he relented over some trivial point. The others he dismissed, and when Willett pressed for conditioning one statement for accuracy, he said emphatically, 'No, no. That's awful. We'll leave it as it is.' Other alternatives were also perfunctorily turned down, even those from Mountbatten though less emphatically.

We rose just before 3 p.m. Willett whispered, 'Do you want to thank Prince Philip?' Swallowing my resentment at being treated as a child, I did so, and prepared for the next ordeal in less than half an hour. 'We'll all be there,' were Willett's last words of comfort. I had been told I was addressing the *men*, for heaven's sake!

No wonder Ferdinand Magellan named this ocean Pacifico. Day after day passed without a cloud in sight and the sea had no more than a hint of a swell. All that we saw was an occasional atoll, too small to be worth charting, like a cartoonist's desert island with a pair of palm trees and a few square yards of grass and sand. Schools of porpoise followed in our wake, easily able to keep up with our slow progress, and terns and gulls sometimes landed on our deck.

Thank goodness I had brought plenty of books for there was nothing to do during the day. I played an occasional game of deck tennis but found it painful on my knee; the swimming pool was out of bounds which seemed a bit thoughtless considering the heat; and I just lay in the sun reading or sleeping most of the day, the only sound the endless soft whine of the rotating radar aerial. In the evening there was bridge and always a film. All ranks attended, the royal party occupying the front row in armchairs. They were mostly old war movies, chosen jointly by Mountbatten and his nephew, who laughed or talked loudly and mostly critically throughout. 'I know for a fact that Clark's *only* aim was to get to Rome first,' commented Mountbatten of the Salerno landings. 'I told Alex that he really ought to tame that incompetent general.'

'Just look at those medals!' Prince Philip roared on another evening. 'He's got the DSO in front of the OBE.'

But on Saturday it was dining-in night, and what a performance *that* was! Tanya Tolstoy and her equally pretty friend and fellow secretary, Amanda, Prince Philip's burly bodyguard, Chief Superintendent 'Jumbo' Thorning, and a rather comic clerk with a facial rash, were the wardroom guests. 'The girls', greatly loved by all, made their entrance in bell bottoms, white blouses and epaulettes, Tanya in Admiral of the Fleet epaulettes loaned by Mountbatten. The effect was a knockout and they were given a stiff drink before retiring to put on long evening dresses for the meal.

Dinner was formal and splendid at a table loaded with silverware collected over the centuries, completed when at length the port and madeira decanters were brought in by the stewards. Coffee and brandy followed, and then, like a naval broadside, battle commenced.

Wardroom games, beginning with special *Britannia* variations on charades and paper games, turned into more active and then violent activities, like walking as far backwards as you could on your hands with ankles slung in loops at the ends of a rope lashed round the switched-off but freely rotating ceiling fan. The next minute we were in two teams, clutching broomsticks between our legs, the girls leading, round an obstacle course.

The evening wore on. With complete dignity, and just an occasional apology, when he got in the way, the surviving steward continued to hand round drinks, but, I noticed amidst the turmoil, they were virtually alcohol free. Then, the culminating key game: a length of nylon string, a key tied at each end, the two teams facing one another. The winning team was the first to hold up the key at each end after it had been passed up and down every single trouser leg. My team cheated by accelerating progress with trousers fallen to the ankles; the other team followed; and there was not an officer in the wardroom who did not reveal the colour of his pants. Tanya and Amanda thought it a great joke, so that was all right.

The next day, Sunday 21st February, was more formal but still fun. We were due to arrive at Pitcairn in the afternoon, and I packed an overnight bag and made sure I had a bottle of whisky. The island might be dry but I was to stay with the New Zealand schoolmaster and his wife. At mid-day there appeared a smudge on the horizon. Soon it developed a shape with which I was familiar from my father's old photos.

We dropped anchor at 4 p.m. on the dot. Bounty Bay! We were above the last remains of Bligh's ship, burned and sunk by the mutineers. Half a mile distant, the shoreline rose, in places with stunning steepness, one sheer hill of almost a thousand feet, Christian's cave, his brooding retreat, a black splash near the summit. Wherever the rock ceased, rich vegetation took over, secondary scrub in the centre, flowering shrubs, bananas, banyans and breadfruit, oranges and limes, lemons and grapefruit, paw-paws, tall gently waving palms – a feast of richness, a palate-full of colour. If this was my dream come true, what must Christian have felt on finding this island after all those months of agonised wandering about Polynesia?

There were bungalows among the trees: Adamstown, built on the island's only plateau. Union flags were flying, and down at the landing point – the only one – a crowd was bustling about the island's two longboats, both flying the flag. They came out through the surf, fully loaded, the entire population of some ninety. Soon we could see that the men were in jeans and shirts, except Pervis Young and Ben Christian, whose ancestors fired the mutiny, in suits. The women and girls wore bright dresses.

I watched them come up the companionway, the children excited, only the youngest women still slim, a few European faces but mainly half or three-quarter Polynesian. I joined the officers as host on the verandah deck, where they arrived after shaking hands, and I mixed in with them, finding them relaxed, delighted, quite unawed, and hell-bent on eating as much of the food as possible in the time.

Mountbatten and Prince Philip were marvellous hosts, far better than with those Ecuadoreans. Prince Philip settled down with a family here, wandered over to join a group of boys there, and I caught a glimpse of Mountbatten feeding ice cream to a tiny piccaninny. The band played on the quarterdeck, and against the background of the lush undergrowth, the towering peaks and rocks, with the sun slanting down the slopes and through the palms, the scene was romantic and moving.

I picked up my bag and joined them as they left, laughing and singing and finishing off the last food they had grabbed. The sea was calm, but even so the break through the surf between projecting rocks called for concentration and precise timing. We went in in one sweep, to the small area of calm water behind the breakwater.

Russell Henry, the schoolmaster, was waiting, a small, bald, cheerful man who greeted me warmly then put me on the pillion of his Honda 90. We spun up the steep dirt track in great style, avoiding and waving to the climbing villagers we passed, then through Adamstown, past the *Bounty*'s anchor and the remains of Fletcher Christian's son's first house. Several times we stopped for introductions to more Christians, another Young, a Warren, and a Clark, most of them descendants of the original doomed community here. They talked a mixture of eighteenth-century English and pigeon Polynesian, without a 'v' between them.

Margaret Henry, polio crippled leg, New Zealand chin, angelic smile, greeted me outside her home, her three children at her side. My host and hostess were to have all the royal party for lunch the next day, and much of the evening was spent helping to lay the tables and polish the silver. There was a break for sausages and eggs, bananas and pineapple, washed down with many cups of tea. Late in the evening we sauntered down to the village to see the worst film, *The Fastest Guitarist in the World*, in the most beautiful setting in the world.

The sun roasted me awake at 7.15. I can't be on Pitcairn! was my first disbelieving thought. Then I opened one eye, and it was true, and there, at anchor directly below my open window, flags and standard flying, was the glistening *Britannia*. By 9 a.m. the entire population was seated in the village square on benches taken from the church, the council members, all male of course, and looking very self-conscious in their ties, facing them on the village hall verandah. Such a lot of trouble had been taken with multi-coloured bunting and strings of hibiscus and other flowers, the Union flag flying from its pole beside the *Bounty*'s anchor.

The dignity and seriousness of the occasion were broken by the arrival of the royal party in the island's two Mini-Mokes at a brisk speed and almost invisible within their own dust. Prince Philip sprang out, obviously relishing the occasion, and was led by the chairman and island magistrate, Pervis Young, up the newly painted red steps to the seats. Everyone stood up, the national anthem was sung. The flag was lowered and Prince Philip's standard was broken, after some technical help from Mountbatten. 'The Queen – she lovely!' remarked my stout neighbour of Lady Brabourne, and a friend behind her agreed.

Pervis Young, tall, dark, one-third Polynesian, began his speech of welcome. This was the moment of his life. 'We wery much welcome the wery royalty family,' he began proudly, 'and their staff, and' – with a glance at Trowbridge – 'the Admiral of all the Fleets.'

This, I mused, must be the first time that a Rear-Admiral has taken seniority over two Admirals of the Fleet within their presence. It went on for rather a long time, but the usually impatient Prince Philip bore it all with a smile, and then responded on just the right note, with a couple of jokes about how many teas were consumed on this most beautiful island.

Tea followed, appropriately, with the consumption of mountains of sandwiches and fresh fruit, and then a tour of all the sights – the school, church, the graveyard ('The dead centre of the island, sir') and so on. I took advantage of this to walk about parts of Adamstown and its outskirts seeking evidence of the sites mentioned in early accounts of the mainly awful things that had happened here long ago.

The royal party changed into informal gear in the Henrys' house, and we tucked into the buffet lunch we had prepared the evening before. Prince Philip brought his plate to the bottom step of the stairs where I was sitting with Tom Christian who operated the island's radio. He sat down between us and asked him where his infamous ancestor was buried.

'No grave. He just disappeared,' the young man replied.

'You know Mr Hough here is writing a book about him. He thinks he was a homosexual.'

I did not think this was very tactful, but Christian just laughed. 'Wery naughty man. But all Christians after wery good.'

Mountbatten was feeling the heat and told his nephew that he was taking a sleep instead of touring the island, so Prince Philip invited me to join him in the first Mini-Moke. The island is only two square miles, but the tracks are so circuitous and the gradients so steep that it took – with halts for photographing and picking fresh fruit – almost an hour of bumping and skidding to reach the highest point. On one precipitous corner, the second Mini-Moke with the pastor on board, stalled. Everyone but the pastor, anxious for his dignity, got out, including Prince Philip from ours, and put their shoulders to the rear. This was perhaps the first time the sovereign's consort has ever pushed a Seventh Day Adventist church leader uphill. *And* I failed to photograph it.

'Jumbo' Thorning (most unsuitably) and Willett followed us up on Honda pillions, and we all rendezvoused at the summit, Up-in-Ti, 1,100 feet. The full glory of the island was unfolded at our feet, and Pitcairn seemed to dominate the whole Pacific. Only the western end of the island was cut off by nearby shrubs. I tried to mount the roof of a small hut, but Prince Philip called me over to a small clearing at the edge of a sheer drop down to the sea. 'You can see almost everything from here.'

I stood beside him, photographing. No assassin could have hoped to work himself into a position like this. 'Do these moments make you worried?' I asked Jumbo, some ten yards behind us. 'Not a bit,' he replied blandly.

Back in the village we were confronted with yet another tea, with speeches and the presentation of a carved shark's head to Prince Philip. Studying it quizzically, he remarked that 'the only thing I can see in common with this shark and Pitcairners is their appetite', which almost brought the roof down.

Finally the pompous pastor, in great voice, led a rousing hymn, and then a curious piece of narrative verse detailing the gloomy drama of how the good ship *Vestris* went down because the captain hesitated, 'and many homes were saddened, and many widows made'. I looked at the Flag Officer Royal Yachts meaningfully, and Prince Philip could not contain himself. 'Well, we'll just have to do the best we can,' he commented, not very quietly.

Down at the landing, it was almost dark, and the floodlit *Britannia* looked rather distant. All the islanders were there to see us off, Prince Philip sitting casually on the engine hatch of the longboat, looking as cheerful and filthy as the rest of us. Just as we were about to cast off, islanders dropped into the longboat, too. Mountbatten looked resigned. 'Another *Vestris*,' he remarked ruefully, counting them. '. . . thirty-one, thirty-two.' There was less than a foot of freeboard and the sea was getting up. There was much shouted advice from the jetty. 'You'll take a wet!' someone said encouragingly, but our helmsman did not seem to care.

At the precisely timed moment – no hesitation – the throttle was opened and we pushed out between breakers into the choppy bay. The Pitcairners sang all the way and behaved as if they had known us for years, without respect or disrespect: just happily. Prince Philip was first off, timing his landing skilfully, and then reaching out for Mountbatten's hand. We were back amid formality, pomp, spit'n'polish, gleaming uniforms and salutes. But we all lined up at the rail in the dusk, waving last farewells to the jolly boat-load.

The anchors were already being raised, the deck began to vibrate, and I remained at the rail after the others had left, watching the spectacular configuration of the island, with its scattered pinpoints of light, fading into the night.

16

Travel Teaches
Toleration

I met Charlotte in the foyer of a Sydney hotel. She dropped her shopping and exclaimed, 'Dr Livingstone, I presume!' She had got to Australia free, after walking into the office of George Gale, then editing *The Spectator*, and offering to write and illustrate a series of pieces about her journey. Very good they were, too. 'Gosh, you are brown,' she said, and glanced down at my stick, and then my right foot. 'What on earth have you done to yourself?'

'I don't know, but something to my ankle.' I told her about transferring back to the *Blue Rover* at Rarotonga. 'The voyage seemed to be going on interminably and I wanted to reach Australia and get on with this damn research and see you. The *Blue Rover*'s third officer, a nice lad, had heard that his father in England had suffered a heart attack. The Navy's very good in this sort of situation and took urgent steps to get him home,' I explained. 'A plane was laid on to take him from Samoa to Fiji, and then back across the Pacific, New York and London. By going with him to Fiji I could be in Sydney in a couple of days.'

But, I told her, the journey flat out to Apia proved fateful. After the space restriction on board the *Britannia*, I had stupidly played an energetic game of deck tennis on the steel helicopter pad, frequently hopping on my right leg to save the pressure on my knee. There had been a crack like a pistol's and I fell to the deck as if shot. I thought my ankle was badly twisted, and one of the officers fixed a cold compress and bandaged it up. No sleep that night, and the next morning before anchoring off Samoa I could scarcely walk. The two flights were fairly good hell, and now here I was with Charlotte, thank God.

Apart from the relief and pleasure of being with her again at last, she fixed appointments with doctors and physiotherapists, acquired a set of crutches and helped me in and out of taxis. I had also to face the press and radio. This was the only occasion when I was publicised before even starting to write a book. My publishers in Australia had let it be known that I had travelled to Sydney by the Royal Yacht with half the royal family on board, and there were phone-ins and photo sessions and interviews in our hotel bedroom.

For the next ten days the pattern of our life was set around the Mitchell Library and the Bligh papers, Charlotte usually reading, writing and sunning herself in the gardens outside; a long visit daily for electric treatment to the wretched ankle; and evenings out with the ever-hospitable Sydneysiders. We loved the place, and the people, but the mobility problem and the state of my ankle were a constant preoccupation. Life would even have been easier if, like Dickens's Silas Wegg, I had been 'a literary man – *with* a wooden leg', instead of dragging this swollen foot around with my inadequate left leg.

I was still determined to find the Great Barrier Reef opening and the island on which Bligh had landed during his open boat voyage following the mutiny. He had written in his log: 'I now expected to fall in with New Holl[and] reefs every hour being determined to look for a passage & take the first opening . . . At 9^h. made for the main reef & disc, an opening ½ mile wide. When in the Passage Land like an Isl^d . . .'

We drove to Brisbane, with two stops on the way, one at an amazingly isolated farm belonging to a complete stranger we met in our Sydney hotel lift, with whom we then had lunch. This gave us a taste of the starkness, richness, variety and sheer size of the continent, and, later, the glory of the Barrier Reef coast of Queensland after we had flown up to Townsville. A launch took us out to many beautiful and unspoilt islands and we worked our way north towards Bligh's island. But in the end we were defeated by the weather, the rain bucketing down day after day, even (we learned) carrying away the coast road.

'Constant Rain – Many Birds & Fish,' ran Bligh's log for one day. 'Storm of Rain. Dismal dark Rainy W^r . . . Rain so heavy scarce able to keep the Boat free by bailing . . .' So nothing much had changed.

It was extremely uncomfortable and disappointing for us, but it did help to imagine what it had been like after crossing half the

Pacific Ocean with scarcely any provisions, and we saw plenty of islands similar to the one he had eventually landed on. My ankle remained in exactly the same condition of disgusting swollenness, in spite of all the treatment, but I found relief in the water where I was more mobile than on land.

Back to Sydney, almost our home city now, and a last dinner with Ros and Peter Grose, who had been so kind and helpful earlier – he an agent and head of Curtis Brown Australia, today a publisher in London. That left Tahiti, the most important of all the islands associated with the mutiny, where Bligh had started off so well intended 'to cultivate a friendship with the natives' – and the friendships became too strong and intimate for too many of his men. It was easy to see why. Before you are out of the airport, you have seen enough of these peerlessly beautiful, tall, dark, well-built young Polynesians to persuade you that there might be worse ideas than to construct a straw hut and settle down there.

Little had changed down at Point Venus where everything conformed to Bligh's account of 25th October 1788 when he sighted the towering green volcanic peaks of the island. 184 years later I wrote in my book on the mutiny:

> The *Bounty* closed the island during the night and by the following morning, a Sunday, they could make out the deep valleys between the shoulders of the mountains, the thick, rich forests, the proud and elegant coconut palms along the sandy shoreline and the natural groves of breadfruit trees.

We rented a little car and drove clear round the island noting the site of events during the too-long stay of the *Bounty*, while the growth of the breadfruit plants matched the germination of the seeds of mutiny. One of the great nineteenth-century idiocies committed by the British was to let these islands go to the French. But, my goodness, they have exploited their gift tastefully and cleverly. All the luxury hotels are as spectacular in their architecture as in their outlook across the sea to the island of Moorea, an equally beautiful miniature of Tahiti itself. Charlotte was becoming as Pacificised as me, and as brown from the sun.

When we flew across the California coast on 30th March 1971, I had travelled some 18,000 miles over the Pacific, by launch, by air, by supply ship and yacht, and had successively been under the jurisdiction of Panama, Ecuador, Chile, Britain, Samoa, Fiji,

Rarotonga, Australia, France and finally the USA. Had it been worth the time, trouble and expense – and injury? I might find the answer when I completed the book I must start when I returned home. As to the mysterious injury, which had puzzled the Sydney medical profession for so long, I dragged my poor old ankle into the consulting room of the orthopaedic surgeon, Rodney Sweetnam, in Harley Street. He was writing at his desk, but before I sat down thankfully, he declared, without looking up, 'Ah, perhaps a ruptured achilles tendon?' No wonder he is today the Queen's orthopaedic surgeon. The two ends of the tendon were far separated by now, and the operation and limping about on crutches for some weeks was a tiresome price to pay for that otherwise strange and idyllic expedition.

My last words with Prince Philip after the last lunch on board the *Britannia* were:

Prince Philip: Why don't you write a history of royal yachts – you know, all of them, Venetian doges, and the Portuguese, had some pretty good ones, too?

Me: Thank you very much for the idea, sir. I'll think about it.

Although his suggestion might be interesting at some time in the future, while I was still working on Bligh and Christian I wrote to Mountbatten when he got back. Could I come down to see Broadlands; and, after all our fascinating talks, would he think about allowing me to write his biography?

He said 'yes' to the first, and named a day, and a guarded 'no' to the second proposal. I drove down one late morning for lunch. Everyone can visit the house now but in 1971 visitors were confined to his family and friends – and I certainly could not claim to be even the second of these, though we seemed to have got on quite well, talking about naval history, and himself, mostly himself.

A maid opened the door to me, and Mountbatten came shuffling out of the drawing room, feet wide-splayed, in dingy slacks and tweed jacket. He led me back into the room from which he had emerged. There were windows on two sides looking out onto the garden, which descended to the broad waters of the fast-flowing Test. There were portraits of his and Edwina's ancestors on the walls, an impressive one of the crashingly handsome, bearded Prince Louis of Battenberg, Mountbatten's father; side tables with family pictures, including one of Edwina in the 1930s with all that side lighting they were so fond of then. There was a desk in the corner at which he had been working, with portraits of his daughters, Pammy and Patricia, in silver frames. The armchairs and sofa were covered in well-worn, faded brocade, and the carpet was worn beyond what any self-respecting housewife would tolerate. Apart from the pictures, the most valuable object was probably the outsize silver cigarette box.

This box was offered to me, revealing three tatty cigarettes nestling in their spilt tobacco. 'Lung cancer, Dick?' He walked over to a well-loaded trolley. 'I don't usually drink before lunch.' He poured me a colossal pink gin, and another perhaps even larger for himself. It went down in a couple of minutes, with no visible effect.

We chatted about the voyage, before and after I left, and he told me his Western Australia property was prospering. (I learned later how very unselfconscious he was about his possessions and property. Once, driving through south-west Hertfordshire with him, he swung his arm from right to left. 'This is all mine,' he said. 'All green belt now, but that won't last for ever.')

I have never known a man so handsome, so accomplished, so charming and amusing with so much need to be liked and admired. I did not discover until later that this was a part of his insecurity, which was deep-set and went back to his childhood when his father was publicly humiliated and thrown out of the First Sea Lord's office in the early, frightful days of the First World War. This insecurity explained many things about this extraordinary man: his boastfulness, his burning determination to excel, his fury on the rare occasions when he did not, his excessive family pride and excessive pride in his past accomplishments. The slightest hint that he was not the greatest destroyer commander, Supreme Commander in war and Viceroy of India in peace, drove him into a frenzy to correct the record.

In Mountbatten's judgement this perfectionism applied to all his family, living and dead. I once wrote that one of the reasons why his father had been forced to resign in 1914 was that he had a marked guttural accent when we were fighting the Germans. Absolutely not, he claimed. But I had heard it from too many people to yield. Years later, having tea at Kensington Palace with, among others, Mountbatten and Princess Alice of Athlone, Queen Victoria's aged granddaughter, he revived the argument and asked her for her confirmation that 'Mr Hough here is utterly wrong'. 'He is absolutely right,' she replied crisply, to Mountbatten's utter chagrin. 'Well, just a trace then.' 'No, very marked, Dickie.'

Mountbatten combined to an uncommon degree guilelessness and wiliness, generosity of spirit with meanness and covetousness. He would go to extraordinary and to anyone else humiliating lengths to get even the smallest discount on – anything: air fares, books, cars, consumer goods of all kinds. And the sustainment and even improvement of the gigantic Cassel fortune which came to him through his marriage to Edwina Ashley was a constant pre-occupation. As I know to my embarrassment, he was a very slow payer of debts. When, to the dismay of the staff, he later decided to open Broadlands to the public, a great notice went up outside: 'Lord Mountbatten's Home'. This infuriated Edwina's family and friends. 'It's never been *his home!*' Edwina's sister exclaimed angrily. 'It belonged to *Edwina.*'

During lunch I raised the subject of a biography, just an interim, I suggested. He made it clear that the family (which really meant Patricia and her husband Lord Brabourne) had decided that this should wait until after he died. I should, perhaps, not have pressed the point but I did so, as delicately as I could, indicating that there were certain advantages in having your subject alive and talking and answering questions and elucidating certain things and correcting others. He was clearly tempted but in the end he would have none of it, only suggesting that he had no control of events after he was dead, something which he repeated several times over the following years.

I was taken over the house after lunch. In his bedroom, where the Queen and Prince Philip had slept on their honeymoon, the curtains were faded, the carpet stained and in my domestic eye there seemed to be a need for a good dusting. He indicated a photograph of a pretty dark girl. 'That is the Grand-Duchess Marie, assassinated by the Bolsheviks. I was going to marry her.'

Going down the beautiful staircase, he pointed out portraits of his Hessian ancestors, Grand-Duke that, Princess this of somewhere unpronounceable. Suddenly he lurched against me and I held his considerable weight steady. We were still near the top and it would have been a long fall. Perhaps if I had not held him, his official biographer might have been chosen sooner than expected. 'Bloody vertigo!' he exclaimed, furious at exposing this disability.

We proceeded cautiously to the enormous muniment rooms in

the basement where every document related to his long life lay in apple-pie order. Models of all the ships in which he had served were laid out in illuminated cases. Drawing on my boyhood enthusiasm, I was able to surprise him with my detailed knowledge of them.

A few days later, I had another letter from him on the heavily embossed Broadlands writing paper. It was very friendly and he invited me to come to see him again. He suggested that, while a biography was at this time impossible to authorise, I might like to consider taking on the task of writing the family history and a dual biography of his mother and father. 'The background might be useful to you later.'

'How exciting!' exclaimed Charlotte at breakfast. 'You will do it, won't you?'

'Will I not!' And I went to my desk to write a letter indicating, not too breathlessly I hoped, that I might be able to find the time.

Domestic life at this time was full and mainly happy, though it would be laughable to claim that you can bring up four daughters without a few crises and worries. I do not suppose that we had more than an average number of these though sometimes it seemed so. Bryony was at Roedean, Debby reading English under Christopher Ricks at Bristol and soon to start writing novels, Sandy now a fully fledged physiotherapist at Westminster Hospital, Sarah with children of her own (Charlotte a grandmother at forty-two) and beginning her career in the country as a children's book writer and artist. Like the first move out of publishing in 1955, my second in 1970 had led to an improvement in our finances, and as well as running houses in the Lake District and London, we were able to go on interesting holidays.

The earlier visit under royal patronage to the Galapagos Islands had been tantalisingly brief, and Charlotte, with her abiding interest in natural history, longed to see this strange archipelago. After a week in Quito staying at the British Embassy and making short expeditions into the Andes, we flew out to the islands with five others. We were supposed to cruise about in a schooner but the engine refused to work so we hired a launch and made day trips to the islands under the guidance of a young Englishman of great charm and knowledge. It was stupefyingly hot and more fascinating every day.

The next year we had a trip around South Africa. Tom Pocock, as travel editor of the *Evening Standard*, asked me to do some pieces on the game parks. We went out in style on one of the very last Union-Castle liner passages. The first-class passengers, almost to a man and woman, spent most of the voyage gambling for high stakes, among them Hugh 'Cocky' Dundas, one of the Battle of Britain 'greats' and, like me, an early Typhoon pilot. He and his wife were agreeable company, and later Cocky was helpful when I was co-writing the Golden Jubilee Battle of Britain book.

We had been told not to fly out to Cape Town as there is nothing in the world to match arriving at dawn by sea. It is indeed a beautiful and moving experience, and it is easy to imagine the joy and relief of those early traders, bound for the riches of the East, sailing their carracks into Table Bay for fresh fruit, meat and water.

We did not do badly ourselves up at the Nelson Hotel in the shadow of Table Mountain before we set off on our travels by courtesy of the benign travel people. First stop was Uppington, a real Afrikaaner town where little English was spoken and beefy, hairy-armed farmers drove in in the morning with their black 'boys', laughing and shouting at the prospect of a day out, packed into the open pick-up trucks.

We stayed in a hotel which, like the shops, reflected in their decor and furnishings the old Dutch mix of extreme masculinity and daintiness. In our bridal suite, the four-poster bed and the chairs were of enormous girth, dark stained wood, with the frilliest of lace-edged cushions and hangings in execrable colour schemes. The bedside Kleenex and even the lavatory roll were fastidiously obscured by multi-coloured lace. No one spoke a word of English and we might have been back in the Netherlands of the Prince of Orange.

Our guide's wife was off at twice-weekly rifle practice when we were taken to his house, and in this town we became for the first time conscious of the Afrikaaner culture, industriousness and defiance; nor had we before seen blacks, who appeared to own half the businesses, so content with their lot. This was fifteen years ago, and attitudes may have changed, but not the tough, defiant element amongst these Boers, who were once the heroes of the Western world in their wars against the British.

We went off in an old Mercedes, air-conditioned thank heavens, towards the Kalahari and the Gemsbok Park. All that day, and the next, we headed north, the track becoming scrubland with scattered thorn trees and not country in which to break down without a radio. Every mile there was something fascinating to see – a giant owl poised in a tree above, a pair of lions stalking a herd of game, a string of ostrich crossing the track ahead of us, one of them laying an egg as a horse might defecate. (We picked it up warm and kept it for breakfast at the next encampment. It provided scrambled egg for eighteen.)

At our final encampment there was an English couple carrying out an extensive study of the brown hyena. They had darted and then fitted collars with a minute transmitter on a number of them. Back in the wild they could be followed in the dark, revealing their movements and habits. We went with them in their Land-Rover one night. They appeared to have built up a special relationship with these unlovely beasts, whose eyes glittered intermittently in the dark when we came close, as in a Walt Disney film.

On the last night the heavens opened and we were treated to a five-hour-long thunderstorm, with rain and hail beating down on the tin roof of our hut. No one calculated how many inches fell, but at dawn, as the storm rumbled away into Botswana, we looked out on a new flooded world. Vast areas had become lakes, tracks raging torrents. We emerged barefoot at mid-day and surveyed the landscape. Already, the desert flowers of many colours had shot up out of sand that, yesterday, had looked as sterile as the Sahara. By the next day the Kalahari had become a carpet, as far as the eye could see, of flowers, many like cultivated pansies, others as tall as foxgloves.

'How long can you stay?' our guide asked after breakfast.

'You mean the roads are impassable?'

He nodded. 'It will be many days.' We were due in Durban in two days for a tightly scheduled tour of several Natal game parks. I explained this to him, and he at once radioed back to Uppington for a plane. There was a small airstrip at this camp and it was not too sodden to land.

The little Piper arrived in the afternoon, the pilot taking a long hard look at the state of the terrain before putting down. We waved to our hyena friends, climbed in and took off. For a bumpy ninety minutes we flew low over the now unrecognisable and largely invisible route we had taken north in the car, now water and blooms the whole way. The Orange River, when we reached Uppington, was a wide brown torrent, banks broken, racing towards Namibia and – in another 250 miles – to the sea.

Durban seemed to us to be like a very hot Brighton, with better hotels, more fruit in the diet, and many more swimming pools. The beaches were still segregated, but none looked very attractive, while day and night the surf riders could be seen far out as dark dots, occasionally springing up to come racing in on the Indian Ocean rollers. Driving along the front on our first day, we caught sight of two friendly familiar figures on the stoep of the old-fashioned Hotel Edward. They were Gordon ('Richard Gordon') and Jo Ostlere putting down gins in the shade. We had both grown ferocious beards since we had last met and that added a certain piquancy and competitiveness to the occasion. We dined together that night, became rather drunk and played many rounds of trick-golf on the seafront playground.

The next day Charlotte and I drove a great distance in the heat towards the borders of Basutoland and Mozambique where we stayed in two or three very five-star game park resorts, air-conditioned kraals and supper round a great bonfire at one of them. These reservations, like the much larger Kruger National Park, did not have the same excitement nor the vivid contrasts of the Kala-hari. But we had pleasant and well-informed guides who knew how to find the game, were good on birds and we learned a great deal; most of it, alas, all too soon forgotten.

I have been back several times to South Africa since that first visit, which I record as being the best bit of journalist's research I ever enjoyed. I have driven from Johannesburg to Plettenberg Bay on the Indian Ocean where Louis Klemantaski's sister-in-law, Yvonne Thynne, offers hospitality and kindness, both on a heroic scale. I have followed young Winston Churchill's adventurous trail to Ladysmith and the battlefields nearby, on Spion Kop finding plenty of evidence of that terrible battle between Boer and Briton. I have travelled over much of Cape Province, seen the Kimberley mines, met Black, Indian, Afrikaans and English newspaper editors and men of power and influence.

Heaven knows, I cannot begin to claim to understand half the manifold problems of that rich and beautiful country. Politically the far right are an odious lot, and the principle of apartheid is against the tenets of any acceptable society, though even at its worst it is better than India's racial intolerance of Moslems and the Untouchables, or the fanatical tribalism of many other African states. Nor would you anywhere hear a Black employee addressed by his boss as 'you fuckin' nigger', the first words I heard in a New Orleans shop recently.

One of the advantages of scratching a living by writing, and especially writing non-fiction, is that you do tend to get around to interesting places, and meeting people. For me this all began in the Admiralty itself, where Lieutenant-Commander Peter Kemp presided over the library in the 1950s. Peter was just about the most useful, kind, generous and well-informed person a young aspiring naval historian could ever hope to meet; and he has remained so to this day. His range of knowledge is breathtakingly wide, and he has written some fine books himself.

Whatever knowledge I had imbibed about the ships of the Royal Navy, I knew next to nothing about the men who served in them. Among the officers Peter put me in touch with were Captain Stephen Roskill DSC, the official naval historian of the Second World War, and Admiral Sir William Tennant, Lord Lieutenant of Worcestershire. Tennant had survived the sinking of his ship, the *Repulse*, when she went down with the *Prince of Wales* off Singapore in 1941, and when I stayed with him lived in a glorious house on the river at Upton-on-Severn. These officers were all immensely hospitable and had kind wives of strong character. One of many was Mary, the wife of Admiral Sir Angus Cunninghame Graham, the Lord Lieutenant of Dunbartonshire and Keeper of Dunbarton Castle in retirement, who lived in another glorious house on the banks of the River Clyde. They wanted me to stay a week!

The Dannreuters were equally welcoming at their weird house like a Bavarian Castle on the clifftops above Hastings. Rear-Admiral Dannreuter, as a Midshipman, had witnessed the Battle of the Falkland Islands in December 1914, and the massacre of the German Squadron; then, in the same ship, HMS *Invincible*, he was in the same fighting top at the Battle of Jutland. He was thrown clear when his ship blew up and was one of only two or three survivors. 'I was picked up so quickly that I scarcely got my feet wet.'

I did stay a week with the Duke and Duchess of Hamilton at their place, Lennoxlove, in Scotland. David, the 14th Duke, had been a prominent RAF pilot who had visited Germany before the war and made contact with a number of Luftwaffe officers. When the demented Rudolf Hess flew to Scotland, ostensibly on a peace mission, he hoped to make friendly contact with the Duke, a slight embarrassment for the family.

His mother had been a close friend of Admiral Lord Fisher, and when I wrote my biography of that naughty but brilliant old boy, it was essential to see the family papers. Lennoxlove was a mixture of considerable style matched by seeming austerity by my middle-class standards. The Duke himself insisted on carrying in my luggage and took it upstairs to my room. On the way there were wonderful photographs of flying in the '20s and '30s, including the summit of Mount Everest – he had been the first to fly over the top on a world-acclaimed exercise.

As I worked up in my garret every morning, I could hear the rattle of guns on the estate, and at lunchtime the guests of the day would appear, great big men in tweeds like armour plate and heavy boots, and tiny wives. 'Mr Hough,' my hostess Elizabeth would introduce me, 'do you know the Duke of Roxburgh? And, perhaps you know the Duke of Buccleuch? And Lady Bowes-Lyon? . . .' There might be a dozen or more, all charming and gentle, and *quite* unknown to me, alas. But I enjoyed the assumption that I *might* know them all.

17

In the Wake of
Captain Cook

In early 1972 I faced the most complex writing task of my life so far. I had on my hands this long dual biography, and history of the Hessian family from which Mountbatten's father had stemmed. On the one hand it was pretty clear that he was going to keep a watchful eye on its progress; on the other hand, his position of power and influence opened every door. In fact, they were like the electronic ones in airports and shops that swing open as you approach.

All the Broadlands archives, including those available to his eventual official biographer, were available to me, together with the services of an able archivist, Mrs Mollie Travis. Everything that I asked for at the end of one visit would be set out next time I came down. Mountbatten would drop in from time to time, tall, but a little bent now in his early seventies, jovial, inquisitive. He might have a rough draft of a recent chapter I had given him, pointing at a marked line. 'Ho! Here's another "Houghler",' he would exclaim in wardroom mock outrage. Then, a bit more quarterdeck, 'I thought I had made clear to you that my Uncle Henry married into the Löwenburg-Sandbürgs [or some such]. That's why the children were called [so-and-so].'

'Yes, of course, sir.' (Later he asked me to call him Dickie, and made it quite evident that Dickie was superior. 'Why on earth do you call yourself Dick?') 'This genealogy does floor me sometimes. But, then, I don't have the privileges of being President of the Society of Genealogists.'

'Then,' he continued, 'if you don't mind my saying so, I don't think you can refer to a male lover – paramour surely.' His eye for detail, even if incorrect, was amazing, but he was less helpful when

Barbara Cartland was drawn into the editing process. It was once thus:

'I showed this chapter to Barbara Cartland last week. She thought it was very good. But paragraphs too long. "You see, Dickie," she said, "the reader's eye is deterred by large blocks of type. Half a dozen lines quite enough – something I learned from Max Beaverbrook."'

Since Edwina's death, Mountbatten craved female company more than ever, and they met at least once a week and often spent the weekend together at Camfield Place or Broadlands. Barbara told me later, bubbling away, 'We are terribly fond of one another – almost lovers.' Then a shrill laugh. 'But not bed, my dear. Oh no, no, no. We're both long past *that*.'

After a while, Mountbatten would slope off, to go for a ride or dictate letters to John Barratt, his secretary. A great deal of time was spent on the telephone when he was at Broadlands. It was seven years since he had resigned from his epochal period as Chief of Defence Staff, but he had become associated with nearly two hundred organisations, electronics and the United World Colleges – a network of international schools – being the most important to him. He derived perhaps the greatest pleasure of all as colonel of the Life Guards, especially on Trooping the Colour day, for which he practised with great solemnity in full rig around the bridle paths of his estate. He took all such tasks seriously and conscientiously, and the time and attention he gave to my book astonished me.

When working at Broadlands, I would be called up to lunch just before 1 p.m., sometimes with Mrs Travis, at others alone. There would either be no drink before the meal, or a gigantic one. There was a good cook at Broadlands in the early days when I was working there, and the food was light and delicious. Mountbatten kept a very keen eye on it in case Mrs Travis or I helped ourselves beyond our share, especially when the cream was going round. He ate heartily and talked throughout with little regard for mastication, in the German manner. You could not claim that he ranged widely over world affairs or anything like that. The subjects were his family as it related to himself and the book. I kept the tape going on the table and the sounds of clinking cutlery, the butler's murmurs and the pouring of wine contributed a steady background epicurean chorus.

It was the summer of 1972 when I was most often at Broadlands, and it must have been a fine one because I have strong memories of progressing to the garden after lunch and sitting with him on a hammock in the sun, continuing lunchtime talk about his life and achievements; naval engagements in which he had been involved, the Norwegian campaign and its follies, playing hide-and-seek with the German bombers off Namsos, then back to peacetime Malta, before the war with Edwina and the girls, after the war with Princess Elizabeth and Prince Philip. He talked often and freely about the Queen, 'the most wonderful woman alive', and 'it may surprise you, but she is the finest judge of a horse in the land – everyone who knows about it agrees'. And I could have written a full account of Prince Philip's younger years from these tapes.

The hammock, I recall clearly, was only just big enough for two, and we both willy-nilly tended to slip towards the centre, thigh to thigh. To emphasise a point, he would sometimes place his hand on my knee, which made me think a bit about all those scurrilous stories. But when I later wrote about him after he was blown up, I made clear my belief that he had never indulged in homosexual affairs, and, rather, his sexual drive took a bad third place to his ambition and achievement of excellence.

'I am going to Germany to stay with Princess Margaret in July,' he announced one day. 'I'd like to show you where I grew up at Schloss Heiligenberg, and I think you ought to take a look at the Darmstadt papers, too, in the old Hessian palace.'

I agreed that would be fun and made arrangements for Charlotte and me to stay at a Darmstadt hotel. Princess Margaret, 'Peg' of Hesse, married Louis, the last Grand-Duke, in 1937. Almost the entire Hessian family was wiped out in an air crash *en route* to England for the wedding. Peg and Lou had no children, and after the war, with their powers much reduced, they lived mainly at the Hessian summer place, Wolfsgarten. This is a magical *schloss* with a lovely garden and some distance from Darmstadt. With the death of Louis, the title died, after many centuries, and Peg continued to live at Wolfsgarten, much respected by the hierarchy of the state of Hesse, though with no real powers.

Charlotte's mother had known Peg when she was a girl, a daughter of Auckland and Isabella Geddes, prominent in politics and diplomacy. When Peg knew that we were coming, she wrote and invited us to stay at Wolfsgarten with the others, and very pleasant it was, too, with drawn baths and heated towels and someone to unpack and pack and provide you with all comforts. The

Brabournes were there, too, with two of their daughters, and one of Prince Philip's German nephews drifted in and out. The Brabourne girls were at an awkward age and there was a certain amount of quarterdeck booming around the corridors, like 'Amanda, do as your mother tells you at once.' For a father of four girls myself, this made reassuring listening.

It was too hot to do much, and we sat in the shade, and took in the wonderful scents of the garden, chatted and read. An air-conditioned large car took me in to Darmstadt to meet the archivist and find out if there was anything useful. There was not. More usefully, I went with Charlotte and Mountbatten to his boyhood home, Heiligenberg on the River Rhine. It had been an institution for some years, but we were able to inspect the house and gardens where Nicky and Alexandra of Russia and half the crowned heads of Europe would gather every year before 1914.

Mountbatten and I strolled about in the heat, he recalling those distant days before assassinations and revolutions and the toppling of emperors and empires. 'There were tennis courts, there,' he said, pointing. 'And all sorts of games like diabolo and croquet. Then we went on picnics up into the hills and we had ponies to ride. In the evenings we had more games. I remember I wore my cutaway coat for the first time, and it was much admired by my cousins and I was terribly proud. There were a lot of us, and it really was just like any other family.' ('Well, nearly,' I muttered under my breath.)

'They were charming, every one of them,' Mountbatten continued. 'Even that crazy lunatic, my aunt the Empress, was absolutely sweet and charming. But I remember my father saying to my mother, "Alicky is absolutely mad – she's going to cause a revolution. Can't you *do* anything?" "Well, I'm doing all I can," my mother replied plaintively.'

Princess Peg was a marvellous hostess, showing us round all the sights and historical Hessian mementoes. There was the beautiful little house in the woods, everything to scale including fine cutlery, built for the spoilt and fated little daughter of the moderately dotty Grand-Duke Ernest, Peg's father-in-law (or would have been but for that air crash). The Queen and Prince Philip often stayed at Wolfsgarten and instead of signing the visitors' book, they and other members of the royal family had etched their names neatly into the glass of one of the drawing-room windows.

At breakfast on our last morning, my mind went back to that solitary German sausage-skin maker down in the Magellan Straits.

There were any number of sliced sausages on the table, particularly relished by Mountbatten who revealed the (I assume) standard method of peeling off the skin by putting the whole slice in his mouth and then, through the conversation, pulling out the skin with finger and thumb in one long, tough string. Very neat, we thought.

At the end of breakfast as we prepared to go and the little Alfa was brought round, shining from a recent wash, Mountbatten fixed a date for me to make another visit, this time to his little house in Belgravia. 'We must arrange some visits for you,' he said mysteriously. If they were anything like this one, I was all in favour.

Without discussing the subject with me, Mountbatten had shrewdly judged that the more 'names' I could cite, and quote, in this dual biography, the more authoritative it would be regarded, and the better the sales. 'It's a pity my father died such a long time ago,' he said. 'But there are a few old admirals still alive who served under him, and I'll write to them asking them to see you.' We were in his Kinnerton Street *pied-à-terre*, our drinks on the glass top of a table tracing all Edwina's journeys about the world, and a fair number of them there had been, more than a few to get away from him.

'My mother's easier than my father,' he continued, 'so don't take any notice of people when they say they can't remember anything about her. Just keep asking.'

The setting up of these interviews was a trivial business compared with running the south-east Asia command, or even commanding a destroyer flotilla, and I expect most of it was organised by John Barratt anyway. But there were a few busy people involved, like Prince Philip and the Queen, and I was amazed at the speed at which telephone calls came in to me from secretaries proposing dates to visit Windsor Castle, Buckingham Palace, Clarence House and Kensington Palace.

It was curious seeing Prince Philip at Windsor Castle. It was rather like meeting again someone you had met by chance on holiday, not usually a wise thing to do. The difference was that he was in his own home, so to speak, and one of the prime purposes of this massive castle, with all its flags and protocol and formality, is to cause visitors (or besiegers in the old days) to feel subservient. Anyway, I felt jolly subservient that morning in July, but also amused to see that, like his German antecedents from Prince Albert on, he had followed British custom and slipped on a tweed jacket with patches at the elbow for Saturday morning.

Prince Philip's own mother, Alice, Princess Andrew of Greece, came prominently into my story. She had been born deaf and had married a gadabout royal Greek from whom she lived apart for much of her life, which, especially in middle age, had been in and out of sanatoria anyway. She was also virtually penniless for much of her life, and later lived at the top of Buckingham Palace until she died in 1969.

Prince Philip talked quite freely about her, pooh-poohed rather fiercely that he might have become a trifle insecure without a family home or steady mother and father, and when I asked what was really wrong with her, had replied, 'Oh, I think she was just a bit loopy.' He talked as freely about Mountbatten's mother, Victoria, who was really his surrogate mother for years, though he was not anxious to see it that way. As a boy he had a room in her chambers in Kensington Palace, and spent part of his school holidays with her. He emphasised to me the masculinity of her mind. 'I liked her very much and she was very helpful. She was very good with children,' he told me. 'Like my own mother, she took the practical approach. She treated them in the right way – the right combination of the rational and emotional.'

Not everything came out on my recorder. The windows were wide open and about every ninety seconds a jet took off over our heads. He went on talking as if there were no intrusion, his lips mouthing inaudible words. I believe all the royal family do the same, none of them being inclined to give way to a mere Boeing.

Princess Alice was a darling, already eighty-nine years old, bright, mobile (with a stick), intelligent, forthright. Her father, a haemophiliac unfortunately, and she a carrier, was Queen Victoria's son Leopold, Duke of Albany, who succumbed to the disease a year after Alice's birth. His mother wrote rather sharply of him, 'For dear Leopold himself we could not repine, there was such a restless longing for what he could not have . . .' Alice of Athlone's memory went back to the time when Mountbatten's father was still only a Lieutenant, and she told me a story about trotting round Windsor Park with the doomed future Tsar Nicholas II on a visit when they were both youngsters. He told her mournfully, 'I don't want to be Tsar of Russia, Alice.' And she replied firmly, 'Oh, but you must, Nicky.'

The Queen Mother was a stickier proposition altogether. I went to see her one wet morning at 11 a.m. in Clarence House. 'Do you think I can take this tape recorder in with me?' I asked her private secretary. 'Well, no harm in trying. See what she says.'

So I did, remembered to call her Majesty and not Royal Highness, and was offered a Regency chair with arms in front of a circular marble-top table, while she settled herself opposite. Her eyes were a startling blue, fresh as a girl's, and her smile – well, there's no need to describe that; hands very pretty, voice very 1920s.

I asked her about the recorder and held it up like an auctioneer.

'Good gracious me, what does it do?'

'It records our voices.'

'Goodness, what a wonder! No, I don't mind.'

'Thank you, ma'am.' And I put it on a low shelf under the table-top in case she took against it, and switched it on.

She had been well briefed on what I wanted to hear, and she began to tell me about Mountbatten's mother, after asking me how he was. She gave me a few quotable bits, but not much I did not know already. There may have been more, but like those damn jets at Windsor, the Horse Guards chose to march past just under the window on their way from the Palace, their bandsmen hard at it. They might as well have been back in their barracks for all Her Majesty took notice of the interruption. As the military music faded, her fluting little refined voice became gradually audible again. I do wonder what I had missed. Not much, I think.

After about half an hour in the same position, my knee stiffened, as it increasingly did, and I crossed my legs. She went on talking as if nothing had happened but those twin blue orbs dropped like hostile searchlights to my knees, held there for enough seconds to make the meaning clear, and carried on smilingly. I recounted this to Mountbatten later, and he roared with laughter. 'I'll tell her you smashed your legs in the Battle of Britain, that'll put things right.'

I saw a king next, the King of Sweden, who was staying at the Hyde Park Hotel, a grumpy ninety-year-old who had obviously been ordered to see me by his brother-in-law. His wife, Louise, was Mountbatten's sister, who had died childless seven years earlier. He made it amply clear that anything I wrote of her, or him, must be checked personally by him. He evaded my questions, and told me virtually nothing, so I left. When I reported to Mountbatten he said he was not surprised and that he doubted if the prohibition would be relevant because he would probably be dead before the book was out. He was.

The Queen herself was much better value than her mother and more relaxing, even commiserating with me over King Gustav: 'Oh dear, what a boring man!' I invited Bryony along, not to see the Queen but to look at the inside of the Palace. Bryony played noughts and crosses with Bill Heseltine, the Queen's press secretary, while I was led up the wide shallow stairs, noting the silence, the neutral, greyish mauveish colours, the regal oil paintings and the beating of my heart.

My escort tapped gently on an enormous mahogany door and without waiting for an answer, opened it. The Queen was sitting at her desk set before the window overlooking the grounds. She turned, arose and walked towards me, smiling the same smile as her mother's. She was dressed in a light tweed suit with a bit of expensive stuff round her neck, and more on her fingers. I did my little bow, began to say Your Royal Highness, and checked to 'Your Majesty . . . very kind of you to spare the time.'

'I do hope you had a nice time in Germany . . . yes, isn't it a charming place, and the Princess so kind . . . Won't you sit here?' She patted the sofa on her left, and off she went. 'Well, I didn't know him, of course. I wish I had done, then –'

I knew this was not going to be any good. She was going to ramble on, delightfully no doubt, but I needed to be in the chair, so to speak. 'Ma'am,' I dared to say, extracting a notebook. 'I have a list of questions here. Do you think we could work through them first?'

She smiled sweetly and sat back on the sofa, smoothing her skirt, waiting for me to begin.

'Tell me first, ma'am . . .'

She had a very good descriptive ability. Of Mountbatten's mother, for example, she said, 'Very manly, in looks and ways. Her voice was a man's voice, and she walked with great strides, like this,' and she used her first and second fingers to demonstrate across the sofa towards me. They were her mother's hands, too, I noticed, beautifully formed, worthy of all those diamonds – and how they glittered!

'And Lord Mountbatten's brother, Georgie, did you ever meet him?' (He had died of cancer in 1938, when the Queen was twelve.)

'I only once talked to him for any length of time,' she told me, 'and that was when he – poor man – found himself next to me at the wedding breakfast for Princess Marina and the Duke of Kent. But I don't think I have ever enjoyed a meal so much. He was one of the most intelligent and brilliant of people. He spoke to me just as if I were grown up. What a tragedy that he died so young!'

We talked briefly of death and she said poignantly, 'One sometimes appreciates the special qualities of people only after they have died. That was certainly the case with me and my father.'

She went on like this for an hour or more, then out of the corner of my eye I saw the door slowly opening as if by remote control. The peace of the private drawing room was shattered by the tumultuous arrival of five corgis and one cross corgi-dachshund, all barking their heads off. Knowing their reputation for ferocity, I lifted my legs as two of them homed in on me, teeth bared. But a sharp imperious order stopped them in their tracks. 'Behave yourselves!' and they did. I had the feeling that this was a palace ruse to remind Her Majesty that her next engagement was imminent. I had asked the secretary how long I should remain, and he had replied, 'Oh, there won't be any trouble about that. It'll be quite clear.' And indeed it was, shortly after the corgi invasion. The Queen arose and wandered over to the window. The lawns were full of people, thousands of them, the men in tail coats, the women in long dresses, some carrying parasols.

'I seem to have some visitors to tea,' she remarked and smiled at me. 'I think perhaps I had better change to greet them.'

'I was one of your guests the day before yesterday, ma'am. Thank you for having me, I did enjoy it.'

'Oh did you?' she replied as if surprised as well as pleased. 'I'm so glad.'

We headed for the door, and I thanked her again, gave my little bow and the door magically opened, with my previous escort on parade again.

Downstairs, the noughts and crosses were over, Heseltine was on the telephone and Bryony was drawing horses. 'Time to go home,' I said. Curious crowds about the gates stared at us, but not for more than a moment. No prince with his princess there, just a small car with anonymous father and daughter.

A few days later, I was summoned to the Palace again, this time to meet two of Prince Philip's sisters, Margarita, Princess Godfrey of Hohenlohe-Langenburg and Sophie, Princess George of Hanover. Margarita was quite old, sixteen years older than her brother, while Sophie was almost a female replica of him, though taller, very vivacious and talkative. For some reason, the curtains were drawn in the large room in which we talked, and the guard was being changed down in the forecourt with all the usual flourish and noise. Sophie could not resist pulling aside a corner of one curtain to take a peek. 'You mustn't do that,' her elder sister admonished, 'all the crowds will see.'

The sisters did give me some anecdotes about their family, especially their unfortunate mother, but of all the royal and titled people I interviewed, the Queen, as the youngest, was much the best. And yet, Mountbatten told me, when she joined her guests that afternoon and he asked her how things had gone, she said apologetically, 'I'm afraid I wasted your friend's time, I'm so sorry.' He rang me from Broadlands that evening, in some anxiety. 'No, she was marvellous, really marvellous. I'll show you my notes next time we meet.'

Slowly the book took shape. Mountbatten drew up some incredibly complicated genealogical tables, which we used for endpapers. He read the second draft as closely as the first, sending them back piecemeal by diplomatic bag from China which he was visiting, and then the proofs. Never for one moment did his interest wane. Some weeks after the proofs had been distributed, I invited him to the publisher's sales meeting. I picked him up from the studio of a friend of mine, Carlos Sancha, who was painting yet another full-length portrait of him in the uniform of Admiral of the Fleet, with nine rows of ribbons, and we drove out to St Albans, where a large hotel room had been hired for the meeting.

The chief executive, who had, alas, superseded the retired Sir Robert Lusty, promised me personally 'to see the book through stage by stage myself'. I had heard nothing from him over the years of work, and since, and he now started proceedings off badly when I introduced him to Mountbatten. 'Did your father serve in the First World War, sir?' Considering Prince Louis was First Sea Lord at the outset, this was perhaps not the cleverest question. But Mountbatten passed it off and began talking to someone else.

After a buffet lunch, the conference was shown jacket roughs of the books they had to sell, my *Louis & Victoria* being first. It was projected in full colour on a large screen, supervised by the woman who had been responsible for jackets for decades and was renowned for her firm ideas. Mountbatten at first greeted the jacket of my book in silence, with all eyes turned upon him. It showed portraits of his parents by de Laszlo with some rather nice lettering and twirly bits. Then suddenly a voice boomed out. 'It's not bad,' he said, head on one side. 'But you must have the portraits the same size. It upsets the balance like that.'

The jacket lady was clearly shocked at this interference. But she did as she was ordered, and very much better it was for the change. The book came out in 1974, accompanied by many and mainly favourable reviews and absolutely no publicity or advertising. I surmised that the new regime at the publishers, including the chief executive who could not be bothered to read it, was anti-monarchical and socialist. If anyone had read it, Mountbatten's socialism and the radicalism of his parents would have been clear. Nor was it very good business as they had paid me a large advance which they never recovered. The non-reading chief executive was sacked shortly after this, but too late for the book.

My dear mother had to spend the last two years or so of her life in a nursing home. She did not want to leave her own home, and it was the most harrowing episode in my life persuading her of the necessity. She was eighty-five and very unsure on her feet. Neighbours came in every day and I would visit her as often as possible, but she was found helpless on the floor several times. Nor would she have a full-time nurse, nor come and live with us in London away from her friends. So I took her to a nursing home off the Dyke Road in Brighton, within a few hundred yards of the little house where she had begun her married life more than sixty years earlier. Once reconciled to the new regime, she regained her old spirits. Our children visited her, and she loved best of all to watch Sarah's children playing in the garden of the home. I often wheeled her round the nearby public gardens or gave her drives around her favourite Sussex lanes.

She loved hearing my tales of Broadlands and the various palaces I visited and the people I met, but of course none of the other inmates believed a word when she told them later that I had been to the Palace to see the Queen, or any of the other stories either. Hector Bolitho, the distinguished royal biographer who knew them all well in the 1930s, and was in the next room, was regarded as an even worse show-off.

In the winter of 1973–4 my mother began to weaken and was confined to her bed, and eventually to a caged bed as she kept falling out. One day, after I had left a message for her that I would not be coming down, I had a premonition that she was close to death. I got a non-stop train, faster than the car, and raced up the hill from Brighton station. But again I was too late, by an hour or so. She died more peacefully than George, and there was a faint smile on her lips when I kissed her cold forehead. I was more affected at her death and at becoming an orphan in middle age than I had ever expected.

While sending me some photographs of her as a child, a cousin wrote a letter of comfort which I have kept. 'This pain of loss that you are enduring is worse for you, as you were affinities, and you came as a great comfort to her after Mollie's death,' Marion Clark wrote. 'Time I find does not help, but if you can understand that the crippling disabilities are over after fourteen years of them (and partial dependence on other people), and old age. Hers was a very young spirit – she literally bubbled over with fun – so it was only a half-life. Now I know she will be with you more than ever – she was very proud of you . . .'

At around this time, I became involved in one of those admirable charities instituted by King Edward VII when he was Prince of Wales, with time on his hands and many rich friends who were expected to support them, quite frequently with a title in mind. One of the closest and most generous was Sir Ernest Cassel, Edwina Mountbatten's grandfather. This one was – and is – called King Edward VII's Hospital Fund for London. Its activities have changed greatly since the introduction of the National Health Service, but the functions of the Auxiliary Hospitals' Committee remained roughly unchanged over the years. We were available for grants for charity-supported homes in London and the outlying area, for, say, a new central heating system or an extension, or a new lift, items running up to three or four thousand pounds on average.

These applications came in throughout the year, and it was our business to make visits, inspect, talk things over, sometimes give advice and then, more often than not, give a grant. You might do a dozen or so visits a year with one or two other members, in the company of the first-class professional secretary, and they were always fascinating – from severely handicapped children's homes to physically disabled or terminal or retired professional homes like Denville Hall for actors and actresses. Here were a number of people you thought you once knew, taking a relaxed view of life in their eighties and nineties, until it occurred to you that, of course, they had been familiar figures on the stage or screen in the 1940s, 1930s and even the 1920s. Just like those film stars of 1941, you felt as if they were old friends as you met them for the first time.

By contrast, I remember one severely mentally handicapped home in south London where, such was the seriousness of their condition, the ratio of nurses to patients was one-to-one. For this most taxing of all nursing branches there is never a shortage of applicants, and it was clear after watching them together for some time that the patience demanded is something few people are blessed with. But the reward of the devotion of these children and the pleasure of making some sort of progress with them was also evident. At the entrance to the dining room there was a blackboard on which the nurses chalked up any improvement, however small, that they could claim for their charge. One of these read, 'Gavin tore paper.' He was fourteen, a big fellow, kind and gentle, the world stacked against him with only his gentle nurse on his side.

It was so utterly different from any other part of my life that I found it most refreshing. Just as my five years were up when I would have had to resign, I was made chairman and enjoyed immensely my ten years' association with this splendid organisation.

In 1977 David Lean bought the film rights to my book *Captain Bligh & Mr Christian*, four years after its publication. I was scything the orchard at Town Foot when the telephone brought this thrilling news. I dropped such bucolic pleasures and raced to London. My agent told me, unbelievably, that he planned the film in two parts, each of three hours, which should have been enough, even for him. I met his producer, Phil Kellogg, at Claridge's, and he told me that the old partnership was to be reinstated, Robert Bolt doing the script. As soon as the contract was signed, Phil told me, they would all be off to Polynesia to seek locations and make arrangements for the film crew's arrival and accommodation, a task of logistics about equal to a Second World War assault on a Japanese-held Pacific island.

'Any chance of your being there?' Phil asked me, in that way which suggests your fare is not going to be paid.

'Yes, I will,' I said firmly. 'I'm writing a book on Captain Cook's last voyage and murder at Hawaii. I'm going out looking for locations, too.'

James Cook, Bligh's mentor, had for long fascinated me, even before Prince Philip somehow got the false impression I was writing about him in 1971. The bicentenary of his death in 1779 was coming up, and there were to be a lot of celebrations to mark the event, especially in Vancouver, which Cook had charted and named after one of his midshipmen on this voyage. There were one or two places he touched which would be impractical to visit, but on this Pacific trip, besides all the Tahitian islands (easy), I wanted to visit the bay where he had wooded and watered off Tasmania, Queen Charlotte's Sound in New Zealand, Vancouver, Cook Inlet in Alaska and as far north as I could in the north-east passage towards the point where Cook was forced back by ice.

'Good – excellent,' exclaimed the admirable Phil Kellogg. 'I'll give you dates so we can synchronise.'

I bought a return first-class air ticket to Melbourne, which would allow me all the diversions I might need, and the near-certainty of getting on any Pan Am plane at short notice, which proved extremely useful, and cost under £2,000. When I took off on 1st August, it was with a single flexible bag (no black tie this time), camera and a pile of xeroxes of passages from Cook's log and contemporary drawings and charts of the places he had called at so that I could photograph them as they are today.

I spent four days in New York, calling on old friends like the Kahn sisters, Mr Shawn at the *New Yorker*, who had not published anything by me recently, and a children's book editor who had published a science-fantasy book of mine. I left her with another one and told her, optimistically, that it was even better. More important, I had lunch with Howard Cady of William Morrow and succeeded in persuading him to publish this Captain Cook project. A few months earlier I had handed over to an editor I knew at Collins in London the manuscript of Debby's first novel, *You Must be Sisters*, and they had taken it enthusiastically. It had then been sent to Viking in New York and I went round to find out the decision and do some salesmanship on her behalf, which was much more fun than pushing your own wares.

Then I set off on this long Pacific trip to join the film crew in Tahiti. In the event, they were delayed and I spent the first day being interviewed by the Polynesian press because the news about the film was creating great excitement locally. There was a large photograph of me, stripped in the sun at my hotel, holding up an American paperback copy of the book, on the front page of *Les Nouvelles*. 'L'Ecrivain du Film que David Lean Tournera à Tahiti Suit les Traces de Cook,' screamed the headline, all in red and black, too.

Then by copra boat or light plane, I visited the islands in the wake of Cook on his last visit to the islands. These were the islands Bligh should have been charting when he was stuck at Tahiti waiting for the breadfruit to mature, instead of leaving his men with the girls to sow dissension, while he sulked on board his ship or made angry visits ashore.

The film team had turned up when I returned to Papeete and I spent several days with them looking for locations. The film was never completed by David Lean, who refused to accept the economies demanded by the studio. Some years later, with Bolt's script, it was made as a single two hours twenty minute film, of brilliant quality, the critics agreed. It was called simply *The Bounty* and starred Anthony Hopkins, at his very best as Bligh, Mel Gibson as Christian, Daniel Day Lewis as the Master and Laurence Olivier in his last film part.

From Polynesia my travels in the wake of Captain Cook on his last voyage took me to North and South Island New Zealand, Sydney, Melbourne and Adventure Bay, Bruny Island, off the south coast of Tasmania, where he wooded and watered. Then to the Hawaiian islands, Vancouver Island and finally to Alaska, where I went as far north as I could by road.

Neither in terms of time nor expense did the trip repay itself for the book sold modestly, and there were times of loneliness, but it was quite an adventure and matching the places today with two hundred years (almost exactly) earlier was fascinating. Twice I chartered launches and light aircraft to photograph the *Resolution*'s anchorages, and used a dramatic photograph of Kealekekua Bay where the foolhardy and by now mentally unstable explorer met his end at the hands of Hawaiian natives, as endpapers.

18

Fickle Fortune

The tragedy of Captain James Cook two hundred years earlier was coincidentally reflected in my personal life. Shortly after my return from this long trip, my mother-in-law, Helen Woodyatt, began a decline in health that ended with her death on 29th November 1977. Her rôle in my life had been of immense influence and importance. Without underrating the part played in my childhood by my own beloved mother, dead for nearly four years now, Helen had introduced me to the intellectualism, sophistication, worldliness and elegance, which I had not enjoyed in my own upbringing. My debt to her was limitless, quite apart from her allowing me to marry Charlotte while she was little more than a child.

Helen had seen us through countless crises and failures and shared our successes for almost forty years. Her unassuming wisdom, her brisk pragmatism, her readiness to listen and offer advice when asked, had all been a great influence for good in the upbringing and young adult life of our children.

Helen had never been far distant and since 1959 when we moved to London she had lived in the annexe to our house, separated by only a single door. There was no way of telling how much she had sustained our marriage for we had never known life without her. Perhaps her constant and close availability was a prop we should have dispensed with in order to secure and test our independence. Perhaps she would have moved if we had suggested it. Who knows? The idea never crossed my mind.

None of this mattered at the time, and even less today, fifteen years later. All that must be recorded is that, with her death, the happiness in our married life which had already declined sank as rapidly as Helen's health over the previous months. While I wrote of that last, fatal voyage of Captain Cook, and of what I contended to have been the breakdown in his mental condition, the compatibility Charlotte and I had enjoyed since 1940 began to wane rapidly. One day in the spring of 1978 she said that she had been to see her lawyer that morning about a divorce. The wheels were set in relentless motion, while friends – after recovering from the shock – rallied round. Among these old friends, Kaye Webb, whose husband Ronald Searle walked out on her some years earlier, sympathetically offered me accommodation in her flat, but for the first and only time in my life I wanted to get away entirely and start some sort of life in the country, retaining only a necessary toe-hold in London.

Our eldest daughter Sarah with her family had settled in a Gloucestershire village, Chedworth near Cirencester, so I bought at auction a cottage with a small garden called the Old Manse at the other end of this village from her and began to organise myself a new country life. Everything was very strange and it was disquieting to wake up in an empty house without even a dog. Before the London house was sold, I had the occasional use of it and then I set about finding a small flat as a *pied-à-terre*, helped by a kind actress, Julie Laird, who was in a similar state of emotional turmoil.

Julie had been out with the David Lean team in Polynesia, among other tasks helping to look after Robert Bolt's child while he began work on the script of my film. She had returned to become Lean's research person on the film in England, and she had naturally sought my help as a key source. Meanwhile, after months of heavy pressure, Robert Bolt himself planned to return home for a break. He got as far as Los Angeles, where he suffered a massive heart attack and was detained in hospital and given a by-pass operation. This did not work, and he ended up suffering a crippling stroke, with the script unfinished, though what I had seen of it was brilliant.

The year 1978 was decidedly an unsettling one. In the midst of all these professional and domestic upsets, I made contact with Judy Taylor, my old friend and fellow office worker at The Bodley Head. I had always been fond of her and watched her rise in publishing with great pleasure. Her children's book list was unsurpassed. In 1971 she had been appointed MBE for her services to children's publishing, and she became deputy managing director to Max Reinhardt among other directorships.

Judy had been away for some time in Canada on book business and I met her by chance at a book gathering shortly after she returned. I took her out to dinner and we began seeing one another with increasing frequency, while I found her calm good sense and amused view of life particularly supportive and engaging at that time. She had a spare room in her flat in Paddington, I cancelled the flat I was going to buy, and took her down to see the Old Manse – and the Garland family.

Judy's ties with my family were already close and I had first met her when she was still a child. Judy was godmother to Sandy and publisher of much of Sarah's work as well as a figure of affection for her children. By high summer my life was assuming a more comfortable and congenial shape, and as far as Judy's professional responsibilities allowed, we were living together, awaiting the divorce. When Judy had to do her usual publishing stint at the Frankfurt Book Fair, I joined her for the last days. Max Reinhardt was being very generous and avuncular over our arrangement, and gave us a last-night dinner, a sort of engagement celebration.

If there is one thing about being a writer, it is always there, like being a meteorologist with the weather. As Winston Churchill once claimed in his young manhood (not very truthfully, I fear), give me a table and some sheets of paper and I am content. I was writing novels again at this time. I had written one terrible sort of allegory which Michael Joseph were foolish enough to publish some years earlier, but I have always enjoyed spinning a tale and had embarked on two trilogies in turn, one about flying in the war, the other about a fellow called Buller who had a pretty active life in the Royal Navy between about 1890 and the end of the First World War. None was particularly profound, in fact not at all profound, but quite racy and the Americans, too, liked them well enough to publish, in hardback and paper. Once plotted, they took only about two months to write.

I also did a life of Nelson at this time which was sold only through Marks and Spencer, along with other biographies by Elizabeth Longford, Martin Gilbert, Christopher Hibbert a future friend, and others of like calibre. And I half completed a book on Royal Yachts.

I was reminded of this earlier suggestion by Prince Philip and asked him now if he would like to collaborate with me. He thought this an excellent idea and I went to see him at the Palace with William Willett to discuss the shape of the book. He wrote me an enthusiastic letter to confirm it. I went ahead, a contract was drawn up with George Weidenfeld, and I began the research, visiting the naval museums at Venice, Paris, Lisbon and of course Greenwich. I collected a formidable dossier, including photographs and paintings, and had arranged a second meeting when I received a letter. It told me, without much preamble or decoration, that he could not do it after all. He was too busy with the Queen's Silver Jubilee preparations to spare the time, and I had better get on with it on my own. No one wanted a book on Royal Yachts by me alone when it was going to be by HRH and me, so the whole enterprise was scrapped, at considerable cost in my time, money and pride.

I was romping through one of my novels when Mountbatten was blown up in Ireland. I was in the garden of the Old Manse, and it was August Bank Holiday 1979 and hot. Judy told me the BBC was on the telephone. 'Have you heard the news,' asked the voice, 'that there has been a bomb outrage and that Lord Mountbatten and several of his family have been killed?'

There was silence, and, 'Hullo – are you there?'

'Yes, hang on a minute.' I was accommodating my mind to a reaction I had not experienced for some years – reaction to sudden violence, close by – at least it felt close by.

'Would you be willing to broadcast this evening? You needn't come to London. We can pipe it through from Oxford if that's all right for you.'

I agreed, and went out to think, Judy of course striking just the right note. She knew what I thought of the old man, by no means reverence, and even respect a tiny bit qualified, but limitless regard for the richness of his personality, the way you felt better for his company and did better in his company. He really did, in that old cliché, 'light up a room', and made you laugh and enjoy the way he was never at a loss for the right word and the sardonic crack. Of course his conceit was mountainous, and it is difficult to know which expression to assume when a man says, with all seriousness, 'I can honestly say that I didn't make a single mistake . . .' – as Viceroy of India, as a destroyer captain, as Chief of Defence Staff, as Supreme Commander South-East Asia, and so on.

However, my affection and admiration were considerable, and I had loved it when I was writing about his family, and it was Dickie and Dick and a great deal of laughter. My mind went back to that time when the Prince of Wales came into the drawing room at Broadlands when Louis Klemantaski (who had been doing some photography) and I were talking to him, and we recognised at once the immediate spark of affection and rapport between great-uncle and nephew that had long since been established. We were on our way out, and it was for only a few minutes; but remembering it then, I thought how devastated Prince Charles would be by this news.

I duly made my broadcast and the next day wrote some obituaries, including a long, dictated one for the *Evening Standard*. I must have been quite severely knocked by Mountbatten's death because it was not for several days that I remembered what I must do urgently. Several times by now, once with Charles Pick of Heinemann and in the presence of John Brabourne and his wife Patricia, I had made a bid to write an interim biography while he was still alive, and each time I had been told by the Brabournes that an authorised biography must wait until his death.

Mountbatten knew that I was not interested in being the official biographer. I told him so many times. He predicted that it would be in three volumes, that it would have to receive family approval. This was not in my style. And I knew that Mountbatten's official biography would require the imprimatur of the royal family and clearance by his daughters, and especially by Lord Brabourne.

To pre-empt any approach about becoming Mountbatten's official biographer, to announce my intentions, and not least to sympathise with him and his wife on their loss of a son, his mother and their own grave injuries, I wrote Brabourne a letter. He wrote back, pleasantly enough, but said he hoped that I would not write what I had made clear was an interim tribute to his father-in-law, and 'nothing to do with the official biography'. It was advice that I chose not to take, confident in my mind – and as Barbara Cartland agreed – that this was what he would have wanted me to do.

Meanwhile, my friend and excellent agent, Graham Watson of Curtis Brown, had fixed up a contract with Lord Weidenfeld. This entailed making contact for the first time with John Curtis, matchless editor, easy to work with, encouraging yet forthright. I needed all these qualities because it was decided from the beginning that this memorial, this extended obituary, must be published on the first anniversary of Mountbatten's murder, 27th August 1980.

I counted the weeks, listed the priority people I must see, calculated that around 100,000 words was the minimum if I was going to give reasonable credit to his long life: and felt properly daunted. Then I looked at a box of records I had kept of the endless hours I had spent with him at Broadlands, in London and in Germany. How the words had flowed! Some of them, necessarily, were about his mother and father, but every mention of them led to himself, his childhood, boyhood, early days in the Navy, his meeting with Edwina, their courtship, marriage and honeymoon, what Charlie Chaplin had said when they called on him in Hollywood . . .

The range and extent of the notes I had made additionally, of comments of people I had seen in connection with the earlier book, from the Queen down to a hapless one-legged survivor of the Dardanelles campaign who had been 'adopted' by Mountbatten's father, was very wide. I looked at all this material and was encouraged. All that was needed was a fast needle to stitch it together.

Through this period of several weeks while the ground work was laid, Judy was professionally supportive. I wanted to get the beginning right and all my efforts were unsatisfactory. John Curtis, deeply anxious as always that things were going well, asked to see my first efforts, and did not much approve. For a while, and for the first time with a book, I lost my nerve and became panicky. Then, one day Judy said, 'You've got to start off with the murder.'

Of course she was right. Start with the murder. We rushed off to Dublin, hired a car and drove to Mullaghmore on the north-west coast, and close to the Ulster border, where it had all happened. Etched on distant hills in huge letters was 'BRITS OUT', which seemed to set the tone. Classiebawn Castle, Cassel's old Irish estate on the clifftops, inherited by Mountbatten from Edwina, looked dour and threatening, like some of the local people. All the staff of twenty had dispersed and there was not even a housekeeper. But there was a field full of ewes and their young lambs, and forgetting the melancholy nature of our mission for a few moments, Judy took up one in her arms and I photographed this poignant evidence of young life by contrast with the evidence of old death we were seeking.

Then we followed the route of the car which had taken the doomed party down to the harbour on that bright bank holiday morning, followed closely by the Gardai escort. We talked to the local fishermen who showed where *Shadow V* had been moored and noted the road along which the murderers with their remote control device had driven, following the progress of the boat out of the harbour.

We talked to a number of the villagers, including a tiler who had been on a roof and had seen, from his elevated position, the whole sequence of events. We came back the next morning to check a few more points. We were strangers in this small community, we were British, and we were asking questions. A note of hostility was now clearly recognisable. A shopkeeper said to me, 'I think you ought to go now.' It was a recommendation rather than an order. We left.

I felt much better with the new opening under my belt, and got on with the book, writing and interviewing simultaneously, while our next-door neighbour in Chedworth, friend and typist, Jackie Gumpert, kept pace with my narrative. I wanted to talk to people, anyone who knew him well socially, politically, professionally in the Navy or among the innumerable charities and institutions he headed, from the Royal Naval Saddle Club (whatever was that?) to the Inner Magic Circle, the Institute of Electronic and Radio Engineers to King George's Fund for Sailors. The Earl and Countess of Longford were wonderful on the human side, emphasising his good points but being sardonically amusing about his frailties and mountainous pride. Frank told of his intellectual insecurity and of how he had once told him, 'You know I am much more intelligent than you think.'

Lord Butler, a most genial old boy, agreed about Mountbatten's consciousness of intellectual inadequacy. 'He felt he had missed the academic and intellectual side . . . One was a little defensive with him,' he added. 'He so liked an argument, and then it all came back in your face.'

Lord Hailsham was excellent value, and so were Harold Wilson and Julian Amery. I had never trusted Harold Macmillan but I thought I ought to get his views and spent an hour with him at his publishing house. I took very careful notes, sent him a draft for his approval, as I did with everyone, and heard nothing from him. I sent a copy of the book, when it was, of course, too late to correct anything, and he protested vehemently that I had misquoted him. But I also had a tape of our conversation. I did not pursue the matter.

A friend, Colonel Colin 'Mad Mitch' Mitchell, had been GSO1 to Mountbatten when he was Chief of Defence Staff, and he was marvellous – lucid, affectionate and very funny. An appeal in the *Daily Telegraph* brought in a flood of letters, some of which were invaluable. A QC wrote to point out the anomalies in the libel case Edwina had been obliged to pursue (she won) against the *People*. An elderly Fleet Air Arm pilot recounted a flight with Mountbatten as a passenger in a two-seat fighter after the *Kelly* was sunk and he wished to visit the hierarchy in Cairo to complain of lack of RAF support: 'When I offered him a parachute he declined to wear it,' he wrote to me, concluding with the strange words 'I'm sure if anything goes wrong you will show me what to do.' A Wren secretary recalled taking shouted dictation outside the door while he splashed about in his bath. There were many recounted incidents even more trivial than this but they all helped to build up a picture.

These several hundred letters also confirmed my own judgement of the man I had known intimately for three years and on and off for five more years. What was particularly interesting about them, which I had also noticed from talking to all manner of people, was that the more humble and less educated people tended to admire him greatly while the higher up the social scale the more marked were the reservations. None of the senior politicians I spoke to held him in uncompromising regard, while several spoke of him with the utmost contempt.

It was all very exciting, and I managed to get a first draft ready in three and a half months. There was still a great deal more work after that, and there were photographs to collect and hundreds of queries to check, but the final manuscript was ready for the printer by the middle of March 1980.

The book went straight to the top of the bestseller list, was everywhere, and in a few weeks had sold, with bookclubs, some quarter-million copies in hardback, and was to sell many more copies in foreign languages and in America, with serial rights earning a further £50,000. I had never had a real 'blockbuster' bestseller before and it was a curious, and I must say highly satisfying experience. I went up and down the country, signing copies, attending lunches as guest of honour, broadcasting, receiving accolades, and all that. I understood for the first time why so many successful writers become spoilt and then, for their publishers and agent, awkward to deal with. My determination not to follow that foolish route was strengthened by my failure to emulate this success, though my biography of Edwina Mountbatten did pretty well, too.

In the midst of all this turmoil and publicity, I had felt several times the tightening of a band round my chest which told me pretty clearly that my heart was giving trouble. There had, for some weeks, been twinges of angina which restricted, among other activities, the distance I could walk our dog. This was more serious and I was carted off to intensive care at University College Hospital where I remained under observation for a week.

Judy and I had married just before the health and legal troubles began, and it was an uncommonly distressing experience for her. Very few marriages can have been tested so comprehensively after only a few weeks. Without her at my side in court, and at my bedside in hospital, I am quite sure I could not have survived that summer of 1980. On the one hand the newspapers and magazines were publishing long reviews and advertising hoardings carried huge advertisements for the *Sunday Telegraph* serial, while I was having to recognise that this could be my last ever book. At least I was going out with a bang.

In the spring of 1981, we flew to New York for the American publication by Random House. I was strictly limited to what I could do in the way of publicity, and it was mostly done with a telephone from the hotel bedroom, to radio stations and newspapers all over the nation. This was certainly less demanding than travelling for TV and radio shows, bookshop signings and talks to women's clubs.

We made one journey only, and that was purely for pleasure and because we had never been there, to New Orleans, and its jazz. Luck was on our side. Glancing through the local newspapers, I spotted a modest announcement that Ella Fitzgerald would be singing at the Fairmount that very night. If only we had known, we told one another. But I called the number and got at once an almost ringside table. Then there was the World's Greatest Jazz Band, with Yank Lawson and co. at the Constitution Hall, which is a wooden hut where you sit on the floor. Then: of course the usual hospitality. The father of my publicist at Random House took us all over the place and dined us at one of his restaurants.

On the strength of the Mountbatten royalties Judy and I had bought a larger house in Chedworth, on the other side of the valley and with views down it. Denfurlong, a seventeenth-century farm-house from which all but about four acres of land had long since been sold, was a typical all-square Cotswold dwelling, with a ter-raced garden, a giant barn and other outbuildings, an orchard, and a meadow. In this meadow we kept for a while two ponies for the Garland grandchildren and felt very country-squireish.

Judy could exercise to the full her new skill in gardening and we had London friends to stay at weekends, and Sunday lunches for friends around, including my old publisher, Sir Robert Lusty, and his wife Babs. At this time, my brother Philip and his wife Peggy left their stud farm in Devonshire for a place nearby, also for health reasons. I had seen sadly little of them over the years, but they became fond of Judy from the first time they met, and for us brothers it was almost like a family reunion. Phil had long since retired from farming, had handed over his second Devonshire farm to his son Peter, and dedicated himself to the arts of drawing, carving and sculpting, previously his hobbies.

On our return from New Orleans, it became increasingly evident that medication was not sufficient to keep me safe from further heart attacks. My life was very restricted. I could not walk any great distance, and I had had to give up bicycling, a lifelong joy. I longed to feel well again, and friends told me I looked awful. Among them was John Vaizey, the authority on the economics of education, virtual founder of Brunel College and political maverick who had been ennobled by Harold Wilson and then became a firm Conservative and supporter of Margaret Thatcher. John was a very clever, very astringent, very funny and very kind man, who had suffered a massive heart attack himself in the Tube. A fellow member of the Garrick got help for him, and he underwent open heart surgery at St Thomas's Hospital. In typical Vaizey fashion, he developed a friendship with his cardiologist, Dr Stephen Jenkins, and became something of an amateur expert on heart disease.

'For God's sake go along and see Steve,' he begged me one day. 'I'll ring him up now. You're past the pills stage.'

So, much to Judy's relief, I did so, and he gave me a cardiac catheter, which tells all. In my case it told of one closed artery, a second more than half closed and signs of the same in the third. No wonder I was not feeling my best. After showing me this bizarre and frightening film, Steve said mildly, 'Yes, I think you would benefit from a bypass.' The surgeon's secretary later told me that there was a nine-months-long waiting list. No one told me I was unlikely to last that long, though they did when it was all over.

Only a few years earlier, I learned, it was a no better than a 40:60 chance-of-survival operation. Now the anaesthetist told me cheerfully it was 97:3; so I surrendered my body with a great deal of relief and not much trepidation and later found myself all right in intensive care with what appeared to be a length of sawn 2″ x 2″ timber down my throat. Judy was there beside me, and I indicated I wanted something to read, which I gathered was not customary in intensive care. I never felt the slightest twinge of pain, only a slight soreness in the chest, hardly surprising in the light of what they do to it.

I went home to the London flat after ten days and as typing was not very comfortable I soon got bored and made my way, quite slowly in a taxi, to the Garrick two weeks after they had cut me about. That cheered me up no end, though it surprised several kind people who had taken the trouble to visit me only a few days earlier. The effects of the operation were remarkable and immediate. Not only could I walk as far and as fast as my increasingly arthritic knee would allow, and bicycle for miles, but the sense of wellbeing was as if I had been reborn, and so it has remained for ten years.

John Vaizey was not so lucky. Constitutionally handicapped anyway, having spent most of his boyhood on his back (about which he wrote a most moving book), and his cardiac condition was more complicated than mine. After a few years, he began to feel rotten and then quite suddenly collapsed with heart failure again. They managed to get him back to St Thomas's and onto the operating table. 'We nearly made it,' Steve Jenkins told me later, but I think a valve had gone and they could not get to it in time.

I ventured back warily into the Mountbatten world a year or two after the publication of the biography. Ever since I first met him I had been intensely curious about his late wife Edwina, about whom he talked to me at length – of their stormy relationship, periods of happiness, long periods of separation brought about by his appointments abroad and her lust for travel. He had once told me poignantly, 'The tragedy of her early death was that we were just getting on better than ever before, and we looked forward to old age together.'

As before, a great number of people helped me, most of all Edwina's sister, Mary. I had met Lady Delamere at Broadlands and she had been kind about *Louis & Victoria*. Mary was a red-head, quite as pretty as Edwina, a few years younger and even more highly charged and emotional. There had been childhood tantrums. 'Edwina was the only one who could manage me.' The two sisters were utterly devoted to one another all their lives. When their grandfather Cassel died, Edwina got two thirds of the mountainous inheritance, Mary one third, but that was quite enough and more to live on, and quite enough to attract numbers of unscrupulous young men, which led to a miserable too-young marriage.

Her last marriage was to the 4th Baron Delamere (not the 3rd, murdered, one) and she lived for years in Kenya before they divorced. She was going to marry again, she told me, a rich Californian of about her age, but he died of a heart attack in the air on the way to the wedding, only shortly before I came to know her well. Mary was a dear but there had been much tragedy in her life, and much pain, too. She had been a daring skier. 'I have broken every bone in my body at least once,' she said. 'This is why I'm in this state.' The arthritis had really got a hold on her and her recent death must have come as a relief. Mary talked to me for hours about Edwina at her home, Cassel's old shooting lodge at Four Mile Bottom near Newmarket.

On my second visit I plucked up my courage and said, 'Look, I feel a bit nervous asking you this, but I can't possibly *ignore* the fact that your sister had affairs, some of them quite notorious.'

She laughed sweetly and her smile hinted at the reason why she had a few, too. 'Oh, of course Edwina had affairs, but not *so* many.' She mentioned a few names and added, 'She told me about all of them. We had absolutely no secrets from one another.'

Even more daringly, I asked, 'What about Hutch, the black singer, and Paul Robeson?'

'I can tell you this for absolute certain, she never went to bed with Paul Robeson though of course she knew him well.' I waited to hear about Hutch but nothing was forthcoming so I left the subject thankfully.

I also went to see, several times, Edwina's lifelong friend Barbara Cartland at Camfield Place, and became increasingly fond and admiring of her. Her award of a Damehood in the 1991 New Year's honours list was richly deserved.

I usually went to see her for tea, and 'the girls' were sometimes still hard at work. These girls were her shorthand typists, and two were required to keep pace with her output. I had the singular privilege once of hearing Barbara dictating one of her romances. She scarcely paused for breath, the amorous sentences pouring forth in an effortless torrent. Moreover, she was revelling in every moment, acting out the parts in her mind and converting them without pause into words like some processing plant.

She was immensely kind and thoughtful of my needs, rattling on about Edwina and her loves with complete indiscretion while dropping bits of cake from the loaded teatable to her Pekinese dog at her feet.

'You *must* have another cucumber sandwich, dear. They'll be so offended in the kitchen.'

Her appearance is too well known to require description, but I have to admit that on every occasion the first sight of those black eyelashes caused me to take a sharp intake of breath. I once took Judy with me and she was as impressed and amazed as me. Judy was writing her biography of Beatrix Potter, whose grandfather had bought Camfield Place as a retirement home in 1866, fancying the handsome low-built house and the fine gardens laid out by Capability Brown in 1800. As a little child from London, Beatrix loved visiting her grandfather's house – 'the place I love best in all the world.'

The walled gardens, according to Barbara, provided part of the inspiration for Mr MacGregor's garden, and we went out with her to photograph it. While doing so, a storm broke over us. At once, Barbara picked up her Pekinese protectively and ran back to the house at the speed of a schoolgirl. (She was born 1901!)

There was no particular pattern to my writing during the 1980s, one book leading to another. After Oxford University Press commissioned me to write that history of the First World War at sea, I wrote a more commercial history of the Second World War at sea for John Curtis. I wrote a history of the Garrick Club, a modest but pleasurable exercise, which concluded spectacularly with a one-night show to celebrate publication at the Duke of York's Theatre. This was organised and directed by Ronald Harwood, featuring the club's most distinguished actors, and Donald Wolfit's daughter, Margaret. A dinner at the club afterwards was chiefly notable for me by not having to make a speech; and Kingsley Amis contributed a neat poem of praise, 'Come to the Garrick . . .'

After this exercise I wrote a sort of multiple biography of George

V and Queen Mary's children, who had always interested me. And then, for the jubilee of the Battle of Britain in 1990, I wrote a joint recounting of that hot summer in the skies of southern Britain with my old friend Denis Richards. Denis in the 1940s and '50s had already written about it for his official history of the air war, and had met many of the great figures of the time, while I had served under a number of them.

Finally, as I write this, I published on the 50th anniversary of Winston Churchill's accession to power and the premiership in 1940, a new biography, with a strong emphasis on his marriage; in fact the book is called *Winston & Clementine: the Triumph of the Churchills.*

For the first time for years the other day I counted the number of books I have published. The total was ninety-five. I am uncertain whether to be appalled or impressed by this figure, which hints of hackwork – or perhaps just 'scribble, scribble, scribble! Eh! Mr Gibbon?' And scribble I do, three hours every morning when at home, revising or researching later in the day. The figure of ninety-five does include several edited anthologies and edited letters, several collaborations including *A History of the World's Motorcycles* with the delightful and frighteningly knowledgeable Leonard Setright. It sold and sold!

It all began with that unsolicited article of little more than 2,000 words for a very early number of *History Today* in 1950, published 1951. Included in this total of books are also a ghosted autobiography of Sir Geoffrey de Havilland as well as *W.O.* There are some very short books for young children among the total, and limited vocabulary readers, and *they* were hard work! Several 'career novels' for children when they were fashionable were followed by science-fantasy novels which I believe are still fashionable, and straight adventure stories under the 'Bruce Carter' pseudonym, historical and contemporary in their setting.

All these, over forty years, were written between the longer adult histories and biographies, with the emphasis on naval and military history. As Samuel Johnson put it succinctly, 'No man but a blockhead ever wrote except for money.' At the same time no one can spend a lifetime writing for money while not enjoying it, and I went on enjoying it until it became the drug it is today.

I could not begin to count the words in those ninety-five books, but, oh my! there are a lot of them – 590 pages in my last book. I suppose I will go on writing while people go on reading my books, and possibly even when they do not. I can see myself following the habit of a lifetime tapping away with my arthritic fingers on this ancient Olympia typewriter at eighty, with pages of unpublished manuscript growing about me until, like those unfortunate old ladies in Kansas with their newspapers, the stacks will collapse and suffocate me.

Around 1987 Judy and I became increasingly aware of the stress involved in keeping a largish house and garden going in Gloucestershire as well as our London commitments. We seemed to be on the road a great deal, wondering if we had left anything behind, and a flat is a rotten place to leave a dog if you are out most of the time. We first sold off the Denfurlong barns which relieved us of a slice of garden, but increasingly we felt that a house in London, with a smaller garden, would be quite enough.

Denfurlong went, with many tugs of the heart, just before Christmas 1986, and we settled in the flat for the time it took to find the right place. Prices were sky high but we had made a bit selling off the barns and then the house, and by extraordinary luck, found just what we wanted on our second reconnaissance expedition: a small, easy-to-run, modern house, with a pocket handkerchief garden, too small really. Two of the children are nearby, the others more distant, in Worcester and Sarah still in Chedworth.

Even Bryony, born after a gap of twelve years, is over thirty years old, married to an exceptionally nice and able schoolmaster, Jim Driver; while the birthdays of the grandchildren – Will, Laura, Kitty, Tom, Lotty, Jack, Roger and Sam – come round like the second hand of a clock.

Good friends have died over the past ten years. The worst loss of all was that of my brother Philip, leaving me the last of the family, the only one to remember those childhood days of the 1920s and 1930s. His death in June 1990 was particularly poignant as he was enjoying real success with his sculpting and had a number of uncompleted commissions; but he had been so effortlessly fit all his life that the crippling heart disease he had suffered for too long made death almost a relief for himself and his wife, Peggy.

Judy and I have celebrated our tenth ('tin') wedding anniversary. It has been an eventful and mainly happy decade, with plenty of variety and travel, and always professionally interesting. Some of the scenes I remember are Judy and me spending an hour with

Mrs Gandhi in her office, her clever, friendly smile as she hitched up time and again her beautiful sari while she told me about her old friend Edwina; the primitive native villages of Natal we drove through in the burning heat of South Africa; the millionaire Indian newspaper proprietor and shipping tycoon who mentioned at the end of our talk in his own skyscraper that he must get home now to Indiatown as the law prohibited him from sleeping in Durban; watching panthers stalking game in the shadow of Mount Kilimanjaro; Las Vegas under snow with unbelieving children on the streets; and, inevitably, the Taj Mahal by moonlight.

I have been more lucky perhaps than I deserve to have survived war and ill-health, to have travelled so far and wide; to have an abundance of family and friends, and above all Judy; and to have been granted sufficient talent to earn a livelihood by writing, now almost on the top of Primrose Hill.

Our house overlooks Regent's Park and the zoo, a great part of central London and, far to the south, Epsom Downs and Greenwich. On the summit of this hill there is a viewfinder which marks the names of some of the buildings on an etched replica outline. From our windows we can see running dogs and bicyclists, loving couples on the grass, young and old kite-fliers, young joggers and old men turning over the rubbish in the wastebaskets.

Primrose Hill is as close to my heart as it is to our home, and the thread of affection and association goes back fifty years. Driving past it with my aged father shortly before he died in 1970, he eyed this green rise of grass and trees and told me, not for the first time, 'When I was a boy at the bank, Mater used to send me off with broken biscuits and an apple for my lunch. On fine days I would walk here, climb the hill and settle down with my paper bag and watch the world below.'

When I was about the same age I saw Primrose Hill for the first time, as I marched and did gymnastics at its foot as a green RAF cadet. It had assumed an aggressive stance, and there was no place for me to eat a picnic on its summit, for as Louis MacNeice had recently written,

> They cut the trees away:
> By day the lean guns leer
> Across their concrete walls;
> The evening falls
> On four guns tucked in bed.

The anti-aircraft gun battery occupied all the top of the hill, and the camp much more of the slopes. There had been barbed wire and patrolling sentries. In one-day-old-stiff uniform, I counted the guns and retired to my barracks beneath the hill. Likening the hill to 'a raft on stormy sea', Louis MacNeice had completed his poem, written a few days before war broke out in 1939, on a prophetic note:

> Some night the raft will lift
> Upon a larger swell,
> And the evil sirens call
> And the searchlights quest and shift,
> And out of the Milky Way
> The impartial bombs will fall.

They had by then already fallen many times, and the cracking, ear-wrecking sound of the guns shot us awake in the night.

A while after peace returned, we had come to live within ten minutes' walk of Primrose Hill, a playground for our children and dogs. And now, another thirty years on, Judy and I have this house just a few yards from the hill. Little more distant are friends, 'The Folks that live on the Hill', to use the title of a novel by one of them, Sir Kingsley Amis. The old houses that once faced the guns have long since been bombed or demolished, and in our garden we still come across broken window glass from the concussion of those guns or the blast of the bombs.

When the war was over, they took away the guns and the barbed wire and the mess huts. But they could not be bothered with the building foundations and the thick octagonal concrete gun bases. They just covered them with soil and sowed grass seed. In dry weather, the octagonal shapes of the bases upon which the big 4.5-inch guns once rested, are indicated by the lighter shade of the thirsty grass. This gives way to daisies which mark their own white war memorial to the dead Londoners of 1939–1945.

I walk to the top of Primrose Hill whenever I can and always derive comfort and reassurance from the view and the associations with the past, while the maturity of the trees planted to replace those Louis MacNeice saw cut down is a reminder that I am nearing seventy and that it was about time to recount these memories.

INDEX